The Surgeon and
the Shepherd

T0326817

The Surgeon and the Shepherd

Two Resistance Heroes in Vichy France

MEG OSTRUM

UNIVERSITY OF NEBRASKA PRESS

LINCOLN & LONDON

Publication of this volume was assisted by
The Virginia Faulkner Fund, established in
memory of Virginia Faulkner, editor-in-chief
of the University of Nebraska Press.
Library of Congress Cataloging-in-Publication Data
Ostrum, Meg.
The surgeon and the shepherd: two resistance heroes in
Vichy France / Meg Ostrum.
p. cm.
Includes bibliographical references and index.
ISBN 0-8032-3573-9 (hardcover: alk. paper)
ISBN 978-0-8032-3641-7 (paper: alk. paper)
1. World War, 1939–1945—Underground movements
—France—Biography. 2. Schepens, Charles L.
3. Sarochar, Jean 1892–1975. 4. Surgeons—Belgium—
Biography. 5. Shepherds—France—Biography. I. Title.
D802.F8076 2004
940.53'44'0922—dc21
2003012629

To my mother and to the
memory of my father

Contents

Illustrations

Acknowledgments

This project has truly been an odyssey, one that has transported me across geography, time, and cultures. Much as I have experienced many memorable visual moments, the human relationships encountered in this long journey have been the most meaningful to me. Now, at long last, I can pay proper tribute to an array of extraordinary people.

First and foremost I am deeply indebted to Charles and Cette Schepens for their endless hospitality, kindness, and patience over almost two decades. The Schepenses' willingness to allow me to probe the public and private dimensions of their lives in detail was a gift. From them I have learned more about goodness and greatness than could ever possibly be contained between the covers of a book.

I must confess that the warm reception that I received by all those I interviewed made the arduous task of doing fieldwork a privilege, and to each and every one of them I owe special thanks. Certainly I could not have accomplished my research in the Pays Basque without the enthusiastic and generous assistance of three key people: Abbé Bernard Erdozaincy, Jean Moretti, and Charlotte d'Anjou. They were continuously willing to serve as guides, go-betweens, or translators, and they all royally welcomed me into their homes. Our ongoing friendship is a wonderful dividend of this endeavor.

I wish to acknowledge the following people as well, individuals who either helped me locate material or gain background knowledge about a variety of research topics: Lilita Dively; Jokin Apalategi; Joxemartin Apalategi; Tom Anderson; Everett Demeritt; Buck Heath; Mary Sue Glosser; Karol Kwakia; Paul and Elise Dauchot; Annie Neumark. I must thank and commend Marcelino Ugalde and his staff at the Basque Studies Library at the University of Nevada, Reno, for making my short time there so productive. I would be remiss, also, not to mention the kindness of those with whom I lodged in far-flung places during the course of my research, particularly Marjorie McClung, Christiane Ardohain, and Muffy and David Vhay, all of whom took special interest in the project and shared their local knowledge.

Beyond those individuals critical to the research work, countless others contributed to the preparation of this book. Because it has been so many years in the making, the refrain, "and your book?" has been a constant in conversations with friends, neighbors, and colleagues. The list of supporters is far too long to enumerate, so let this stand as a blanket expression of my sincere appreciation for their interest and insights. Similarly, I wish to extend a collective thanks to the staff of the University of Nebraska Press for their enthusiasm for the manuscript and their diligence in shepherding the book through the publishing process.

Certain people must be singled out because of the time they invested or the wisdom they lent, and without whose help I would not have been able to advance this pursuit from research project to publication. The literary and networking skills of my family have been invaluable. Their involvement and gentle prodding furthered my resolve to see this challenging endeavor to completion. With pride and great pleasure I express my heartfelt thanks to my dear mother, my brother Alan, and my sister Mollie.

It has been my good fortune to enroll Deborah and Nicholas Clifford as advisors. Their deft coaching over a dozen years gave me confidence, and their thoughtful critiques of both an early and a later draft of the book were vital to advancing the work in progress. I treasure their collegial generosity.

I appreciate, as well, the encouragement and suggestions of Anna Ginn, Andi Pepper, Stephen Jacobs, Mal O'Connor, Ellen Lovell, Veronica Ryback, and Christophe Lissarrague, all of whom read chapters or the full manuscript at various stages of completion. I am particularly grateful to Joe Kirkish, Richard Rabinowitz, and Robert Zaretsky for their meticulous and insightful editorial assistance.

In the final — publishing — phase of this marathon I have been generously assisted by the following people, who lent advice or performed a variety of technical tasks: Upton Brady, Roger Conover, Judy McCulloh, Tim Newcomb, Agnes Sector, Michael Katzenberg, Bill Jaspersohn, Michael Melford, Tim Kahn, Mark Weinstein, Amy Trubek, Andy Kolovos, and Diane Hood.

Finally, I want to highlight the immense contributions of the three people who from the start have been both witnesses and participants in the saga of the book's creation. Del Sheldon, initially my traveling companion in the Basque country in 1983 and then an exemplary friend and champion, listened patiently and perceptively to my stories, my quandaries, my frustrations, and my successes. Little did folklorist Jane Beck know that helping me find Charles Schepens in 1984 would immediately recruit her as "project sage" to guide my work as a novice fieldworker. Nor did either of us know that one day we would be working side by side at the Vermont Folklife Center. Since 1990 this project has added another dimension to our professional collaboration, and I have benefited enormously from her enthusiasm, wisdom, and understanding of my need to disappear at various junctures. My husband, Tom Leytham, took on a long list of roles—chauffeur, mapmaker, and technical consultant, to name a few—but it was his companionship and humor that sustained me through the project's evolution. To Del, Jane, and Tom go my admiration and appreciation: without their steadfast support I could not have taken on this ambitious endeavor, nor finished it.

Introduction

What happens to a war hero when the war ends? When and how does an outsider become a giant of legend, and when does living memory turn into mythology? These were the questions that I could not chase from my mind after a chance visit to Mendive, a Basque border village in the French Pyrenees, almost twenty years ago.

I landed there in mid-November 1983 as a misguided off-season hiker. On a gloomy, overcast afternoon my American traveling companion, Del Keppelman, and I donned our hiking boots and left our hotel in St.-Jean-Pied-de-Port. Our destination was the Forêt d'Iraty, described in a type-written tourist brochure as a magnificent beechwood forest in the nearby mountains. Despite the less than ideal weather we were eager to walk off the accumulated loginess of several days' confinement riding through southwestern France in Del's rented Citroën Deux Chevaux.

After forty-five minutes creeping up the narrow, winding mountain road, we had not yet reached the designated trailhead and it was already two o'clock. Del was concerned about the trustworthiness of the car's brakes and beginning to feel vertiginous. What's more, the sights we were encountering — vultures circling overhead, precipitous slopes dropping off from the roadway, and theatrical shafts of sunlight illuminating lonely stone huts — lent an ominous mood to our outing. It took little discussion between us to agree to cancel the excursion, and we started back down the mountain.

As we retraced our path I reread the tourist brochure. When I proposed that we try a shortened version of a walk up toward the Pic de Behorleguy, the highest of the mountains ringing the valley, Del agreed. The vaguely written instructions for this alternative destination indicated that "hikers should park their car by the village church, and begin the trek on the dirt road." As we were putting on our daypacks, from the second-story window of the parsonage opposite the church came a man's voice asking if we needed assistance. I replied in French that we were two Americans visiting the area, and we wanted to go walking up toward the Pic de Behorleguy. Immediately the face of the beret-clad priest turned from curiosity to concern, and he implored us not to make the dangerous journey because the mist already was starting to descend. He then came down to greet us formally, and during the ensuing discussion we discovered that we were in Mendive, not Behorleguy, which was actually a few kilometers farther up the mountain.

Abbé Bernard Erdozaincy wanted to know more about these two thirty-ish women who had strayed into his parish. He invited us up to his spare living quarters for coffee — unexpected hospitality that we readily accepted. When we explained that we lived in the northeastern part of the United States between Boston and Montreal, his countenance changed once again, as if he had had a revelation that we were not lost wayfarers but a delegation of distinguished emissaries. The word "Boston" had prompted his reaction and set him to narrating a tale of World War II resistance set in Mendive. The hero of the story was a Belgian eye surgeon who had moved to Boston after the war. The abbé disappeared into his bedroom, and in a minute returned with a posed black and white photo of a man known by his pseudonym, Monsieur Pérot, with a few of his colleagues. According to the abbé, they had returned to Mendive in the late 1960s to place a commemorative plaque on an important mountain chapel. The abbé also told us that the plaque dedication ceremony had taken place early in his tenure, and that he was very proud to have played an important role in the event. He offered to take us up to the mountain chapel to see the plaque, so off we went in his station wagon.

En route we stopped by the former site of a large lumbermill that Monsieur Pérot had used as a base of operations for his resistance activities. As we surveyed the pasture full of grazing cows, the priest's account seemed to us a modern folk tale, especially the dramatic description of how this man had pulled off a daring escape when the Germans came to arrest him. When we reached the Chapelle St.-Sauveur we viewed the memorial and took several photos of the priest standing next to it.

Our return to the valley led to introductions to several villagers in the midst of evening chores. Each encounter was a chance for us to hear a conversation in Basque; for our guide it was an opportunity to chat with his parishioners and inquire whether the person could remember Monsieur Pérot's real name. Unfortunately no one could help him, but it was evident to us that all pronounced his nom de guerre with awe.

As we neared the Mendive church and parsonage our guide proposed one additional stop: a trip up the mountain to the church in Behorleguy. Once there we were completely charmed by its interior, and Abbé Erdozaincy was delighted when we inquired whether it would be possible to attend a service that weekend. I also indicated to him that if he wanted to write a letter to Monsieur Pérot I would be glad to hand-deliver it, since at the time I was making regular trips to Boston for treatment of a corneal condition at Massachusetts Eye and Ear Infirmary, and was certain that in the next few days he would be able to remember the physician-hero's true name.

Abbé Erdozaincy beamed when he spied us sitting among the thirty-odd parishioners in the little church that next Sunday. After the Mass he greeted us outside under the portico, then pulled out an envelope from his pocket and began reading his missive out loud to us and to a few villagers who had lingered after the service. With everyone nodding in approval of his expression of longstanding admiration and of hope for a return visit, I ceremoniously accepted the letter, realizing with amusement when I glanced at the envelope that my offer of being a messenger was going to entail some detective work: unable to recall the Belgian doctor's name, the priest had simply indicated the addressee as "un oculiste d'origine Belge exerçant à Boston" (a Belgian ophthalmologist practicing in Boston).

Three months later I met the fabled Jacques Pérot. Immediately after my return to the States a casual conversation with Jane Beck, a close colleague, serendipitously yielded his true identity: Dr. Charles Schepens, the eminent retinal surgeon who had saved her eyesight! Although she knew little more than the fact that he was Belgian and had served in the resistance in the south of France during World War II, Jane was certain that Dr. Schepens was the mysterious figure whom I was seeking.

The ballroom of the Ritz-Carlton Hotel in Boston was the unlikely setting for our rendezvous. In my initial phone conversation with Dr. Schepens he had indicated that his schedule left little time for nonmedical appointments but that he would be pleased to have me as his guest at an upcoming afternoon concert to benefit his medical research institute. To my great surprise Dr. Schepens was dressed for this glamorous social event in the same unassuming dark blazer and striped tie that I remembered from the photo taken at the plaque dedication in Mendive. This courtly, seventy-ish man better fit the mold of an elder university professor than an illustrious hero.

Dr. Schepens seated me at the head table with an international mix of

people, placing me next to his wife, Cette. Immediately after he introduced me to her, he excused himself and headed back to the lobby. Mrs.
Schepens and I began chatting in French, and I was struck by her simple
elegance and demure manner. She thought it was amazing that I had been
in Mendive and had been able to trace her husband. I pulled out the
photos that I had brought along. As she studied them I asked if she had
ever been to the village. She looked at me with consternation, saying,
"Why, what do you mean? I lived there, too, during the war!" I was both
embarrassed and taken aback, because from the story I had heard I had no
indication that Monsieur Pérot was married at the time. I apologized for
my faux pas and started to tell her about some of the people I had met and
my first impressions of this sleepy Basque community.

When her husband returned to the table she showed him the photographs. I noticed that a few turned his owlish countenance to a more
relaxed expression. When I handed him the letter he smiled as he read the
address on the envelope but had to pocket it when he saw the conductor
moving to the podium. During the concert I saw him take the letter out
and read it discreetly in his lap, but I could not see his reaction. Just as the
last note was played before the intermission he stood up and left the room.

A few minutes later a woman approached the table and identified herself as the assistant director of the development office at Dr. Schepens's
institute. She had come to tell me that Dr. Schepens, who normally expressed little emotion, had been truly touched by the priest's words. When
I indicated my interest in learning more about his wartime exploits in
Mendive, she volunteered to send me a copy of a chapter from a book
written about the Belgian resistance that she was sure would satisfy my
curiosity.

Within a week the promised photocopy from the book, *Histoires des
Résistants*, arrived. At last, reading the chapter entitled "Il n'y a plus de
Pyrénées," I began to comprehend the boldness of Dr. Schepens's undertaking and its strategic importance in the efforts of the Belgian underground in occupied Europe in 1942–43. However, the account, written by
William Ugeux, one of the leaders of the Belgian underground, was somewhat different than the tale I had heard recounted in the village. Another
set of perplexing questions filled my mind: Why were there discrepancies
in the written and oral accounts? Why was there no mention of Madame
Pérot the first time I heard the tale in Mendive? Was Dr. Schepens natu-

rally guarded, or only when it came to talking about his wartime experiences? My curiosity, rather than being satisfied, only grew. It occurred to me that in writing a short travel tale about seeking a mountain adventure and instead finding a "lost" war hero, I might be able to make sense of the fantastic series of events that had begun at the humble village church in Mendive and led me to the Ritz ballroom in Boston.

It was clear that I needed not only to do background research on Basque culture and resistance activities in the Pyrenees but also to meet privately with Dr. Schepens. After the concert he tentatively agreed to be interviewed, so on several occasions I contacted him well in advance of my planned trips to Boston, but my timing never seemed to be convenient. On one visit I was able to arrange a date with Cette Schepens for tea at a Beacon Hill cafe. She brought along two family photos from their stay in Mendive and gave them to me. It was evident that talking about the experience was not easy for her; she candidly admitted that it was a black period in her life that she had tried to obscure, and I recognized that it would be far better to save my questions for her husband.

My persistence was rewarded in December 1987. Earlier that year, hopeful that I might meet some older inhabitants of Mendive and the surrounding villages who had firsthand recollections of the war years, I decided to make a return visit to the Basque country as part of a three-week trip to Europe. Abbé Erdozaincy introduced me to Monsieur Pérot's former neighbor and a man who had been an employee at the lumbermill, both of whom had vivid memories of the Pérot story. From them I heard a repeat of the priest's version of Pérot's escape, but more important I learned many fascinating details about the relation of this Belgian couple to the people in the village during their residence. Also, during my brief visit the proprietors of the local hotel and restaurant gave me another book by Ugeux. A quasi-fictional memoir–spy tale written in the 1960s, *Le Passage de l'Iraty* gave an even more dramatic and detailed account of Monsieur Pérot's secret mission in the Pyrenees.

Apparently it was my persistence in researching the story that finally convinced Dr. Schepens to agree to set a date for a private audience at his seaside home north of Boston. The extended evening began with a gracious dinner with Dr. and Mrs. Schepens in their grand formal dining room. For almost three hours afterward Dr. Schepens and I sat alone in their finely furnished European-style parlor as I quizzed him — sometimes in French, sometimes in English—on the questions that had been accumulating those many months. I used Ugeux's chronology to structure our discussion and to learn more about Monsieur Pérot's relations with the Basques, the Germans, and other *résistants*. During the course of our interview Dr. Schepens also traced his escape route for me on a Michelin roadmap that I had brought along.

My first encounter with Charles Schepens at the Ritz concert had given me a preview of his soft-spoken, self-effacing manner. His modesty was confirmed as I listened to his straightforward description of his service in the underground, which was decidedly different from Ugeux's self-aggrandizing posture. As the former Pérot narrated the stories his reserve occasionally melted into more animated facial expression and gesturing. But throughout the interview Dr. Schepens downplayed his heroic role. He repeatedly talked with praise about the extreme bravery of others, particularly one Basque shepherd named Jean Sarochar (who had also been mentioned by Ugeux). Dr. Schepens indicated with sadness that the shepherd had passed away a dozen years ago.

Afterward, as I reflected on Dr. Schepens's version of the story compared to the others I had read and heard, I began to realize that there were the makings of something far more compelling and complex than an accidental traveler's tale. From my preliminary investigation I sensed that many stories relating to the evolution of Monsieur Pérot's career in the resistance and to life in Mendive before and after the war were yet untold, and that a web of relationships had not been explored or recorded.

To reconstruct this obscure war story posed several challenges, however. First, as a museum professional trained in the study of art history and material culture, my accustomed method of inquiry was not oral history interviewing. Nonetheless, I knew that whatever the source material was—artifacts, documents, or oral testimony—authenticity is the common underlying issue in researching the past. My inability to speak Basque proved not to be a problem; rather, it was the dearth of other historical evidence and the death of some of the key personalities that complicated the process of corroboration. But the most critical challenge to this project was the reliability of the memories of an aging set of participants and witnesses who were now almost fifty years removed from the events of the war.

This hiatus actually played out to my advantage. Social scientists have discovered that the process of "life review" for an elderly person, far from yielding only a sketchy biographical picture can often elicit highly detailed recollections of earlier epochs because there is an unprecedented interest in remembering.[1] Like so many World War II veterans, Dr. Schepens had been eager to put the war behind him and get on with his life and thus, ever since his arrival in Boston, he had spoken, both in private and in public, in only general terms about his involvement in the resistance movement. Only as he neared retirement — when he had achieved his medical ambitions in America and gained international recognition for his advances in ophthalmological research, diagnostics, and surgical techniques — was he willing to talk in depth about this earlier, undisclosed chapter of his life.

Still, the question of credibility lingered, especially since war stories are a genre notorious for producing distortion. We began by reexamining elements of Dr. Schepens's edited story. The coherence and consistency of the unrehearsed version of his biography along with his dispassionate manner earned my confidence early on.[2] He also genuinely seemed to enjoy the cross-examination process that interviewing affords. He never refused to answer a question but would admit frankly if he had forgotten a name or detail or if he had never known of a person or situation. I interpreted as a further positive sign his continual readiness to give me leads and provide overtures to others still living in the Basque country or in other parts of Europe who could be helpful in supplying information on specific topics.

In all I interviewed Charles Schepens more than twenty times, including once on a daylong tour around Belgium to visit several places that figured prominently in his biography. On several of my visits to Boston, Cette Schepens sat in on our interview session, occasionally breaking her attentive silence to volunteer lively details or perceptive commentary. These spurts of recall surprised her, and eventually made her both interested and willing to be interviewed separately.

While Dr. Schepens's personal narrative was the focus of my research, there were also many gaps to fill in as well as the necessity of cross-checking facts and sequences. During six return visits to Mendive and other locales in France and Belgium from 1990 to 2001, I located more than thirty people with direct, if fragmentary, knowledge of what one called "the epic of Iraty."[3] Some of these informants had never spoken in depth, even to their own families, about their wartime activities, but all were eager to contribute vivid anecdotes of an epoch that clearly had importance in their personal, family, or local history.

Gradually I came to realize that retrospective interviewing yields the possibility of learning not just about an external frame of events but also about the internal—and long-term—imprint on the consciousness of individuals and a community.[4] To successfully probe the psychological meaning of memory, however, an interviewer must both *hear* the story and *listen* to the narration.[5] Only after several years of shuttling between Boston, the Pays Basque, and Belgium did I develop this interpretive skill. Through the triangulated process of substantiating testimony, as well as becoming adept at identifying the lore entwined in the story, I was finally able to understand the central truth of the drama: for the residents of Mendive and those involved in the secret operation of the sawmill, the shrewd Jacques Pérot was the living legend, but for Charles Schepens the true superman was the boundlessly courageous Basque shepherd Jean Sarochar. To tell the tale anew—accurately—both points of view had to be presented.[6]

As an afternoon excursion had turned into an extended research expedition, thus did my plan to profile a World War II resistance hero evolve into a compound study of a hero and a hero's hero. Yet beyond this brief explanation I must also add a few caveats. Though *The Surgeon and the Shepherd* is a more thorough documentation than previous accounts, it is incomplete: absence and silence, along with inevitable memory loss, leave some unanswered questions and unsolved mysteries that may puzzle the reader as they have puzzled the author. As a tale of happenstance the book may also disconcert readers expecting the linear narrative structure typical of a historical monograph. As a composite of many perspectives and untold experiences it is likely that this more complicated chronicle will surprise those who somehow claim knowledge of or participated in Monsieur Pérot's exploits. Ultimately, both for those already familiar with the story and for those who are not, I hope this book will yield greater insight about how World War II transformed ordinary citizens into daring *résistants* and their complex identities and unlikely alliances. I hope, too, that it will provoke thought about the unpredictable ways that heroic service is recognized—or not—once victory is declared.

Oculiste d'Origine Belge,

exerçant à Boston

The Surgeon and
the Shepherd

Occupied France

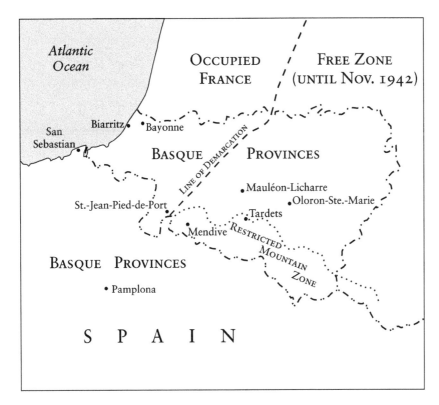

Basque France, WWII

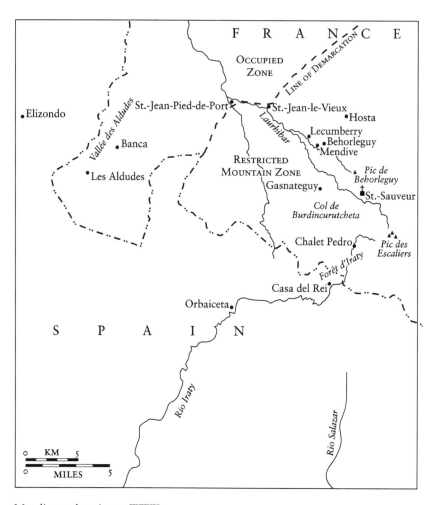

Mendive and environs, WWII

Part One

The Valley of Legends

(*Previous page*) The Mendive sawmill, c. 1930.
(photo courtesy Jean Moretti)

Chapter 1

Given his limited prospects for the future, Jean Sarochar likely regretted the end of the Great War and with it the termination of his service as a soldier in the French army. The return to Mendive, his native village in the Basque country, held few opportunities for one such as he, beyond the pleasures of a hero's welcome or once again ranging freely over the emerald pastures of the Pyrenees with his family's flock of sheep. Decades of indenture in his own household were certain to come.

When Manech (Basque for "Jean") left his pastoral mountain valley for the western front, his life had just begun as a shepherd-in-residence to his older sister and brother-in-law. Longstanding tradition in rural Basque society was a system of inheritance that transferred all of a family's ancestral assets—its homestead, furniture, land holdings, and rights—to one offspring.[1] Usually the eldest child became the resident *jaun* (lord) under whose roof the rest of the family lived and worked. Other siblings simply received a monetary bequest to stake out their futures. Emigration to the Americas, preparation for the priesthood, or apprenticeship as a village artisan were the alternative avenues for Basque sons seeking independence and opportunity away from home, while lifelong security, servitude, and bachelorhood were the realities for those who stayed behind. Lacking ambition, Jean remained in the family fold.

Like the other young men from the neighboring villages of Lecumberry and Behorleguy called up in 1914 to serve in World War I, for Jean leaving the Laurhibar Valley must have been an adventure in itself. Until then his peasant geography was circumscribed by the landscape that his feet had traveled since boyhood: leading flocks from the valley to high pastures for the annual *transhumance*; crisscrossing animal paths along the upland meadows with the sheep in search of food; traversing the border in the dense, beech-and-pine Forêt d'Iraty on occasional nocturnal smuggling missions into Spain; or guiding oxen to St.-Jean-Pied-de-Port, the market town approximately ten kilometers (six miles) away. Until Manech left the only official political division he knew was the path taken by the Rio Iraty, a short stretch of which formed the border between France and Spain.

Moving out of his familiar realm meant crossing into a foreign country, which according to a popular Basque proverb was "a land of wolves." He was no longer able to see the landmarks that served as his spatial coordinates—the stony crest of the Pic de Behorleguy towering above the surrounding peaks of the Basses-Pyrénées, the semicircular apse of the ancient Chapelle St.-Sauveur protruding from the brow of the mountainside, or the small streams veining the ravines—and could not easily judge distance. Surely he was not the first shepherd-soldier en route to the trenches in northern France to mistakenly believe he had landed in Paris upon his arrival in Bayonne (a bustling, river port city sixty kilometers from his valley).

Manech's adolescent years spent learning to survive the hardships and isolation of mountain life had hardened his mind to both physical danger and death, and fashioned him into a fierce and determined warrior. Captured during battle and taken as a prisoner to Germany, Manech escaped, intent upon rejoining his unit. His limited reading and orienteering skills, however, had set him on a northerly trajectory to (officially neutral) Holland, where an unlikely band of "wolves"—a group of schoolchildren—discovered and reported him to their teacher. He narrowly escaped capture during a manhunt organized by the Dutch schoolteacher, and once in France he immediately requested a return to the trenches. By the end of the war his physical feats of courage and sense of duty had earned him several military honors, including a croix de guerre, the highest accolade that could be conferred on a combat soldier.

Jean turned out to be a model soldier and patriot in more than one way. As a boy growing up in Mendive in the last decade of the nineteenth century he had formal schooling that probably lasted until he was only ten or twelve years of age, but during the winter months he received a continuing education through his family's *veillées* (nightly gatherings) to husk yellow corn. Seated with the elders around the hearth Jean listened for hours to descriptions of the pantheon of supernatural beings who tested the physical strength, religious faith, and cleverness of the human population of the Basque provinces or revealed the origins of the mysterious sites that dotted the region. Many of the stories, localized to a particular hamlet or village, told of the *Laminak*, the benevolent little people who lived in holes and caves, hoarded treasure, or would perform household miracles for a price. Other stories featured the giants, the *Mairiak*, responsible for the formation of a variety of monumental stone structures: dolmens, menhirs, cromlechs, chapels, bridges, and even chateaux. The list of their handiwork included the round stone that capped the dolmen of Chuberrasain-Harri (situated in the midst of a mountain pasture above Mendive). According to ancient legend, the boulder's placement was the result of a throwing contest between the superhuman Roland and a Basque shepherd. The shepherd won because, when it came to his turn, the object that he had thrown into the air never landed—it was not a stone, but a bird! The carnivorous and powerful Wild Ogre and Wild Ogress who inhabit the somber forests also figured prominently in numerous Basque myths. By turns comic and moralistic, the fables and folk legends repeated two central themes: the triumph of Christian belief over the forces of evil, and the heroism of a clever Basque shepherd in outsmarting a superior force.

Extended stays up in the high country tending the sheep during the summer months no doubt allowed Jean to absorb an additional collection of fantastic tales. During the occasional gatherings that broke the long periods of solitude, he would have heard the older shepherds reveal the source of the swirling mist, of the distant cries from the forest, of the terrifying landslides of boulders. As he sat huddled among them in the crude, smoke-filled stone shelters, he would have heard as well the stories of human encounters with talking animals and capricious spirits who terrorize the sanity of men living in the mountains—all told, of course, as gospel truth.

Jean Sarochar drew upon these tales of magic and miracles to maintain his own alertness in the trenches and to relieve the anxiety and boredom of others in his regiment. By narrating Basque legends for an audience of other peasant Frenchmen (unfamiliar with the terrain and the culture of his homeland), Jean discovered his gift as an entertaining raconteur. For hours on end the animated banter of the diminutive shepherd with a ferretlike mien could amuse the other *poilus* nearby. If his delivery failed to produce the intended response Jean likely recited the disclaimer invoked in Basque oral tradition: "There was once a crow, a very black crow. He had one wing that was much longer than the other; and if the short wing had been longer, so would this tale!"

Four years of outlasting the misery and suffering in the trenches and exemplary action on the battlefields earned Jean Sarochar new status among his French comrades-in-arms as both a hero and a storyteller. He was one of the lucky ones who emerged from the relentless artillery bombardments with a single permanent scar of a minor shrapnel wound in his leg. Unlike the men whose homecoming would be noted by an engraved marble memorial honoring "Enfants de Mendive, Morts pour la France, 1914–18," prominently placed on the church portal where all attending the daily or Sunday Mass would be reminded of their sacrifice, Jean returned with a pension and a chestful of medals. Just as important, he bore a new collection of dramatic stories in which *he* was the brave and resourceful protagonist who had outfoxed the powerful enemy.

But why was a decorated shepherd-soldier who was returning from the Great War met with such a disappointing reception in his own village? Perhaps it was too painful for those who had lost family members to hear the stories of Jean's exploits. Of the twenty men from Mendive killed in the war, twelve were under thirty years old and the rest between thirty and forty-two. They were not youths but rather the village's fathers and fathers-to-be, comprising more than 5 percent of the village's population. So great was France's loss — 1.5 million dead and an even greater number nonfatally gassed or seriously maimed — that during the postwar years, honoring the fallen took precedence over recognizing the still living. Only on the national holidays of Quatorze Juillet or Armistice Day, when veterans' groups assembled for the large parades in St.-Jean-Pied-de-Port, could a soldier like Jean enjoy the full glory of his achievement.[2]

Perhaps the repeated tales of a war in a faraway "land of wolves" led to waning interest by Jean's neighbors. Perhaps they considered his moments of valor and daring exploits nothing more than simple demonstrations of manhood. In the Basque border culture, where smuggling was both sport and livelihood, eluding one's captors was a basic skill learned in youth. Perhaps Jean's monologues did not sit well with listeners accustomed to a narrator as transmitter of wisdom rather than narrator as protagonist.

Jean's credibility was also a problem. His efforts to promote a new image as the hero-storyteller most likely only confirmed the villagers' sense of him as a blagueur and buffoon. It is unclear whether or not he was given the epithet of *le grand menteur* (the big liar) before his departure, but his status as the local misfit was probably already well established. Jean's tall tales lacked the verbal genius of the bard-storyteller so admired within Basque culture. Of numerous ancient oral traditions, Basque *bertsolari* (improvised poetry) was considered the ultimate art form. Usually staged as a verbal sparring match that involved two contestants spinning out spontaneous verse on a given subject, the *bertsolari* was an entertainment fixture of formal social events such as weddings as well as everyday, informal gatherings at the local inn. Topics could be serious (the life of a married man versus the life of a bachelor) or frivolous (the respective merits of a hoe and a scythe). The audience thrived on the humor, imagery, and frequently caustic repartee, and would listen for hours to these displays of wit.

Jean's storytelling style and his eccentricities alternately amused and annoyed people in the village, particularly his quixotic mind and his lackadaisical attitude toward work. His habit of constantly talking to himself — a defense mechanism he developed to survive the stress of the trenches that he could not shed — was viewed as another irritating idiosyncrasy.

The local population attributed these character flaws to his lineage. In Basque tradition social identity derives from association with the family house. In the province of Basse-Navarre the physical household was such an essential organizing element of community life that many houses bore a decorative stone lintel, inscribed with the property name, over the entry.[3] Gravestones in the church cemetery, etched with the same designation, grouped families across generations. Officialdegia (translated as "home of an artisan") was the domain of the Sarochar family tragically marked by a history of mental problems. Manech's youngest brother, Raymond, was considered a harmless simpleton. His older sister Marie was mildly retarded, and her marriage to Louis Etchepare, a man known for his raging temper, only added to the family's woes. In the words of one of the neighbors, the family was "un peu sauvage" (a bit brutish).

The brother-in-law's unpredictable outbreaks of violence made life in Officialdegia difficult for the other occupants of the household. It is not surprising that Manech found the spare comforts of his family's mountain dwelling a more inviting home upon his return from the war. Indeed, its second-story sleeping loft was a rare amenity in a rustic shepherd's hut. When other men would migrate back to their families in the valley, Jean chose to stay on through the winter months, descending to the village only on occasion.

Jean relished this elevated vantage point where, unobserved and unsupervised, he could constantly survey the distant movement of humans and animals in the vast mountain landscape: the caravans of men and mules heading up to the Iraty Forest, the drift of the sheep from pasture to pasture across the valley, and the aerial ballets of vultures circling and ready to devour some dead animal. There, perched on high and guarded by a faithful sheepdog, Jean could pretend to be lord of the terrain. In fact, were it not for the arrival in the valley of two enterprising brothers in the early 1920s, Manech might have contentedly lived out the rest of his days as a bachelor-shepherd, wandering the ancient hills at liberty to let his imagination spin a cocoon of heroic fantasies.

Chapter 2

Mendive, France, lies at the heel of the Laurhibar River Valley, the southernmost of a string of small villages spanning a broad alluvial terrace that stretches from St.-Jean-Pied-de-Port to the foothills of the Pyrenees. Of the geopolitical divisions of the French Basque province of Basse-Navarre, the Pays de Cize is perhaps the most richly endowed with archaeological and artistic stonework; of the region's three major valleys the Laurhibar boasts the premier collection of ancient monuments. The dolmens scattered on the hillsides above Mendive attest to the arrival of a pastoral culture around 2000 B.C., a people whose seasonal migration from the lowlands to the mountain pastures established the rhythm of *transhumance* that continued to shape the lives of the valley's residents in the twentieth century. Were these waves of Neolithic peoples of Indo-European origin from farther east on the continent the ancestors of Jean Sarochar? While no conclusive proof ties these Iron Age emigrants to the Basques, without doubt they blazed the routes across the mountain passes of the Pyrenees that would be used by later European peoples seeking access to the Iberian peninsula.[1]

The Pays de Cize first became a strategic site during the Roman empire, both because of the relative ease of passage over the mountains there and because of the region's abundant supplies of clay and wood. St.-Jean-le-Vieux, a village situated at the heart of the plain six kilometers northwest of Mendive, was a major depot and fortification on the road connecting Dax to the north and Pamplona, Spain, in the south. Beginning in the tenth century Christian pilgrims on their way to Santiago de Compostela also traversed the valley, making St.-Jean-le-Vieux and other surrounding villages a stopover point.[2] Wayside stone crosses, various houses identified as "*Ospitalia*," and a hospital operated as an infirmary and shelter by the religious Knights of Malta in St.-Jean-le-Vieux evidence their passage. Mendive's St.-Sauveur, originally a sacred pagan site and then a small Carolingian sanctuary, evolved into the "hospitau de Laurhibarre" in the thirteenth century to harbor exhausted wayfarers.

In the seventeenth century the region drew the interest of numerous empire-building monarchs, not as a transportation route to Spain but for its rich forest resources available in the wall of mountains above the valley. The humid, rainy but mild climate of the inland section of the Basses-Pyrénées, together with the relatively low altitude of the peaks (few rose above 1,200 meters, or 4,000 feet), provided an ideal growing environment for pines, oaks, and beeches. The Forêt d'Iraty, an 180-square-kilometer (45,000-acre) virgin timberland that blanketed the south-facing flanks of the Pyrenees along the France-Spain border, was a cache waiting to be exploited. The French navy, which had already depleted the timber resources farther east in the central Pyrenees, considered the vast stands of old-growth pine of particular importance. In 1629 officers of the royal navy visited the region and more than sixty giant pines were felled and sent to the shipyards of Rochefort to the north for use as ship masts.[3]

For two hundred years the Basque shipbuilding industry used the Iraty Forest as a source of beech and pine.[4] Geography actually favored Spain: 150 square kilometers (37,000 acres) of the forest lay in Spanish territory, while only 30 square kilometers (7,400 acres) lay on the French side. Moreover, the headwaters of the Rio Iraty, a tributary of the Ebro River, were in the forest, thus allowing the Spanish to float the wood via a series of manmade locks directly down the waterways to the Aragon plains. Mountain chains make imprecise international borders, though, and beginning in the eighteenth century the competition for timber sparked a series of disputes between France and Spain.[5] In 1856 a treaty to avert war finally resolved the conflict, which delineated a portion of the Rio Iraty as the official boundary.

In the nineteenth century local demand for beechwood for charcoal for the iron forges in the region (including one in Mendive) supplanted the preeminence of the naval market.[6] From 1847 to 1866 extensive cutting took place in certain sections of the forest. However, by the time of Jean

Sarochar's birth in 1892 there had been neither the large-scale logging in the surrounding mountains nor industrial activity in the valley for more than twenty-five years. Easy availability of pine from other lowland regions had essentially eliminated the market for wood from the forests of the Pyrenees, and the depletion of mineral deposits and competition from larger metalworking plants had led to an economic downturn. Mendive reverted to an isolated backcountry community of scattered farms, and the period of natural regeneration within the French portion of the Forêt d'Iraty took over.

The most prominent vestige of the valley's former industrial activity was a dirt road that paralleled the twisting course of the Laurhibar River from St.-Jean-le-Vieux to Mendive, which had been constructed in the first half of the nineteenth century as part of the economic development of the region. This transportation corridor caused a second commercial hub to spring up away from the traditional node of the community — the parish church, parsonage, and cemetery — in both Mendive and Lecumberry. The road, running right in front of Officialdegia, in turn brought a new breed of pilgrim to the village in the first two decades of the twentieth century. While the Atlantic coastal resorts of Biarritz and St.-Jean-de-Luz and the nearby thermal springs of Cambo-les-Bains were the principal attractions of the Basque country to European notables and fashionable travelers, excursions farther inland to visit authentic mountain villages had a certain appeal for more adventurous tourists. Mendive and Lecumberry served as a staging ground for guided packtrips to more remote mountain sites. As a boy living just down the road from the inn and outfitting service operated by Dominique Esponda, Jean Sarochar observed the departure and return of numerous small parties and their donkey porters as they traveled to and from Ahusky, a mineral spring known for its curative powers for kidney ailments. For centuries Ahusky had been a pilgrimage destination for Basques from the provinces of Basse-Navarre and Soule to the east. The combination of the new vogue for exploring the Pyrenees, train service from Bayonne, road access from St.-Jean-Pied-de-Port, and lodging at one of the rustic hotels at Ahusky had widened the tourist possibilities of the region to include well-heeled cure-seekers and coastal residents alike.[7]

Hardy backroading visitors to the Basque hinterland likely would have been surprised to discover that Mendive also boasted one of the earliest local electric generating plants in France. Monsieur Ardohain, known by the nickname "Bainam," owned property on the right bank of the Laurhibar just below the main road, where he built a dam to operate a small-scale power station. By the time Jean left for the trenches electric lights were flickering in the more prosperous homes and establishments in proximity to the road from Mendive all the way to Ahaxe, three kilometers up the valley.

Following the First World War a dramatic population exodus occurred from the inland towns and villages in the Pays Basque, especially to the chain of cities from Bayonne to Hendaye along the Atlantic coast.[8] Mendive, however, was an anomaly in this demographic trend: due to the establishment of a major new timber business in the valley in the 1920s the number of inhabitants increased by nearly one-third. This industrial enterprise fell far short of its economic promise in the early years of operation but later would play a vital — and unexpected — role in World War II resistance efforts in the Pyrenees.

In 1923 two Frenchmen came to the backwater village of Mendive to start planning the construction of what would become the longest mountain cableway in Europe. The entrepreneurial Pédelucq brothers, Alexis and Paul, had established a network of lumbering and milling operations in the Landes, a vast area of pine plantations just to the north of the Basque country.[9] The brothers envisioned the new venture in Mendive as a major addition to their expanding empire in the Pyrenees that had begun with the recent construction of a sawmill in Oloron-Ste.-Marie, a town situated in the province of Béarn (to the east of the Pays Basque).

In the dispersed but small world of the wood products industry to which the Pédelucqs belonged, directors and managers of lumber companies in Europe had not forgotten that Europe's largest beech forest was growing high in the mountains above Mendive. Each year representatives of local, regional, national, and international logging companies competed at the annual spring and autumn auctions for timber rights to parcels selected by the Service des Eaux et Forêts (forest service) for harvest.[10] The gatherings, held in regional centers such as Bayonne and Oloron-Ste.-Marie, were highly charged commercial events as well as occasions to socialize and swap gossip about the success and failure of various timber-cutting projects.

Among the legendary high-risk ventures that had failed was the construction of a funicular to convey the wood from the Forêt d'Iraty down to Mendive. Since the waning years of the nineteenth century a series of Swiss companies had attempted to engineer a cable railway but had eventually abandoned their efforts, due to the tremendous investment and the difficulty of constructing tracks on the terrain. The inaccessible location of the forest on a high plateau within the mountain chain seemed to pose an insurmountable challenge for renewed large-scale commercial logging.[11]

The growing market for railroad ties in the 1920s and the rot-resistant character of beechwood were strong incentives to the Pédelucq brothers to conquer nature's obstacles. The pair contacted Hans Bernard, director of the most recent Swiss firm to attempt the construction of a mechanical relay system, and enlisted his technological expertise in erecting an aerial cableway. Bernard dispatched "Maître Jean," a serious but amiable pipe-smoking engineer, to assess the possibilities of such a project and design a suitable installation. Maître Jean proposed a tri-cable system — an ingenious configuration of wires and pulleys that would rely on counter-balance; through careful calculation the weight of the logs descending from a mountain loading station would in effect pull the empty trolleys back up the mountain once the logs were removed at the valley terminus.

By 1924, convinced of the merits of the approach and having easily secured a contract from the forest service to harvest portions of the remote woodland region, the Pédelucqs began recruiting the international work-force necessary for the ambitious undertaking that came to be known as Compagnie d'Iraty. Maître Jean became company engineer and director of operations. Among the first specialists to be hired were the three Moretti brothers from Bergamo, Italy, all of them renowned cable operators. Maître Jean had previously worked on projects in the Alps with the Morettis and knew the value of their experience and teamwork for the daring and dangerous installation. Led by François Moretti, the senior member of the clan, they used only the most basic of surveying equipment to plot the course and erect the pylons for the ten-mile cable course from the valley floor to the Plateau of Iraty, in addition to a small network of secondary feeder lines located at sites deep within the surrounding forest.

Equally critical in the start-up process were the lumberjacks to fell the enormous quantities of timber needed for the various structures to be built in the mountains. Spanish Basque woodcutters from the Salazar Valley on the south side of the Pyrenees were a ready source of labor—they were well organized crews with decades of experience harvesting the beech and pine resources of the Iraty Forest.[12] In 1924 the Compagnie d'Iraty began contracting with Senor Zabaleta, who recruited nearly 150 men for the logging work.[13] During the three years of start-up Zabaleta's crews of burly woodsmen constructed the upper cable terminus and relay stations, the colony of post-and-beam buildings for company employees on the plateau, and a rustic cabin deep in the forest for the forest rangers.

Occasionally their families came up to visit the crews, but almost never did the Spanish Basques descend to the Laurhibar Valley to socialize. Though they shared a common language and heritage with the French Basques, their lifestyle seemed primitive to the shepherds of Mendive who only had contact with them during the summer months when the Frenchmen pastured their flocks high in the mountains. Especially curious to the local shepherds was the Spanish lumberjacks' practice of carrying spoons on their belts and using them at mealtimes to eat from a communal pot. Clannishness was so deeply ingrained in the Basque *mentalité* that each village felt superior to its neighbors and even a fellow countryman was likely to encounter suspicion. Indeed, distrust of outsiders ran so deep that a Basque proverb warned, "Who goes far to marry is either fooling or fooled."

From his family's mountain hut Jean Sarochar would have had an excellent lookout to watch the progress of the installation of the pylons up the slopes on the opposite side of the valley toward the Chapel of St.-Sauveur, one of the key relay sites in the cable system. By 1926, in the meadow just below Officialdegia in Mendive, an even more dramatic transformation was underway. The Pédelucqs had purchased for their new sawmill complex a flat, roughly four-acre site that bordered the main valley road on the east and the Laurhibar River on the west.

The Pédelucq brothers envisioned the sawmill of Mendive as one of France's most modern and efficient facilities. Once again it was a matter of engaging a well-respected team of technicians that could both build the structures and operate the machinery. The disappearance of lumber enterprises from the valley in the nineteenth century had led to the lack of a local workforce of skilled sawyers.[14] As the cable installation neared completion Paul Pédelucq drew on his contacts with independent and multi-talented sawmill operators from the Landes, who worked as blacksmiths, mechanics, and carpenters.

In contrast to the years it took to first survey the land, clear a path, and erect the cable system, the collection of factory buildings on the valley floor took only months to construct. The company purchased much of the pine and oak necessary for the post-and-beam truss construction of the sheds and hangars from Mendive landowners whose property lay in the path of the cable. A resident of Mendive remembers her grandfather selling fifty oaks to Paul Pédelucq for the new installation. To the Basques, who loathed the notion of debt, harvestable trees represented a savings account to be tapped for major expenditures, such as a marriage dowry or the financial settlement to be made between an "anointed" new *jaun* and the "unanointed" siblings at the death of their parents.

The local Basque population played a relatively minor role during the complex and lengthy construction process of the sawmill. The Compagnie d'Iraty did enlist the assistance of carpenters, masons, blacksmiths, and other artisans from the valley for construction of a boardinghouse for the workers in Lecumberry and for a new house for Paul Pédelucq's young family just across the road from Officialdegia. Only when it came time to haul and raise the lines of cable up the mountainside did men from the valley leave their farms to join the monumental effort. François Moretti and his team installed the thirty-six kilometer (twenty-two-mile) moving cable in sections along the series of relay points — first to Partida, then to St.-Sauveur, then up to the highest point at the Col de Burdincurutcheta (nine hundred meters, or three thousand feet), and then down to the plateau (seven hundred meters, or twenty-four hundred feet). However, the two heavier stationary lines, each eighteen kilometers long, could not be segmented. Hundreds of men carrying the steel cable on their shoulders, in addition to dozens of teams of mules and oxen, formed a rhythmic caravan from the valley floor up the mountain slopes. Not since the twelfth century, when legions of pilgrims had trooped through the valley, had there been such a spectacle.

Residents of the valley quickly recognized that most of the benefit from the new lumbermill would be derived by supplying secondary products and services — property or building material for the Pédelucq factory, provisions for animals, or spirits for the employees to the *maketoak* (Basque for "strangers"). The younger generation especially appreciated the excitement and worldliness that the foreigners brought to their isolated village. Aurélie Erraçerret, daughter of the local innkeeper in Lecumberry, remembers an Italian orchestra, made up of Pédelucq company employees, would march from Mendive to Lecumberry and provide music for Saturday evening dances—much to the horror of the local clergy. Constantly vigilant for outside influences that could dilute ethnic identity or threaten the control of the Catholic Church, the priests only sanctioned choreographed Basque folk dances as proper social activities.[15]

While the *maketoak* never became integrated into the tightly knit fabric of the communities in the valley, certainly an indication of their acceptance was the courtship and eventual marriage of Henriette Esponda, daughter of Mendive's mayor and innkeeper, to François Moretti's son, Angèle. By 1927 the Compagnie d'Iraty had more than 400 people in its employ: 150 in the woods, 50 on the plateau, and 200 in the factory. Mendive, long the cradle of ancient legends and mysteries, seemed on its way to rebirth as a modern industrial center.

Chapter 3

The last component of the logging enterprise to be completed, and the first to make use of the beech logs relayed down the mountain via the cable from the Forêt d'Iraty, was a private railroad line running from the factory to St.-Jean-Pied-de-Port, the commercial junction for the region. Once it purchased a log hauler (a combination steam traction engine and steam locomotive) and flatbed trailers for transporting the stock to the depot, the company possessed both a delivery system for the raw material and a shipping mechanism for its finished products. It was time to celebrate.

The formal inauguration of the plant, held just before the 1928 spring *transhumance*, drew people not only from the Pays Basque but from all parts of France, including the project's financiers from Paris, departmental authorities from the forest service, and a variety of political officials from the region. Participants in the festivities gathered for a special Mass at the church in Lecumberry, a two-hundred-year-old edifice more spacious than Mendive's modest seventeenth-century structure. In a fashion typical of the Basque country, the interior of the Lecumberry parish church combined architectural simplicity with lively folk carving. To an outsider the almost theatrical presentation and the quantity of wood would have made a striking impression, but the seating arrangement was probably even more memorable to the non-Basques in the crowd: the women, cloaked in their almost full-length black crepe mantels, occupied the ground floor while the men sat in the second-story wooden gallery that projected from the back of the church.

Monsieur Mendury, the parish priest, officiated at the service, which combined a medley of prayers in Latin and hymns sung in Basque—the women's warbling voices initiating the melody, then amplified and layered by a male chorus of two- and three-part harmony that boomed from the gallery above. Though reserved in their conversation, Basques could be emotional in song. So magnificent was the responsive singing that it mattered little that the Pédelucq family and the other *maketoak* could not understand the Basque lyrics; all felt honored and blessed. The rousing tunes of the Moretti family's accordions at the feast held afterward at Dominique Esponda's inn in Mendive—music that was enjoyed by all but the village priest—provided a rousing finale to the day.

Photographs show Jean Sarochar among the Basques attending the inauguration ceremony. Despite the proximity of the Sarochar property to the new sawmill, Jean had been only a spectator throughout its construction process. It is doubtful that he joined in the march up to the Iraty plateau for the installation of the cable. His independent spirit felt little interest in tasks that demanded both sustained exertion and close supervision. Watching flocks of clouds float by from atop his mountain perch was far preferable to carrying forty to sixty pounds of steel cable on his shoulder for several hours.

Jean instead relished his new assignment as the substitute postman for the valley. His status as a wounded World War I veteran earned him the job, which entailed delivering the mail (a few newspapers and letters) on Sundays. The cap he got to wear, the bicycle he was given to ride and, most of all, the opportunity to entertain the people on the route with his collection of tall tales all were more important than the job's monetary compensation. When asked about Jean's performance people in the village today raise their eyebrows and chuckle about the peculiarities of the storyteller-postman. As one longtime resident remarked about him, "He was a comedian. An idiot? No. Crazy? Yes."

To Jean the greatest dividend of the arrival of the Compagnie d'Iraty must have been the presence of newcomers in the valley, particularly a small collection of young children. The majority of transplants were single young men or others who had left their families at home in another part of France. A smaller contingent of the company's employees, however, did come as family units; each of the Moretti brothers, for instance, had five or six children in tow. Within a few years of settling in Lecumberry and when their grown sons and daughters had married, three generations of the Moretti family were living in the community.

Paul Pédelucq and his wife also put down new roots soon after their arrival, then welcomed the birth of their son, Léon, in 1924, Henri in 1926, and daughter, Cilotte, in 1929. Jean most likely had his first contact with the Pédelucq family as the mail carrier, and probably instantly charmed the youngsters with his humor and mischievous antics. The village jester had at last found an enthusiastic and captive audience.

Paul Pédelucq directed the plant's production and marketing with the same relentless energy and drive he had shown during the construction of the factory and cable system. Several regional railroad companies (which in the later thirties became a part of the national railroad corporation, the Société Nationale des Chemins de Fer or SNCF) were the principal customers for the lumber. Besides the performance of the cable, the efficient choreography of the workers, and the skill of the sawyers in maximizing the use of the raw lumber, several external forces had an important influence on the company's success.

A set of charters established during medieval times that delineated property rights for common pasture and woodland within a region or *pays* was still the law of the land.[1] The Iraty Forest, designated as public land, belonged to two of these ancient political divisions. The Pays de Cize, encompassing Mendive and nineteen other communes, controlled 1,050 hectares (2,500 acres) in the forest; the Pays de Soule, a union of forty-three communes, controlled 1,250 hectares (more than 3,100 acres). The French forest service managed the land's resources and the two districts each received a percentage from the sale of the harvest.

Each year a team of rangers, under the direction of a forest service inspector, spent several days marking the trees that could be cut. Good relations with the inspectors and their teams were vital to ensuring a generous marking of trees ready for harvest. Also according to the centuries-old charter the first six meters of each tree belonged to either the Pays de

Cize or the Pays de Soule, which meant that the further down the trunk the designation of the six-meter length, the more wood would remain for Compagnie d'Iraty. The company's construction of a mountain cabin for the forest service to use (or enjoyed by the mill owner's family) clearly was a calculated gesture of good will toward these civil servants.

It was equally important to curry the favor of the procuring agents of the railway companies.[2] Before an order could be shipped an agent would arrive at the factory to verify the correct dimensions and quality of each railroad tie. One by one a team of company employees would rotate the piece of timber, each weighing over two hundred pounds, so that all four sides could be inspected. Once marked by the agent with a brand, the workers restacked the ties by category. It was a tedious task that the mill's owners made more agreeable by providing copious hospitality at the local inns. The more cordial the relationship between the company and the agent the less likely pieces would be rejected and the greater percentage of stock would be classified as superior quality.

No matter how carefully crafted these public relations strategies were, however, the wild card was always the weather. The combination of the region's proximity to the Atlantic Ocean and the terrain of the Basses-Pyrénées created a temperate but temperamental atmospheric condition. Heavy snowfall in the forest in November could shut down the lumber camp, and the mules would refuse to work if a hailstorm hit. Mendive and the surrounding mountains experienced a range of temperatures related to the seasons, but it was the winds that governed the calendar and the locals' daily life. Each type of wind had a special name and personality. For the Basques the harsh south wind from Africa that howled for days on end during the autumn and winter months not only could wreak havoc with its strong gusts, it was feared, too, for its disorienting effect on human emotions.

The gusty winds, the violent mountain thunderstorms that erupted in the summer, and the extended rainy periods in the spring all added a further challenge to the smooth operation of the thirty-six-kilometer cableway. The winds were of greatest concern to the Italian cable crew; indeed, sometime during the first months of operation a runaway log that had been dislodged from the lower cable en route from St.-Sauveur to Partida crashed into the pylons there and necessitated a complete reconstruction of the Partida relay station. The veteran workforce was undaunted by the mishap, and no other major disaster snared the ambitious plans of the company during the first season of operation.

By the summer of 1928 the factory was in full production mode. What had once been a pasture had been transformed into a dense labyrinth of hangars, sheds, and stacks of lumber. The sounds and smells of the mill permeated the valley. Nearby residents were awakened by the mechanical chant and clatter of the equipment and engines rather than cries from the barnyard.

To assure smooth functioning of the company's three dispersed activity zones, almost every day Paul Pédelucq journeyed up to the Plateau d'Iraty. With no road to follow he crawled and bumped his way up and down the slopes in a custom-built vehicle fitted with automobile wheels in the front and a half-track tread in the rear. Occasionally he would load his family into the vehicle and head for an excursion up in the mountains. The ranger's hut provided overnight lodging for these expeditions which, of course, thrilled Pédelucq's young children. Even the 1928–1929 Michelin guide to the Basque country made mention of the unusual all-terrain rig. Despite the efforts already underway to exploit the resources of the forest, the guide touted the Forêt d'Iraty as a virtual wilderness still populated by bears, wolves, and boars. (In fact, during the construction of the cable system the Morettis had come face-to-face with some of these mountain creatures.) The guide gave a one-star rating to an excursion from Mendive up to the mysterious forest, indicating the possibility of catching a free ride up the mountain with "M. Péageluc" as a faster alternative to the three- or four-hour guided pack trip organized by Dominique Esponda.

The cable became a phenomenon worthy of interest in itself. Surviving from the early years of the sawmill's history are a collection of picture postcards — souvenirs purchased by company employees, residents, and tourists alike — that include images of the sawmill's aerial transport system in operation and several of workers in the mill. The cable system became a landmark noted on Michelin maps of the Pays Basque.

Paul Pédelucq, confident of the success of the Mendive plant, then undertook construction of another mill to exploit the beech and oak in the Forêt d'Hayra farther to the west along the chain of the Basses-Pyrénées. Located in Banca, a remote mountain village in the narrow Vallée des Aldudes, this plant was smaller and simpler, but like Mendive's it required construction of a railroad line to export the wood products. By the end of the decade the Pédelucq brothers' lumbering empire included five plants. Alexis oversaw the mills in the Landes and Paul managed the three operations in the Pyrenees.

The first setback to the company occurred in the summer of 1928. The Mendive sawmill used charcoal, which also was produced up in the mountains, to fuel the steam generators. The Spaniards prepared it by slowly burning the branches and limbs in deep trenches; the charred wood was then chipped into small pieces that were loaded into jute sacks and relayed to the mill via the cableway. One day a very hot fire broke out in the steam boiler of the electric generating plant. Creosote buildup, a hazard of burning this type of combustible material in a very humid environment, was probably the culprit. Miraculously, the capricious winds that so dominated the valley's weather were absent that day, and the fire was contained to a small area within the mill. In a matter of weeks factory workers had cleaned up the ruins and rebuilt the company's power station.

A year later disaster struck the operation. To avoid breakdown of the cableway system, every day the Morettis inspected the lines to assure proper tension and to check for any damage or weakness to the support structures. Men were also always in position at the relay stations to respond to any overhead malfunction that might occur during the cable's daily operation; the company installed a telephone line to facilitate communication between the stations and the two cable terminals. Work stoppages did occur on a frequent basis since the loaded carriage could and often did derail from the moving line as it passed up and over the glides on the cross-members of the pylons. The force of the mountain winds, especially the south wind, also could cause the apparatus to twist and became disconnected from the moving wire. A snarl in the system could force the line to jump off the pulley wheels at either terminus. Early in the morning of 9 July 1929 Maître Jean, Paul Pédelucq, and Angèle Moretti were troubleshooting a problem in the flow of the moving cable line around the pulleys at the valley station. While attempting to fix the equipment Pédelucq got his shirt sleeve caught by the cable as it moved between the two pulleys. The force of the turning wheels pulled him against and under the machinery and he was instantly crushed to death.

More than seven decades later the tragedy still is painfully etched in the memories of the children of Paul Pédelucq. News of the director's death was so vivid and shocking that even today those who were children at the time in the village (sons and daughters of factory employees as well as those of local farm families) can remember where they were when they heard about the accident. Pédelucq's death was a tremendous loss to the young company. His dynamic leadership had been crucial to its early success. Alexis Pédelucq was convinced, however, that the Mendive plant and the other mills in the Pyrenees were well enough established that he could direct them from afar. Alexis therefore appointed Maître Jean as the manager of the operation in the Laurhibar Valley. Throughout the early 1930s production at the Mendive sawmill remained relatively strong, but each year profits decreased. As the worldwide depression took its toll the company saw the number of orders dwindle. By 1934 the company, still facing repayment of the enormous capital investment, was in serious straits.

Paul Pédelucq's death also left his wife — a widow at thirty-one years old — with three children under five years old. After the July accident Madame Pédelucq returned to the family villa near Peyrehorade in the Landes. To maintain a family presence in Mendive, though, she and the children vacationed in the mountains in the summers from 1930 to 1934.

Trips up to Jean Sarochar's hut were a favorite activity for the youngsters. Depending on the season, a visit to Jean's enclave could promise a hunting expedition in the woods for mushrooms, chestnuts, or berries and, of course, nonstop narration of stories. Though Jean had a standard stock of Basque legends and World War I tales, he frequently would spin out a yarn based on incidents he had witnessed or experienced in the mountains. Jean also took great delight in leading games of hide-and-seek around the small mountain property. Henri Pédelucq remembered that during several visits Jean prepared for the children a dish of *taloa*, a grilled cornmeal cake dipped in fresh sheep's milk that was a staple of the Basque diet. Henri would watch in wonder as Jean would remove an iron nugget heated in the open fireplace of the hut and then, using a pair of tongs, immerse it in the pot of liquid — a cooking practice dating back to the Iron Age. For young Henri this simple shepherd, whose blue eyes were the only bit of color surrounded by sooty, dark clothing, was an enchanting storybook character come to life.

Madame Pédelucq, however, was not completely at ease in Mendive. Though the villagers and employees treated her with respect she still felt isolated and exposed as a female *maketo*. Thus Jean's role as playmate and babysitter for her children soon took on another dimension. On numerous evenings the children of the Moretti and Pessenti families who lived nearby in the village would gather at the Pédelucq house to be entertained by Jean's storytelling. His comedic talents mesmerized the children and sent them into peals of laughter. Images of this twinkle-eyed, sprightly man standing on a table spinning out tale after tale are firmly fixed in the memories of those who participated in the fun-filled gatherings.

Jean's regular visits made him the natural candidate for the watchman Madame Pédelucq was seeking. At her request he would spend the better part of the night on guard at their house once his soirees with the children had concluded. In the early hours of the morning he would leave and sleep for a few hours at Officialdegia and then ascend back to his mountain home. If for some reason he could not make it to the Pédelucq home he would send his brother Raymond as his substitute.

Facing imminent bankruptcy and suspecting general mismanagement, Madame Pédelucq decided to take a more active role in the family business. The Pédelucqs thus extended their annual stay in the Basque country and spent the fall, winter, and spring of 1934–35 in Mendive. Over that year the mill shut down and then reopened with a much smaller workforce. Railroad ties continued to be the company's principal product, but the factory also was now using scrap to make chair parts, wooden shoes, and furniture squares (uncut blocks for shaping finished products). However, the scaled-down routine and the intervention of Madame Pédelucq were not enough to salvage the overextended company. In the final days only a dozen or so workers were on site to operate the saws and shaping machines. By the end of the decade the mill went idle.

During the dozen years of the sawmill's activity the local communes had completed paving the main valley road. Along its course a cluster of small shops, grocery stores, and bakeries had sprouted in Mendive and Lecumberry. In 1931 Pedro Hernandez, a Spaniard new to the area, had founded a thriving business serving meals to the workers from the nearby factory in the hotel formerly owned by Dominique Esponda. The shutdown of the plant and the departure of most of the workforce meant an uncertain future for his and other local enterprises.

Surprisingly, a large influx of Spanish Civil War refugees into the Laur-hibar Valley did not come on the heels of the exodus of the factory workers in the late 1930s. Of the five hundred thousand exiles that had fled into France after the war, almost one hundred thousand were Spanish Basques.[3] And, despite their ethnic ties, their arrival in the French Basque provinces was greeted with limited sympathy if not outright resentment. Especially among the conservative, devoutly Catholic communities of the rural Pays Basque, the alliance that their Spanish brethren had made with the Communist and anarchist forces in defense of the republican cause was regarded with great disdain.[4] Concern that Basque cities and towns were being overrun by dangerous political and criminal elements was also openly expressed in the press and by public officials.

Nevertheless, schools for refugee children were established in several locations in the French Basque country, including a facility at an abandoned chateau in St.-Jean-Pied-de-Port. Many new arrivals to the Pyrenees were housed in provisional camps and drafted into the Groupement de Travailleurs Etrangers (Foreign Workers Groups) to be laborers on French government projects in the mines and forests.[5] Though the Iraty Forest was not among these work sites, the outbreak of World War II soon brought the next wave of *maketoak* to Mendive—and, among them, a Belgian with an audacious plan to revive the defunct mill.

Part Two

Man of Vision

(*Previous page*) A portrait of Charles Schepens
that Cette painted of her husband during
their six-month residence in England, 1936.
(courtesy Mrs. Charles Schepens)

Chapter 4

Before dawn one morning in mid-October 1940 two Nazi officers arrived at 72 chaussée de Haecht in Brussels, Belgium, to arrest Dr. Charles Schepens. Dr. Schepens remembers that as they rifled through his home and medical office, they commented on the "beautiful porcelain and the orderliness of the rooms, which convinced them that my wife must have been German." Dr. Schepens was charged with owning a bus that ferried Allied pilots out of the country, and was taken to the ancient prison fortress at St.-Gilles on the outskirts of the city. At the prison he was placed in a small cell, completely out of contact with his wife, Cette, who had just given birth to their second child, Luc. During his imprisonment Charles was interrogated twice at the Gestapo office on rue Traversière, just two blocks from their house. After ten days he was abruptly released with no explanation.

Dr. Schepens had not yet begun his work in the Belgian underground service, but the incident propelled him into action. His arrest capped a year of uncertainty and upheaval that had begun with Hitler's invasion of Poland on 1 September 1939. King Léopold III had immediately declared Belgium's neutrality and mobilized the country's defenses to insure the inviolability of its borders. Charles, a twenty-eight-year-old ophthalmologist and reserve air force medical officer, was among the 50 percent of the country's male population between the ages of twenty and forty called for active duty. That fall several alerts about an impending invasion (all of which turned out to be false alarms) had sent Lieutenant Schepens off with his unit to a secret airfield at Neerwinden near the German border.

During what came to be known as the eight-month "phony war," officials of the Reich continued publicly to reassure the Belgian population that the country would not be attacked as long as it remained neutral.[1] Despite intelligence reports of German troop movements and even the capture of plans for an invasion, Belgians misled themselves so effectively that during a dinner party in Brussels on 9 May 1940, an erudite friend of Charles and his wife, a lawyer who prided himself on reading six newspapers a day, could definitively pronounce that there would be no war. The next morning what had seemed inevitable to Charles since September came to pass: without a declaration of war the armored tanks of the Sixth and Seventh Division of the German army swept into Belgium and followed much the same path through the central section of the country that the German kaiser's forces had taken in 1914.

Despite recent attempts to fortify its defenses, the Belgian military was no match for the technologically superior forces of the Third Reich. The small Belgian air force was put out of commission in one week. Within eighteen days the Germans completely occupied the country. During the fighting Charles's unit, which initially comprised one thousand men, moved from the airfield near Neerwinden to Brussels, on to Ghent, then to Ypres, and finally south into France. So ill-equipped were the Belgian troops during the chaotic retreat that Charles used his own car as a means of transport.

Also on the run were members of the Belgian government cabinet, who broke with King Léopold III when he refused to change the policy of neutrality to join the Allied opposition.[2] The government-in-exile first set up its headquarters in Paris but was forced to relocate further south as the Germans continued their relentless advance through the French provinces. While the ministers were temporarily in residence in Poitiers, Charles and others from his unit, which had arrived in nearby Tours, met with representatives of the mobile government, but no plan of action had yet been formulated. A few days later, when the government officials fled to Bordeaux, the unit sent another delegation to receive new orders. "No answer, no orders, no planes" was the frustrating message they carried back.

Belgium's armed forces and ministers were not the only ones in flight. More than 1.5 million people, almost one-quarter of the nation's population, fled to France in mid-May 1940. They scattered to relatives and friends in cities and villages throughout the country, or anywhere they could find safe shelter. Cette Schepens and the couple's two-year-old daughter, Claire, joined Cette's parents and other members of the Vander Eecken family in Ghent; traveling in a small caravan of cars they made it as far as Niort, a city west of Poitiers, in mid-May. They sought out a local *notaire* (solicitor) who helped them find temporary shelter in an empty house.[3] From other Belgians passing by on their way southward Cette learned that Charles and his brother Yves, also a member of the Belgian military medical corps, were both alive in France. The same information network of Belgians on the run informed Charles of the whereabouts of his wife and child, and he briefly stopped to see them when his unit went through the area.

On 28 May 1940 King Léopold III capitulated to the Germans while the French vainly tried to stem the invasion. Charles's unit continued to evacuate as far south as Moissac, near Toulouse, where many Belgian civilians and military personnel were congregating. Finally in mid-June the unit's commanding officer, whom Charles characterized as "an instrument of the book of regulations," determined that since the Belgian army had surrendered they should follow suit.[4] Charles and three others in the unit could not accept being taken as prisoners of war. When they refused to comply with the colonel's order he reported them as deserters from the regiment.

The four officers in Charles's car headed to Port-Vendres on the Mediterranean to procure passage to various foreign destinations. On their trip southward they came upon a new Sabena airplane abandoned in a vineyard. The discovery was tempting to the group of veteran pilots, but they ultimately decided it was too risky to try to use it to escape out of the country. They pressed on and when they reached the coast two of the men immediately found French fishermen willing to take them aboard. In their concern about the Italian navy patrolling the area Schepens and his friend and colleague, Anselme Vernieuwe, reconsidered their escape plan — and their caution proved sound because they never heard from their former comrades again. Though close to the Pyrenees and determined to get out of France to continue fighting against the Germans, the two opted to return to Belgium instead. Once on familiar turf they would volunteer their services in the underground war that they were confident their countrymen would mount against the Nazi occupiers.

Charles reunited with Cette and her family, then returned to Brussels in mid-July. To their surprise the Schepenses found an elderly couple who had been left homeless by the invasion squatting in the Schepens residence. Since Monsieur and Madame Dieu were friends of friends and clearly desperate, Charles and Cette agreed to let them stay as houseguests in the top floor rooms.

When Charles fled with his unit in May the capital was a city in chaos. When he returned two months later the flags of the Third Reich flew from the buildings and reconstruction of the damaged infrastructure was well under way. The Germans had sought to demonstrate to the defeated population the benefits of the new Nazi regime by returning to an appearance of normalcy as quickly as possible.[5] At the outset of the occupation the German authorities had attempted to win the sympathy and collaboration of the Belgian people and to prove, through a variety of strategies, that the policies of the Reich were not the same as those of their brutal predecessors in the previous war. They insisted on the polite deportment of their occupying troops, conducted propaganda against the Allies and the former Belgian ministers in the press and on the radio, allowed the early release of some prisoners, and made general promises about Belgium's future once the New Order was achieved.

By the fall, however, Belgians began to comprehend the impact of the German occupation. The shortage and rationing of two essential elements — food and fuel — had the most significant impact on their daily lives.[6] Before the war Belgium had mined and burned coal, and although prewar production had recently increased with the development of the Kempen fields near Antwerp, the country had imported additional quantities to supply its domestic and industrial needs. Beginning in September 1940, when 75 percent of the coal production was diverted to Germany and the British blockaded Belgian ports, a serious fuel deficit arose. Factories, short of coal and other raw materials, were forced to reduce production and lay off workers.

Obtaining food posed an even greater problem. As one of the most densely populated countries in Europe, Belgium had long relied on imports, particularly wheat, meat, and butter, to help feed its population. Early in the occupation the Germans imposed a rationing system for the purchase of basic commodities, which cut in half the caloric consumption of a daily prewar diet.[7] Fat and protein were reduced to minimal levels. Bread (225 grams) and potatoes (500 grams) were the staples of the new food regimen, although at times even these two basic items were not available in stores. The daily allotment for meat was 25 grams, including the bone. Only young children, nursing mothers, pregnant women, and the ill were allotted small portions of eggs and milk.

Thus, despite the Nazi policy of appeasement during the early months of the occupation, the food shortages, the restriction of personal liberties, and the institution of new discriminatory policies brought home to the Belgian population the bitter realities of living under the Third Reich's police state.[8] Gestures of resistance appeared as early as late summer: anti-German graffiti began to appear on walls in Brussels and underground newspapers published their first issues.[9] By September, though it was forbidden under the threat of imprisonment, Belgians were listening to programs produced specially for them on the BBC.

For those like Charles Schepens who sensed that it was going to be a long engagement, involvement in resistance work was not a matter of heroism but of personal honor and decency. "You just can't accept that kind of situation," he said. "Medical friends, people who were in the same air force regiment, people I went to school with — most of them helped in one way or another." For the first few months after his return, though, Charles decided to steer clear of any military contacts since technically he was a deserter and should have been considered a prisoner of war. He believed that by resuming his private medical practice he could take the time necessary to assess the possibility of participating in the Belgian underground service. The absurdity of the charges against him and his treatment by the Germans during his ten days of captivity, however, fueled his determination to act.

His motivation to join the opposition, in fact, had deep roots. His experiences as a child on the front during the First World War had left an indelible imprint. Indeed, those are Charles Schepens's first memories. Born in 1912 in Mouscron, a Walloon textile and manufacturing center near the border with France, he can remember returning from his grandparents' home in Bruges fifty kilometers to the north when war was declared in August 1914. He did not see his grandparents for four years, until the end of the occupation. Charles vividly remembers a room on the ground floor of the family residence that he and his two older sisters and three older brothers were forbidden to enter. The room held a cart that could be loaded with essentials and eight rucksacks that his mother had packed in case the family was forced to evacuate on sudden notice.

The pounding cadence of the exploding cannons at the front less than ten kilometers away — sometimes a muffled sound, sometimes thunderous — was a constant backdrop of Charles's early childhood. For the four Schepens boys the ongoing overhead air battles held both fascination and fright. Charles can recall the pleasure his older brothers took in being able to identify the different models and nationalities of the aircraft. The planes often flew only 150 meters above them and they could see the airmen shooting rifles and handguns during engagements. Once the action was so close that Charles recalls seeing the bloodied hand of a wounded Allied pilot as the plane plummeted to the ground.

Charles spent hours playing in mock war games organized by his teen-age brothers Yves, Edouard, and Gustave, within the walled parklike grounds behind the family residence on the edge of the town's business district. To the Schepens boys the towering pine, beech, and ash trees provided a miniature forest within which to stage their heroic attacks and ambushes. As the war dragged on, however, the boys watched as their backyard haven was appropriated for other uses. Their parents ripped up most of the lawn to plant a field of potatoes, and food was so scarce that the family was forced to guard the plot at night. Their forest was further diminished when several trees were cut down, some for their own fire-wood and some requisitioned by the Germans.

These reminiscences are tempered by other more troubling memories of the impact of the fifty months of war and occupation. Four of Charles's older cousins (the youngest one only sixteen years old) escaped from Belgium at the outset of the German invasion; one of them was killed in battle, one came back deaf, one had been gassed, and only one returned unharmed.

The war years proved to be an informal apprenticeship in civilian resistance for Charles. His father, one of the town's four physicians, not only treated wounded soldiers escaping from the front but also issued to young workers health certificates that ostensibly made them ineligible for conscription by the Germans. In addition, during the four years of occupation the Schepens family hid one of their hired hands and a Belgian carpenter, both of whom had been injured and who were trying to avoid capture as prisoners of war. Among the many dangers of living near the front were the nocturnal house-to-house searches conducted by the Feldgendarmerie (German military police) looking for escapees from the trenches to fill the ranks of the forced labor crews building new railroad links and fortifications behind the lines.[10] Charles learned later that had the Feldgendarmerie discovered these deserters in their home, his father could have been shot.

The patriotic education that Charles received throughout his youth as a member of the Boy Scouts reinforced the stories his parents told and retold of the isolation, deprivation, and resistance of the Belgian people during the First World War. The lessons he learned from the sacrifices made by his parents and the humanitarian service of citizen heroes such as Adolphe Max (the mayor of Brussels), Cardinal Mercier, and the historian Henri Pirenne, left a permanent impression. Conversely, the residue of the war produced a lasting bitterness toward the Germans who had turned from protector to aggressor and had inflicted inhuman levels of suffering on prisoners and the population at large. Like other Belgians Charles also harbored a strong distrust of the Dutch, whose stance of neutrality had proved to be an illusion when they allowed German troops to transport war material through Holland to the front.

Two decades later Charles's year of internship in the military hospital in Brussels (1935–36) forced him to confront once again the destruction caused by the Great War. The war had left ninety thousand wounded Belgian veterans. He remembers now what was so striking about these combat veterans: their multiple wounds and stories of repeatedly being returned to the front for duty rather than being allowed to fully recuperate. As he recalls, "I'll never forget. One patient I saw had been wounded sixteen times."

For Charles and for others of his generation, the catastrophic defeat and rapid occupation of Belgium in 1940 served to rekindle the personal and collective memory of destruction and suffering endured during the 1914–18 war, and a terrifying recognition that the imposition of the repressive New Order could mean the end of their country (which only ten years earlier had celebrated its centennial).[11] At the same time his decision to participate in the resistance was a major departure from his apolitical lifestyle of the previous decade.

The 1930s had been a time of mounting tension in Belgium. Long-standing religious, political, and social conflicts not only factionalized the population and the government but also siphoned attention from the more serious threat of a full-scale war on the Continent. Brussels became the crucible for much of the unrest.[12] Although the currents of modernity were abroad, and the city's boosters were eager to promote its cosmopolitan amenities, the capital was nevertheless a bastion of conservatism.[13] After all, as the administrative and financial center of the country, Brussels was a city dominated by bureaucrats and bankers with entrenched attitudes about politics and power. To the increasingly militant Flemish nationalists the nation's capital was a symbol of the insensitivity of modern-day Belgians and of the effort of the French-speaking Walloons to marginalize their language and cultural heritage: until the *Flamingants* successfully advocated several linguistic reforms in the twenties and thirties, French was the official language used in governmental affairs.[14] Moreover, in the mid-1930s Belgium saw the birth of Vlaamsch National Verbond (VNV), a Flemish nationalist organization that promoted a fascist ideology within the concept of a greater Netherlandish state (that included the Netherlands and the Flemish part of Belgium). *La question flamande*, especially the demand for increased political autonomy for the Flemish provinces, was a continual focus of parliamentary debates in Brussels in the 1930s and the subject of endless newspaper articles and editorials.

Charles Schepens entered medical school at the State University in Ghent in 1930, where he was subject to one of these new linguistic reforms. The Nolf Law required that students of certain faculties had to take either the Flemish program (in which two-thirds of the courses were taught in Flemish and one-third in French) or the French program (two-thirds in French, one-third in Flemish).[15] Though his parents were bilingual, Flemish had been the language spoken within the Schepens family until Charles was five years old. The family's bilinguality abruptly changed toward the end of the war when his father learned that a close Flemish friend had been exposed as a German traitor. Thereafter Charles spoke French both at home and at school. He resented the Nolf Law and regarded its compromise approach as an unnecessary complication, but he was not among the students who protested the policy.

As a medical student and throughout his specialized training and the beginning years of his clinical practice in Brussels, Charles had little interest in or time for involvement in national politics. Though he was not oblivious to news of the day, his career ambitions consumed his energy and intellect. While his father's humanitarian service as a "people's doctor" had inspired him and his brothers to go into medicine, he was also eager to harness his own talents for engineering and physics to work on new scientific inventions. He accelerated his university studies, finishing the normal seven-year stint in six, and managed to complete the coursework needed to receive a special diploma in mathematics.

During medical school Charles had decided that he wanted to practice as an ophthalmologist since the eye seemed to offer the best opportunity to apply and advance his knowledge of optics and, as an anatomy professor urged, the field offered many research possibilities. Some serious obstacles interfered with the pursuit of his intended career, however: Belgium, like all the countries of western Europe, was in the depths of the depression and the Belgian franc had already been devalued twice. Charles had very little savings and could not rely on his brothers and sisters, who had their own struggles in sustaining their medical practices and their young families. At the time no place in Belgium offered formal training in ophthalmology so he decided to enlist in the medical corps' reserve, which would pay him a salary as well as allow him to pursue advanced training abroad after a year of internship in general medicine at the military hospital in Brussels.

Soon after his marriage to Cette in the summer of 1936 the two traveled to London where he served an internship at Moorfields Eye Hospital, which at the time was considered the finest center for eye research and surgery in Europe. A second, shorter residency in 1937 took the pair to Utrecht, Holland, where Charles worked for three months under Professor H. J. M. Weve, an internationally recognized specialist in the treatment of retinal detachments. Dr. Schepens's training in Holland was cut short, however, when he was unexpectedly called up for duty and assigned to the Third Regiment of Aeronautics of the Belgian air force. After Germany's unchallenged annexation of the Rhineland, King Léopold III and his ministers decided they could no longer rely on a mutual aid pact with France and England and that the best strategy for the country's protection would be to declare its neutrality and increase its own military defense. Charles and Cette's fast-paced honeymoon, an eighteen-day trip through numerous cities of Germany, Austria, Yugoslavia, and Italy, had alerted the young doctor to the growing menace of German nationalism; a year later his air force unit's mobilization confirmed his fear of an impending war on the Continent.

This new round of military training complicated an already full medical schedule. When Charles finally inaugurated his clinical practice in Brussels he divided his time between a number of offices: still under contract with the military medical training corps, he continued to serve as a general practitioner at the Military Air Force complex at Evère, near Brussels, three days a week; his employment at the Clinique St.-Jean and Elizabeth, a nine-century-old private medical center in central Brussels, gave him the first real opportunity to develop his surgical skills under the guidance of Dr. Léon Hambresin, an eminent eye surgeon, and the ability to conduct new research on diseases that affect the optical nerve and retina. Charles spent his mornings at the clinic and left the afternoons and evenings open for consultations with patients in his own office on the chaussée de Haecht.

While the first acts of German expansionism in the late 1930s hampered his professional plans, the course of events from May through October 1940 definitively sidetracked Dr. Schepens's promising career. His arrest, furthermore, opened his eyes to the danger that his own countrymen — half a million of whom were unemployed — could pose. As part of the occupation the Gestapo set up the Geheime Feldpolizei, a counterespionage organization that relied on paid informers recruited in part from the Belgian fascist parties Rex and VNV. Just as important, the Gestapo promoted at-large spying by citizens and promised German deutsche marks for denunciation of resistance activities. Charles Schepens never knew the identity of the person who reported him but suspects it was a soldier to whom he had refused a health certificate for military leave.

Charles also was leery of actively working as an agent for resistance cells operated by former military personnel.[16] Since Belgium had developed no professional secret service, resistance activities initially were conducted by independent grassroots groups scattered throughout the country's different regions.[17] Secrecy was essential, so few knew the identities of others in a given organization; individuals worked at the behest of a leader or contact who was usually known by a false name. Most participants carried out tactical actions against the Germans in their local areas but not according to any coordinated plan. Stories of patriotic resisters who had been caught and killed because of inexperience and carelessness had already spread by the time Charles decided to volunteer his services after his own false arrest in late October 1940.

An overture by Anselme Vernieuwe, his trusted air force colleague, had inspired Charles to enroll. After his return to Brussels in the summer of 1940, Vernieuwe had joined a network under the leadership of a "Colonel de Saule," a Belgian former officer of the French foreign legion who was living in unoccupied France.[18] Because he spoke five languages de Saule was appointed by the Vichy government to be head of an intelligence unit based in the Jura region. At the same time he was operating a variety of unofficial and clandestine services for the Belgian underground. Vernieuwe, a courier using the aliases Jean Villeneuve or Jean Vernon, shuttled information between the German-controlled Low countries and the unoccupied Southern Zone of France. Eventually he hoped to escape and become a pilot for the RAF. He and his wife Loulou lived in Brussels with her parents above their restaurant, but Anselme's periods of residency in the city were usually brief.

When Anselme approached Charles to become involved in the network the ophthalmologist did not have full confidence in de Saule's corps of volunteers — several had been caught due to their indiscretions. "They were full of good will," he reflects, "but totally unprepared for that kind of job. They were talking much too much." He instead decided to participate in a limited capacity in the group's activities: he let Vernieuwe use his medical office in Brussels as a station for delivery and pickup of packages and documents. Every few weeks a Flemish-speaking "patient" would make an appointment and bring along a brown satchel filled with secret documents that the ophthalmologist hid in the thick ivy on the wall at the rear of the property until Vernieuwe could retrieve it. From the beginning of his service as an information conduit Charles operated on the principle that "the less knowledge, the better." He never knew the contents of the parcels (which in reality were microfilmed documents, maps, and diagrams about troop movements in the region, lists of arriving parachutists, escaped pilots, and underground agents who had been exposed), nor did he discuss his activities with Cette, although she knew he was assisting Vernieuwe.[19]

Charles undertook several cautionary measures as well. First he installed a platform a few meters down in an existing well in the middle of his backyard garden to provide a hiding place for one or two people. He bought some rabbits, which he kept in cages in the garden to avoid attracting the suspicion of curious neighbors who might see him, bundles in hand, making frequent visits back and forth between the house and the backyard. Finally he plotted a potential escape route over the garden wall and through the adjoining properties should the Gestapo reappear.

Chapter 5

A common feature of photographs taken of war-time Brussels is a long line of people, mostly women, waiting to buy provisions with their ration cards. The reality, however, was that often there were no goods to buy. According to Cette Schepens, "It was potatoes that saved the population of Brussels."[1] Because of the deprivation, moreover, food was a constant and primary topic both of conversation and fantasy. Charles recalls that the simple pleasure of tasting chicken could become the subject of a lengthy monologue.

The family did employ a maid to help with the children, which freed Cette to go on the necessary but time-consuming shopping expeditions for food. The Schepenses' situation was also somewhat eased by Cette's family's connections to farmers outside of Ghent. Once a month Charles, Cette, and their two young children traveled by train to visit the Vander Eecken family, who fed them well on locally produced butter, eggs, milk, poultry, and meat. The vegetables they ate there came from the gardens that Cette's parents had installed on the once-manicured grounds of their country property, the Chateau de Gavergracht — the same lawns that had been the site of the daughter's grand wedding reception in 1936.

To augment the meager rations that the family received in Brussels, Cette's mother sewed a vest into the interior of an extra large, long Loden coat for Charles, which she would load with bags of wheat and buckwheat flour. On one return train ride to Brussels he remembers "overhearing two women gossiping about the thin-faced man with the mismatched, large body." Even this kind of simple subterfuge could lead to a fine or arrest, so he was careful to maintain a state of vigilance during their trips. Watching a man carry a carpenter's bag that was leaking rolled oats across the Gare du Nord was certainly a reminder of the trouble in which he, too, could find himself.

Except for their monthly visits to Ghent and rare excursions to Mouscron, the Schepens family no longer ventured very far from their neighborhood in Brussels during the war years. Charles confined his periods in the public eye to walks with Cette and the children in the nearby botanical gardens and to short transits through the railroad station. The cultured life the family had known before the war was a closed chapter.

Despite Charles's demanding military and professional obligations, when they settled in the capital in 1936 the newlywed couple had established an active social schedule. Brussels was a European city with a vibrant cultural scene. On virtually every street corner the colorful posters and broadsides promoting performances by national and international stars in the cinemas, concert halls, theaters, and cabarets provided an ever-changing montage of current and coming attractions. Charles remembers art patrons and art critics gloating that many new theater productions premiered in Brussels rather than in Paris because it was less costly to do so. Going to exhibits and concerts was the Schepenses' preferred form of leisure, and both nostalgically remember frequent cultural outings during those years.

As newcomers to the capital the couple's social circle consisted mainly of family and family friends. Cette's uncle was a Brussels banker who, along with her patrician parents, provided important introductions to the city's old guard. They regularly saw Charles's older brother Edouard and his family, who lived not far away. Contacts made through Charles's military service soon enlarged their social network and included Anselme and Loulou Vernieuwe. The Schepenses also counted two influential newspaper editors — William Ugeux, whom Charles had known from his university days, and Victor Zeegers — among their sphere of well-connected friends. Once established, Cette and Charles particularly enjoyed entertaining in their elegant nineteenth-century townhouse that she had stylishly furnished with beautiful antiques and fine fabrics. Her painting easel was a firm fixture in their living room, and many admiring guests eagerly volunteered to be subjects for her portraits.

Among the longtime friends whose visits they most eagerly awaited were two remarkable Russian brothers whom Charles had known since adolescence and who were now living abroad. Their friendship, which soon proved to be fateful for his resistance work, had begun when all three were enrolled at a Belgian boarding school. After Charles's parents died within three months of each other when he was just thirteen, his older siblings had determined that their lanky, affable brother should be sent to the Jesuit high school in Namur where all the Schepens brothers had conducted their premedical studies. In addition to being considered the top academic institution in the country, the school offered an unusual scholarship program for Russian refugees who had fled after the Revolution. The year Charles entered the school Oleg and Cyrille Pomerantzeff arrived as new students; Oleg was Charles's age and Cyrille was a few classes behind.

The brothers were dark-haired, dark-eyed, and exotically handsome. For ten years prior to their coming to Namur the two White Russians had been on an odyssey across Europe, including living for a time at an orphanage for Russian refugees in Czechoslovakia, where their widowed mother had sent them while she was en route to France. When Madame Pomerantzeff eventually reached Paris she contacted a relative living in Brussels, who knew about the scholarship program in Namur and helped arrange the boys' acceptance.

As Russian Orthodox rather than Roman Catholics, Oleg and Cyrille were initially regarded with distrust by the Belgian students. The boys, who had received very little formal education, were truly a curiosity among their more cultured classmates, but Charles's status as an orphan likely made him more sympathetic to the predicament of the foreign students. He attributes his more liberal social attitude to his participation in the Boy Scouts, which had taught him the importance of valuing talent over background.[2] His mother Henriette, the scout leader, had consciously organized a troop comprised of her own four sons and boys from the poorer neighborhoods of Mouscron; the troop held its weekly gatherings at the Schepens residence. Thus Charles and his brothers were compelled to interact with a group of boys completely different from their middle- and upper-middle-class schoolmates at the local private Catholic school. Charles discovered a hardiness and tenacity of spirit among the workers' sons that he had not previously experienced among his other friends.

Oleg's talents first captured Charles's interest—and envy—at a school concert. As a choir member Charles had a fine singing voice, but he was awed by the Russian's ethereal vocal talents. Yet it was their shared passion for physics, mathematics, and engineering that cemented the bond and friendly rivalry between Charles and Oleg. Charles, who graduated with top honors, had to work diligently to achieve academic success, while Oleg could comprehend complex theories and abstract principles with little effort. To the amazement of faculty and students alike, in just three years Oleg completed six years of study, graduating first in his class. In fact, he finished high school a year ahead of Charles. Charles remembers the Jesuit faculty as gifted teachers and scholars who motivated students to a high level of achievement, but credits Oleg's brilliance for truly inspiring him.

Charles and Oleg had remained close friends, though separated by distance, during their university days. To his disappointment Charles was unable to convince his Russian friend to join him in his choice of professional study. Oleg believed his homeland would eventually need engineers in a future post-communist era, and instead enrolled at Catholic University of Louvain, where he secured a full scholarship. On several occasions during this period Charles stepped in to help the impoverished Russian. He remembers repeating to Oleg that "a real friend is someone I wouldn't hesitate to walk to the North Pole with." For example, Charles gladly hosted Oleg in his tiny, spartan cold-water efficiency apartment when his friend needed food or lodging, and once lent him his motorcycle to get to a summer job. In 1932 Charles even organized the Bal des Russes, a benefit dance held in Ghent to raise money for Oleg and other Russian émigré students.

Like Charles, Oleg accelerated his university studies and graduated early, at age twenty-three. Immediately he was hired by a Belgian investment firm to direct a new mining operation in the mountains south of Belgrade, Yugoslavia. Not coincidentally, Yugoslavia was also the adopted country of his new wife, Irène, a fellow Russian émigré student at the University of Louvain. Though Charles was somewhat reassured knowing that Oleg would not be a total stranger while working abroad, he was also well aware of Oleg's naïveté and feared that his friend's gullibility could be dangerous in a country of violence and political turmoil (the Yugoslav king had been assassinated one year prior). Just before his friend's departure Charles bought Oleg a pistol and gave him a doctor's kit filled with medicines.

After Oleg's emigration Charles saw his best friend twice before the war broke out: during a brief sojourn on his and Cette's honeymoon through Yugoslavia, and two years later when Oleg and Irène spent a month as their guests at chaussée de Haecht. Charles cherished their spirited reunions, but after hearing stories of his friend's grueling work schedule and the exploitative attitude of his employer, he continued to feel uneasy about Oleg's situation.

In the later 1930s Charles kept abreast of Oleg's activities through written correspondence and occasional phone conversations, and through Cyrille's periodic visits to Brussels to see his uncle. Cyrille was brilliant like his brother, but his passion was philosophy. In fact, during their days at boarding school in Namur, Cyrille's serious expression and love of debate on arcane subjects had earned him the nickname "starik" (the old man) among the other Russian students. Charles did not know Cyrille as well as he knew Oleg, but was drawn to his creative intellect and felt the kind of fraternal relationship that boarding schools can engender among students of different ages. Their casual friendship deepened as a result of Charles's summer trips to France during his medical school days.

Charles's eight-year involvement in the Boy Scouts during adolescence had engendered a strong interest in outdoor leadership. Later he discovered an innovative fitness program developed by a retired French military captain named Georges Hébert, who had watched French peasants (such as Jean Sarochar) outrun and outlive athletes during World War I. Hébert's training course emphasized the development of survival skills in rugged, natural settings. Charles learned that a disciple of Hébert's named Robert Lafitte had opened a training center at Verberie, outside of Paris. Eager for a break from the medical laboratories in Ghent, Charles enrolled in the open air school first in the summer of 1931 and then again in 1932. He left the center muscled, mentally toughened, and deeply inspired by Lafitte's pioneering program.

Each time he was en route to and from Verberie, Charles spent a few days visiting Cyrille and his mother, who were then living in a modest apartment in Paris. After spending a short period at Louvain following his graduation from Namur, Cyrille moved to France to be with his mother. Her employment sewing for a French lingerie firm supported them while Cyrille pursued a degree in philosophy at the Sorbonne. Madame Pomerantzeff's tenacity made a strong impression on Charles, who remembers her indomitable spirit: "She had belonged to the intellectual class in St. Petersburg. In Paris she was a tireless worker and determined to give her boys an education." During his visits Charles came to realize that Cyrille would make an ideal teacher at Lafitte's new school for underachievers. With Charles's encouragement Cyrille applied and got his first teaching position at Verberie.

Hence, when Cyrille visited the Schepenses in Brussels, Charles was eager to hear news of Oleg and to hear about Cyrille's experiences as a teacher and then principal of the school in Verberie. Cyrille's enthusiasm and unconventional motivational strategies, despite his meager pay, intrigued the doctor. News of the school's bankruptcy at the end of the 1930s was a great disappointment and source of worry about his friend. Having watched Oleg and Cyrille establish careers, however, it was becoming apparent to Charles that "money meant nothing to them." Clearly the notion of a challenge nourished their resilient and idealistic spirits.

After the German occupation Cyrille's visits to 72 chaussée de Haecht ceased. Moreover, social gatherings hosted by the Schepens family were few and far between and only for family and close friends. Charles never discussed his resistance activities, even with his relatives. As Cette says, "We were living in an unnatural state. You had to distrust everyone."

The complexion of the capital city rapidly changed—instead of the bold, colorful advertisements of the previous decade, Nazi propaganda papered its windows and walls—but, more important, the rhythm of life changed. Travel reverted to its pre–World War I state in which trams and bicycles once again became the principal means of transportation (since gasoline was virtually unavailable).[3] Trains continued to operate but on much-reduced schedules; the Germans had seized two-thirds of the rolling stock, leaving behind only the most outdated engines and coaches.

For the Belgian population one of the big differences between the occupations of the First and Second World Wars was the absence of foreign aid to supplement the diminished supply of food.[4] During the 1914–18 war the American Commission for Relief in Belgium, headed by Herbert Hoover, had provided critical rations of bread, rice, coffee, canned meat, fish, starches, lard, cheese, and milk—all vital to everyday survival. From 1940 on (until the Liberation) Belgium was completely cut off and had almost no access to any such resources. For the Belgians, especially for those living in cities, the scarcity of food verged on famine. Resentment about the poor quality of the goods and inadequate supplies was heightened by the fact that German civilians residing in the country were given double allotments, and the five hundred thousand German soldiers stationed in the country received triple rations.

In the face of starvation and economic paralysis the Belgians inevitably developed an extensive black market.[5] Brussels became the center of the black market in Belgium, and for all of occupied Europe as well. While traffic in foodstuffs dominated the trade, every imaginable commodity — from shoes to medicine to steel — could be purchased through under-the-counter negotiation and barter. Indeed, bartering became a fact of life and all social classes participated. After family savings were exhausted, people sold their possessions to obtain the high-priced necessities. Those on the lower end of the economic scale simply funneled their earnings into the illicit transactions necessary for basic survival. Even people working in the government offices — and responsible for policing the food ration system — relied on the black market for provisions. The Germans used it to acquire goods and materials for their troops in Belgium. As the war progressed the pressure of competing buyers caused prices to skyrocket. Luxury items such as coffee and chocolate were selling at ten times the prewar costs; soap could cost as much as eighty times more.

Nazi repression and persecution increased as the war evolved. By May 1941 more than eight thousand pages of official decrees regulating every kind of social encounter — even down to the type of funeral service a priest could conduct for an executed citizen and the number of people who could attend it — had been compiled into *The Official Gazette*.[6] In the first two years of the occupation several measures also were enacted to segregate Jews from the rest of the population, such as prohibiting Jewish children from attending public schools or allowing Jews to travel by train only by special permission.[7] A second set of ordinances issued in May–June 1941 confiscated bank deposits from Jews and forced them to publicly declare their property.[8] Belgian Freemasons and labor unions were singled out for harsh treatment as well, including property destruction, arrests, and deportations. The Free University of Brussels was shut down in 1941, and libraries were forced to remove from their shelves both anti-German literature and works by Jewish authors.

Resistance and subversion simultaneously gained momentum at every level. As in World War I, harboring the persecuted and the hunted — whether Jews, prisoners of war, downed airmen, or resistance fighters — once again became commonplace on farms, in convents, and in city backstreets. Like his father during the First World War, Charles's brother Yves, now a doctor in Bruges, contributed to the clandestine war effort by treating wounded partisans. Moreover, Belgian citizens en masse defied Nazi orders to turn over all used metal knowing that it would be melted down and turned into armaments. When the Germans, who were short of nickel, decided in 1941 to remove the country's five-franc piece from circulation, Belgians hid the coin to the point that less than ten percent of the minted stock was collected. A paper drive was equally unsuccessful when word spread that it would be recycled into Nazi propaganda and newspapers. Industrial sabotage, work slowdowns, and strikes, as well as the destruction of German communication lines, regularly occurred.

The underground press proliferated.[9] Since the BBC broadcasts provided daily reports about events taking place beyond Belgium's borders, much of the content of printed publications described resistance efforts and the severe German reprisals taking place within the country, including death, imprisonment, deportation, and fines, not to mention the ever-harsher regulations. (A measure of the scope of the Belgian underground service in the Second World War is the fact that more resisters were arrested in the first eighteen months of the occupation than in the entire four years of the previous war.)[10] The countless underground journals reminded readers of Belgium's traditions of liberty and freedom by publishing article after article that glorified the bravery of World War I heroes and described the current feats of RAF pilots. Jokes and satirical accounts about *les boches* (a slang term for the Germans) were regular features.

With the war's progress came more coordination among the specialized but dispersed resistance groups. By 1942 a variety of evacuation lines and information networks connecting Belgium to the Free Zone of France and the neutral countries beyond the Pyrenees had been established. The largest and most important of these networks were two based in Brussels — "Zéro" and "Luc" — and three Belgian-directed operations based in France — "Sabot" in Montpellier, "Comète" in Paris, and "Caviar" in Roubaix. Former journalist William Ugeux, whom Charles had not seen since the outbreak of the war, had become the second leader of Zéro;[11] under directions from the Belgian government-in-exile in London, Ugeux had been drafted late in the winter of 1942 to set up the Poste du Commandement Belge (PCB) in Grenoble in order to maintain communications among the various Belgian underground groups operating throughout Belgium, Holland, Luxembourg, and France. Ugeux also coordinated efforts with the secret services of Britain and the United States in London.

In his leadership role Ugeux enlisted the cooperation of Colonel de Saule, through whom he had met Anselme Vernieuwe. Vernieuwe recognized the advantages of working with and through Ugeux's London connections, so in early 1942 Vernieuwe became an operative of the Zéro network. Under Ugeux's direction Vernieuwe continued his service as a courier and took on the additional role of escort for the evacuation of underground agents whose identities had been divulged.

Vernieuwe's new affiliation with Ugeux, however, was not enough to persuade Charles to alter his level of involvement, who instead preferred to maintain his low-key profile as a Brussels mail drop. A young Belgian woman who worked as a secretary in the nearby Gestapo office on the rue Traversière aided their efforts. She often informed them of the names of people on the Gestapo's list for interrogation or arrest, so Vernieuwe could help engineer their exit in advance of the Gestapo's appearance.

The few hours Cette Schepens could devote to painting provided a much-needed escape from the gloomy and tense atmosphere of the capital during these first years of occupation. One canvas she completed during the period is a tranquil, impressionistic interior scene that shows young Claire and Luc at play in the airy salon of their townhouse. The focal point of the small painting, which she painted in April 1942, is a large bouquet of lilies, a gift from Cyrille Pomerantzeff delivered as an Easter present. Fresh flowers were one of the few commodities still freely available and, given the dark mood of the times, an especially appropriate symbol of hope and regeneration.

The Schepens family, however, did not spend the 1942 Easter holiday together. Just before Easter weekend the network's mole at the Gestapo office relayed bad news to Charles: his and Vernieuwe's names had appeared several times on the list of individuals under surveillance and they must depart at once. The two immediately left for Paris, where both had contacts they could rely on for temporary protection while planning their next moves. A stopover in Mouscron with Charles's brother Gustave, who at the time was living in the Schepens family residence, would provide an intermediate safe house along the way. Charles's impending arrest meant that Cette and the children must also disappear, so he sent them off to stay with Cette's parents in Ghent.

The day after Charles fled to France the Gestapo arrived at Chaussée de Haecht for the second time, only to discover the sole occupants in residence were the bewildered and terrified Monsieur and Madame Dieu.

Chapter 6

Although Charles had not seen Cyrille Pomerantzeff since before the war, he knew from their intermittent correspondence that after the Verberie school closed in 1938, Cyrille completed eighteen months of compulsory military service in France and then became involved in some kind of commercial enterprise. When Charles arrived in Paris in April 1942 he was astonished to find Cyrille at the head of Trait D'Union, a prosperous new brokerage firm. It appeared that Cyrille had become a rich man almost overnight.

As a Russian living in Paris without a passport Cyrille was uncertain about his political sympathies at the war's beginning, because a German victory could possibly have meant an end to communism in his homeland. But personal survival was his more immediate concern. He and his mother sold flashlights, which were in great demand because of the blackout imposed by the Germans. Their surprising profits on the black market soon encouraged Cyrille's entrepreneurial ambitions, particularly in serving the needs of the newly arrived German military administration in France. With no capital and a lot of bluff he founded Trait D'Union as a jobbing business that solicited orders for cheap office furniture and then commissioned French factories to produce the items. His meteoric success was due both to the scarcity of materials and ready-made goods and to his audacious and effusive personality. When he saw his friend in action Charles realized that Cyrille was "a born salesman" but also a schemer who could always deliver the goods no matter how difficult the assignment.

Cyrille had taught himself German, which gave him a distinct advantage in negotiating with his Nazi customers and in obtaining the papers and permits he needed to source manufacturers and market his services. His well-tailored suits did not go unnoticed by his clients, and he made it a point to introduce them to his Parisian haberdasher. The Germans tried to interest him in working under their auspices, where he probably could have made even more money, but he declined so as to preserve his independent status. Cyrille, in fact, was careful to establish commercial connections and friendships among the French civil authorities as well, including the prefect of Paris.

At the offices of Trait D'Union, located at 121 rue St.-Lazare just a few blocks from the Gare St.-Lazare, Charles met a dozen employees — almost all of them friends from the expatriate Russian community living in Paris. Among those on the payroll were Nicolas Rosenschild, a Namur classmate of Cyrille's hired to be the company's accountant. Cyrille was eager to help Charles in his predicament and immediately drafted Charles into service as a Trait D'Union traveling salesman.

Cyrille's newfound wealth had enabled him to purchase a handsome chateau in St.-Brice, a village on the northern outskirts of Paris. For a month the chateau served as Charles's temporary home, where he was one of several transients in residence surrounded by Russians whom Cyrille was aiding or supporting. One of the few non-Russians he met while staying at St.-Brice was a struggling Frankfurt-born composer named Jacques Spengler. Cyrille had become Spengler's patron and even had underwritten a concert of Spengler's compositions at the Salle Pleyel, a major performance facility in Paris. Knowing of the Belgian's plight, Spengler gave Charles his French identity card, which Charles proceeded to modify: because Spengler was an illegitimate child Charles filled in the name "Pérot" in the blank space for the father's name. Dr. Charles Schepens thus became Jacques Pérot-Spengler, sales agent for Trait D'Union.

Charles was uncertain how far the Gestapo in Belgium would extend their manhunt for him so he was only too glad to leave the city on sales assignments. The trips proved to be the first test of his resourcefulness as a self-taught undercover agent, since travel across the Line of Demarcation separating the occupied and unoccupied zones of France required special identification papers.[1] Because Cyrille did not want to record the name Pérot-Spengler on any kind of official list, he did not obtain a travel pass (*ausweis*) for Charles from the German authorities in Paris — which meant that Charles had to rely on his ingenuity to make the border crossings. Luck was on Charles's side when he made his first passage over the Line of Demarcation to a town in central France. From Paris he took the train to a neighboring town within the Occupied Zone and there learned from a local cafe owner when the border guard duty shifts changed. He timed his crossing of the bridge between shifts and had no problem proceeding to his destination. Charles's second business trip — to Toulouse — was more complicated. From a priest on the train from Paris he learned how to get a fake identity card that would designate him as a resident of Chaussin, a village in eastern France in the Free Zone. He skirted the official checkpoint into Chaussin by wading across the nearby river and then headed to the town hall. Following the priest's instructions he told the mayor he was trying to get to the Belgian Congo, then bribed him with five hundred French francs. The mayor instructed the clerk to record Jacques Pérot-Spengler's signature in the town records — in pencil — then issued the document. Though the trip to Toulouse proved to be a wild goose chase for Trait D'Union, Charles now owned identity cards for both sections of the country.

Cette's father sent word to Charles early in his stay in Paris that under no circumstance should Charles return to Belgium. Remembering the tragic end of a friend caught spying for the resistance in World War I, Vander Eecken feared a similar fate for his son-in-law. Yet it was clearly evident to Charles that staying in Paris was no long-term solution to his situation. The presence of German soldiers and the prevalence of French collaborators made him very uneasy. The only difference he could perceive between the occupations in Brussels and Paris was that "the French seemed more lighthearted about their situation, and willing to openly mock the Germans." To his surprise and disappointment Lafitte, the founder of the school at Verberie who was now living in Paris in very modest circumstances with his wife and teenaged daughter Bernadette, did not openly welcome him. Lafitte was strongly pro-Pétain and believed that the revered World War I hero would be France's salvation.

Despite Cyrille's hospitality Charles could not envision living in the bosom of the Russian émigré community indefinitely. Charles's practical nature made him impatient with the seemingly endless abstract theological and intellectual discussions that frequently distracted Cyrille's circle of friends. "They could spend hours debating the sex of angels," Charles recalls, shaking his head. Two years had elapsed since his refusal to become a prisoner of war in Moissac; because of his interim service to the Belgian underground he found himself back in France, this time as a foreign resister. Like so many others who were "first resisters," Charles Schepens had originally joined in the grassroots opposition in occupied Belgium because of a defining incident — an arrest — that gave him firsthand exposure both to the Germans' harsh, summary treatment of citizens and the weakness of his own countrymen.[2] Charles's decision to affiliate with a friend and fellow military officer (Anselme Vernieuwe) was characteristic of most early *résistants*, who chose to work with and for trusted peers only.[3] Most important, the increasingly repressive German regime and his near-arrest the month before had deepened his determination for more active engagement.[4] In his words, "Survival was not what I was interested in. I was looking for something meaningful."

When they arrived in Paris that April, Schepens and Vernieuwe discussed the possibility of continuing their work in the Pyrenees, which Vernieuwe knew was the final and most difficult relay point in the chain of escape from northern Europe to Lisbon and Gibraltar. Enrollment in the emerging French resistance, however, was not something Schepens considered.[5] Like the active opposition in Belgium, in occupied France from the summer of 1940 through the spring of 1942 the movement was largely an urban phenomenon conducted by only a tiny percent of the population working through a dispersed patchwork of grassroots cells.[6] Some were antifascist and some were anti-German, but personal ethical principles as much as political ideology often spurred the involvement of these pioneering French and Belgian resisters.[7]

Like their counterparts to the north, the first resisters in France usually emerged from a common social milieu and their principal activity was publishing underground journals.[8] (Some also volunteered their services to the specialized evacuation and intelligence networks). The addition of Communist party members in the second half of 1941 (after Hitler invaded Russia) had a marked impact on the nature of the resistance movement in both countries: new organizations emerged, the political and social base of the opposition widened, and open violence against the occupier increased significantly (which until then had consisted of isolated acts of vandalism and military sabotage). In Belgium in the fall of 1941, communist partisans tripled the number of daily sabotage actions;[9] in the same period in France a rash of assassinations of Germans began in Paris and spread to other cities.[10]

Some important differences in the development and growth of the opposition in the two countries in this pioneering phase should also be highlighted. By 1942 Brig. Gen. Charles de Gaulle had gained a following through his broadcasts from London and in the broadening recognition that his Free French Forces were the rebel troops that could lead France's emancipation from the Germans;[11] no comparable charismatic leader emerged as a symbol to the Belgian population from among the exiled military or government officials living abroad.[12] Yet Belgium had one clear advantage: experience in the use of opposition tactics, learned during the country's occupation by the Germans during World War I.[13] Although amateurs, many Belgian *résistants*, like Charles Schepens, were second generation citizen-activists informally schooled in a tradition of insurgency. Moreover, the territory of the Belgian resistance stretched far beyond the country's borders: from the beginning months of the occupation the Belgians (like the Brits and the Poles) had rapidly established extensions of their own information and evacuation networks in both zones of France.[14] By 1942 the coordination of these secret operations into a unified structure was already in progress.[15]

Interestingly, when he arrived in Paris Schepens knew very little about the indigenous French opposition movement or the London-based Gaullists.[16] The month he spent in the capital and traveling the countryside, though, confirmed Schepens's impression of the French as too open and indiscreet; he had no interest in seeking out or participating in a French-led cell of resisters.[17] His continued service in France could only happen through a renewal of his affiliation with the Belgian underground there and, more specifically, only in association with his colleague, Anselme Vernieuwe. Schepens thus headed to Poligny in the Jura region (at the edge of the Free Zone) to rejoin his friend who had gone there in search of Colonel de Saule's temporary protection.

Charles Schepens traveled to Paris in April 1942 dressed in his Loden overcoat and carrying the German-made 35mm Leica camera that Cette had given him as a wedding present, in the hope that the items would identify him as someone of German or Austrian background. When he left the city in mid-May as businessman Jacques Pérot-Spengler, bespectacled and sporting a mustache, he departed with his two fake identity cards and a one thousand dollar bill concealed in his shoe. (During his stay in Paris he had obtained the black market American money through a friend working for the French Stock Exchange.) It was a huge sum, the equivalent of twenty-five thousand French francs — and an indispensable bank account for someone on the move.

Charles left the city assured that Cyrille could be counted on for financial assistance and support during his next round of undercover work, so long as it was far removed from Paris. Cyrille's beneficence towards

Spengler and his hospitality to the many temporary residents and visitors to St.-Brice, as well as Cyrille's willingness to aid a friend turned fugitive, convinced Charles that success "had not spoiled my Russian friend." Indeed, when he and Cyrille spent the night on a bench in a railroad station while on one of their sales trips, Charles realized that his companion had lost neither his skill at improvising nor his sense of adventure. Moreover, during his Paris interlude Charles discovered that Cyrille was funneling some of his profits into his sister's expensive psychiatric care at a private mental institution in France. It was clear that prosperity simply enabled him to be more generous and that at heart the Russian was a "joyful philanthropist."

In order to rendezvous with his colleague Vernieuwe in Poligny, Charles once again had to cross the Line of Demarcation near Chaussin. When he encountered the Vichy border police they detained him for questioning. Fortunately he had Colonel de Saule's telephone number, and through the official's intervention the guards let him go. When he met up with Vernieuwe he learned that the two had been assigned a mission. During a dinner at de Saule's house attended by Ugeux, Vernieuwe, and Captain de Hepcée (another Belgian aviator who, like Vernieuwe, had originally worked for de Saule and then joined the service of Zéro), the four had discussed both the specific problem of reuniting the Schepens family and the general need to develop new sites in the Pyrenees to use as escape routes south. Ugeux, who had just returned from a secret trip to London, was concerned about the increasing number of downed Allied pilots who needed to be ferried out of France, as well as the growing number of resistance operatives who had been exposed and the potential saturation of the existing Belgian evacuation networks that were operating through the coastal cities along the Atlantic and the Mediterranean coasts. Ugeux assigned Vernieuwe and the former Schepens to a reconnoitering expedition with the Belgian consul in Lyon, a center of the French resistance, to collect intelligence about activity in the western Pyrenees.

The pair's brief junket to Lyon is memorable to Schepens both for his lack of confidence in the consul and the covey of agents there and for the admiration he gained for his colleague Vernieuwe. Their unexpected overnight lodging spot was a vacant sleeper car in the central railyard. In the rush to depart the following morning Vernieuwe failed to pick up a satchel filled with confidential material that he had carefully stowed underneath his pillow. When he realized his mistake he was determined to retrieve it before departing the city, so the two went back to find a porter. An SNCF employee at first told them there was no way to find such an item, but the quick-thinking Vernieuwe decided to convince the worker otherwise. He motioned as if he was going to flip back the lapel of his coat, a gesture that he knew was the cue made by the Vichy Milice, which instantly sent the man off looking for the lost leather case. The worker returned moments later, case in hand. The encounter, all carried off with "relaxed nonchalance," confirmed Vernieuwe's superb self-taught skills — and proved to be an excellent model for Jacques Pérot-Spengler, apprentice spy.

The twosome returned to Poligny convinced that only through their own reconnoitering in the region could they assess the possibilities for new passage points in the mountains. Almost immediately they started south, heading by train for Oloron-Ste.-Marie, a town on the eastern edge of the Basses-Pyrénées. Vernieuwe brought along a prewar Michelin map by which, after careful study, they discovered a tiny red line stretching from the village of Mendive several kilometers into the mountains. Curious to see what kind of transport system the marking might indicate, they decided to investigate.

After a bus ride and then a four-hour trek late in the afternoon of a sultry spring day along the back roads from Mauléon, Jacques Pérot-Spengler and his "assistant" arrived in Lecumberry. Fortunately, much of the forty kilometers had traversed flat terrain in the neighboring river valleys to the east, although for the final stretch from Hosta they followed the narrow mountain road over the hilly ridge forming the eastern wall of the Laurhibar Valley. As the two stood for a rest on the top of the ridge they scanned the picture-postcard landscape below: clusters of tiled roofs, whitewashed Basque farmsteads punctuating a vibrant patchwork of tiny pastures, and cornfields and vineyards that carpeted the valley floor and climbed far up the opposite hillside. "We thought we had entered a different country," Pérot recalls thinking on first sight of the valley.

Moving down the hillside toward the center of the village the men found themselves threading an alley-like course among the tightly spaced farmyards. As they passed by, women and children looked up from their afternoon chores, momentarily stared at the two travelers dressed in suits, and went back to work. When the travelers finally reached the intersection with the main road they came upon what became their base of operations:

the Hotel Chateauneuf. After they booked a room the hotel's owner, Monsieur Chateauneuf, directed the wilted pair to a swimming hole in the nearby river to bathe after their exhausting hike — postponing their exploration in Mendive until the next day.

To their complete surprise, one kilometer down the road from the little country hotel they found an aerial tramway, an enormous sawmill, and a railroad bed — all in ruin. As they wandered among the deteriorating complex of buildings and sheds they discovered machinery still in place and many of the cable's upright metal structures still standing. Following on foot the course of the cable as it climbed through the valley they noticed dangling pieces of steel cable and pylons that were either missing or in disrepair, but not beyond repair.

Monsieur and Madame Chateauneuf proved to be a ready source of information about the abandoned mill. Vernieuwe and Pérot-Spengler claimed to be representatives of a wood products firm based in occupied France that was looking for new locations for its factories.[18] From the innkeepers they learned the miraculous history of the construction of the eighteen-kilometer cable system that stretched from the valley floor to the Plateau d'Iraty in the 1920s — including the installation of state-of-the-art equipment, two water-powered electric generating stations in the mountains, and the vast quantities of railroad ties that the Compagnie d'Iraty had exported via the private railroad line. They also heard a gruesome account of the accidental death of Paul Pédelucq and the gradual demise of the enterprise. The company was now in bankruptcy but still owned jointly by the brother and wife of Paul Pédelucq. Monsieur Chateauneuf mentioned, as well, that despite the difficulty of traveling between the Occupied and Free Zones, every summer Monsieur Pédelucq's widow and her children came from their home in the Landes to their house just opposite the factory.

In the course of the conversation the Chateauneufs spoke about the infusion of workers from all parts of Europe that had animated the community for almost a dozen years, and about their sad departure. Their description of Lecumberry and Mendive as "Petit Paris" was in striking contrast to the Belgians' first impression of these Basque villages as backward peasant enclaves. To the former Charles Schepens, familiar with the prosperous Belgian and Dutch farmers surrounding Cette's parents' country estate (who already owned electric milking machines), these Basque communities seemed as primitive as the Yugoslav villages he had seen on his honeymoon. The hotel owners also spoke about the impact of the war on their business, noting that though they were glad their hamlet was located in the Free Zone, the Line of Demarcation at St.-Jean-Le-Vieux had effectively cut off all travel from St.-Jean-Pied-de-Port to the Laurhibar Valley.

After two days the scouts left Lecumberry buoyed by their findings and bearing the address of the Compagnie d'Iraty in Peyrehorade. If the plant could be renovated and the cable reestablished, they were convinced that an enterprise operating from Mendive would make an ideal front for passing people and documents out of France, and a place far enough from occupied Belgium where Pérot-Spengler and his wife and children could take up residence.

What possessed the former eye surgeon to cast himself in this ambitious new role? It was one thing to pose temporarily as a traveling salesman for Trait D'Union, but to volunteer to take on the long-term responsibility of managing a large logging and milling operation was something altogether different. Yet to Charles Schepens the crossover did not seem that far-fetched. Charles had gained rudimentary knowledge of forestry practices as a Boy Scout. Indeed, beginning at age ten when he joined the troop, a camping trip to the Ardennes had been the highlight of every summer. Hiking and practicing woodcrafts and living outdoors for two weeks in one of the country's few true forests were the rewards for the boys' months of fundraising, training, and preparation. Henriette Schepens had helped to organize the expedition for the thirty-member troop with the thoroughness of military maneuvers including, with the help of her sons, a reconnoitering trip each spring to select a site (since the Boy Scouts did not operate their own private campgrounds). After his mother's death, every summer from 1925 through 1929 Charles and his older brothers had taken the troop to the Ardennes to carry on her legacy.

From his teen years onward Charles also proved his talent for organization and his willingness to take on assignments that daunted others. For example, after his mother's death the troop members undertook a campaign to raise money to buy land so that they could build their own local center. Their ambitious goal of thirty thousand Belgian francs (approximately one thousand dollars U.S.) took several years to accomplish. Under Charles's leadership the boys solicited private contributions and organized a raffle. In addition, Charles and four other scouts spent part of their summer vacations working as local farmhands during the flax, wheat, and barley harvests.

The operation of a sawmill was not completely unknown to him either. The platforms that his brothers had constructed in the trees for their backyard battles also served as strategic places to observe activities in their neighborhood in Mouscron. Of particular interest to Charles was the small sawmill next door, owned by the LaMotte family. He remembers as a boy sitting and watching for hours, mesmerized by the sawyer's surgical precision and the speed of the mechanical equipment.

The two Belgians quickly devised a plan to implement their vision: Vernieuwe would return to Poligny to brief de Saule and Ugeux about the scheme while Pérot-Spengler would travel to Paris to propose to Cyrille that the financier purchase the bankrupt mill. The Belgian knew that the realities of Nazi repression had changed Pomerantzeff's political sympathies and was confident that his Russian friend would be receptive to backing the venture.

Trouble set in on their return trip to Oloron. As they approached Tardets, a town fifteen kilometers to the west of Oloron, the Vichy police arrested the men because they were not carrying a special pass issued for travel within thirty kilometers of the Spanish frontier. Vernieuwe and Pérot-Spengler were taken to the local jail. Vernieuwe successfully pressured the Vichy authorities to contact Colonel de Saule. However, after doing so only Vernieuwe gained his freedom. Pérot-Spengler was unable to claim the same protection and spent the night in jail. The following day he was taken to a military barracks in Pau. He told the military authorities that he was Belgian and wanted to go to the Belgian Congo. The authorities offered several choices of punishment: "You can stay in prison, we can send you to a work camp in unoccupied France, or you can be drafted into the French foreign legion." He chose the French foreign legion and signed the enlistment papers because "it meant that at least I would be sent to North Africa, which was okay." He spent the night awaiting his deportation and plotting his escape. Early the next morning he was left alone in a large room in the barracks, the door of which he realized was not locked. He simply walked outside into an exercise courtyard, jumped the wall, and disappeared into the back alleys of the city.

Pérot-Spengler waited several hours, then decided to risk passing through the railroad station in Pau to buy a ticket and board a train. Before departing he called Vernieuwe in Poligny, who told him that if he should be stopped while making any of the transfers to Poligny, de Saule would vouch for him. The young Belgian doctor now held a card that indicated his status as a member of the French foreign legion. Jacques Pérot-Spengler, the Boy Scout–turned–undercover agent, was becoming adept in the techniques of dissimulation and escape.

Part Three

Theater of Resistance

(*Previous page*) Jacques Pérot's identity card.
(courtesy Dr. Charles Schepens)

Chapter 7

By early June 1942 the former Charles Schepens and Cyrille Pomerantzeff were in Lecumberry negotiating for the purchase of Mendive's sawmill. This time the train passed through Bayonne on its way from Paris to St.-Jean-Pied-de-Port, a more direct route to the Laurhibar Valley but one that entailed crossing the Line of Demarcation at St.-Jean-le-Vieux. They booked a room at a cafe-hotel on the main square in St.-Jean-Pied-de-Port and made known to the wife of the owner their need for passage into the Free Zone. As the Belgian had learned from his recent travels in France, although identity papers were frequently checked on board the trains and in the railway stations, it was relatively easy to move about within either zone of the country; getting back and forth across the dividing line between the territories, however, required finesse.

Madame Etchendy, the innkeeper's wife, agreed to help the travelers, but because the Germans were frequent customers of her cafe she insisted that the two stay upstairs while she did so. The men sat there for almost two days until, as Charles recalls, "she instructed us to walk to a farm between St.-Jean-Pied-de-Port and St.-Jean-le-Vieux that night, and there ford the Laurhibar, where our ride would be waiting on the other side with a wagon." He and Cyrille arrived at the Hotel Chateauneuf sitting atop sacks of flour that Monsieur Biskaichipi was hauling to his bakery in Mendive.

As Charles had hoped, Cyrille enthusiastically agreed to invest in the project but he wanted to see the setup for himself. In fact, it had taken little effort to sell the proposal to his supersalesman friend when Charles finally returned to Paris in early June. He had appealed to Cyrille's altruistic nature and his love of risky, new ventures; in buying the mill Cyrille would be reviving an economically depressed region and assuring the security of Charles and his family, while at the same time he would be expanding the supply of raw materials for Trait D'Union. Moreover, just as Cyrille had switched from teaching to commerce, Charles asserted that with his own leadership and organizational skills he, too, could retool himself from eye surgeon to lumber plant manager — with the proper technical personnel under him.

Before they left Paris Cyrille had contacted Alexis Pédelucq to inquire about purchase of the mill and discussed meeting later in Mendive in mid-June. Cyrille first wanted personally to inspect the plant and cable system, however, to assess the renovation costs before he was willing to make an offer. In advance of their meeting with Pédelucq, Charles and Cyrille spent a few days carefully surveying the remnants of the former lumbering operation, including taking a hike all the way up to the Plateau d'Iraty. During their visit Cyrille particularly endeared himself to the daughters of Monsieur and Madame Chateauneuf: at night the irrepressible teacher adopted the role of math tutor to help them with their end-of-term examinations.

Negotiation for the mill was accomplished in a matter of hours at Alexis Pédelucq's late brother's house across from the plant. They discussed the factory's former production levels, the company's marketing and distribution system, and the contractual relationships between the forest service and the Compagnie d'Iraty. Charles remembers Alexis as an aging businessman whose low asking price indicated that he was ready to make a deal. After very little bargaining Cyrille agreed to pay five million French francs (equivalent to two hundred thousand dollars U.S.) for the acquisition of the operation. They shook hands and Cyrille promised to forward a check as soon as he returned to Paris.

Given the shortage of materials and workers in the wartime economy, rapid renovation of the mill likely would be almost as challenging as its initial construction had been. Charles and Cyrille decided that railroad ties would again be the company's principal export, but it would also market furniture squares and other rough-cut blocks to factories throughout the country. Dimensional lumber, broomsticks, chair rungs, and wooden shoes would be sold within the region. They knew it would be impossible to operate the plant at its original level of production so instead planned to undertake only a partial reconstruction of the facilities (that is, no repair of the railroad bed or the electric generating stations in the mountains). It was clear they needed outside consultation to implement the project, so they agreed that Cyrille would seek advice in Paris while Charles looked to hire personnel for the plant.

One of Charles's first acts as the director of the Compagnie d'Iraty was to obtain an identity card for Jacques Pérot-Spengler that would indicate his status as a permanent resident of the valley and prevent another arrest. He remembers the momentary hesitation and suspicion of Monsieur Gastélu, a schoolteacher and the part-time secretary of the commune in Mendive, since Charles was not truly domiciled there yet. Nevertheless, Gastélu conceded to Charles's demand because "he didn't want to make waves with the new boss of the factory." In fact, Charles intended to use the official card only to facilitate his travels back and forth across the Line of Demarcation. Just as he had worn the Loden coat as a symbolic garment when he left Belgium, he believed that a hyphenated French-German name and a card indicating Frankfurt as his birthplace would give him an instant measure of status with the German border guards. To the residents of the valley, however, he planned to be known as "Jacques Pérot" or "Monsieur Pérot." His scheme worked: even today he is remembered by his nom de guerre.

Because most of the company's specialized workers had left the valley in the late 1930s, Monsieur Pérot faced the same recruitment challenge that the Pédelucq brothers had faced twenty years earlier. After buying a bicycle for local transportation and new work clothes in St.-Jean-Pied-de-Port (including a pair of sturdy hiking boots, a Basque beret, and espadrilles), the first order of business was setting up a temporary office and enlisting clerical help. In order to be closer to the plant Pérot moved to Auberge Pedro in Mendive and adapted his room to serve as both a living and a working space. He turned to Monsieur Goyenetche, the priest of Mendive, for assistance in finding a secretary who could take dictation and type. The priest recommended Thérèse Esponda, who not only had the requisite background but whose family connections proved to be indispensable in the company's startup — her sister Henriette was married to Angèle Moretti. Through Thérèse's efforts Monsieur Pérot was able to rehire several members of the Moretti family who had left the valley to work on cable installations in other parts of France.

Finding an experienced engineer to work as director of operations — and who could be trusted as a co-conspirator when the time came — was critical to the operation. After a brief search Pérot hired Marius Pelfort, a man whose training, career, and character made him an ideal choice. Before the war the native of Toulouse had worked as a civil and electrical engineer for a number of national companies and government agencies and had served two stints in the army, first in the mid-1920s as an officer in an artillery regiment and later, when he was called up for the reserves in 1937, as a project manager for construction of a cluster of new French military aerodromes in Normandy. After the armistice in 1940 Pelfort joined the staff of a Chantier de Jeunesse in Arudy, a youth work camp in the central Pyrenees, where he was employed as the director of operations.[1] During his interview Pelfort told Jacques Pérot that he "did not subscribe to the Pétain ideology being promoted at the Chantier de Jeunesse," and that instead of being transferred to another site where he would be directly supplying the German war machine he had decided to look for work elsewhere.

Pelfort's experience and his understated manner impressed Pérot, who early on got a taste of his new assistant's capacity for boldness in dealing with civil servants. Among the assets Cyrille acquired when he bought the company were the logging rights in the Forêt d'Iraty that the Pédelucqs had obtained in the 1920s from the French forest service. To restart the exploitation of the forest the rangers were obliged to mark (or sometimes remark) the trees eligible for harvest and to gain permission from the Pays de Cize and the Pays de Soule to proceed with the cutting. In order to renew the production of the plant the company (now under the jurisdiction of Vichy departmental authorities) also needed to receive a permit from the prefect of Pau specifying the nature of the company's operations. The authorization would allow the Compagnie d'Iraty to obtain coupons to purchase hardware and other basic supplies that were subject to rationing because of the war. The prefect's office also would be indispensable in channeling orders for lumber. Pérot and Pelfort prepared the necessary paperwork and bicycled several hours on the back roads to Pau to obtain the prefect's signature.

Pérot and Pomerantzeff were just launching their enterprise as increasing doubts began to arise about the ability of the Vichy regime to preserve French sovereignty within the Free Zone.[2] Recently reinstalled prime minister Pierre Laval had negotiated a policy in the spring of 1942 which stated that for every three people from unoccupied France sent to work in the German war factories the Reich would return one prisoner of war. From conversations with Pelfort, Pérot realized that the reopening of the plant would be well received if properly presented, since the regional government officials were experiencing pressure from French citizens to protect their sons and daughters from deportation. Pérot and Pelfort planned to petition the prefect's office using the half-true arguments that the company would provide employment to residents and that the materials produced would be for the benefit of the local population.

When they arrived for their appointment they were told by his secretary that the prefect was not in his office that day, and that they would have to obtain the signature of the mayor of Mendive before the application could be approved. Pelfort was determined not to let Vichy bureaucracy impede their progress, so after cajoling and teasing the secretary he forged the mayor's signature and then charmed the secretary into stamping the document. They departed for the strenuous trip back to Mendive, Pelfort chuckling about his minor coup and Pérot assured that his amiable, unflappable assistant was going to be an excellent front man for the company.

Once Pelfort had been hired in the late summer Pérot turned over much of the recruitment work to his assistant, particularly the hiring of specialized technicians and tradesmen. The renovation of the cable was the most important and extensive task in the startup period, so they decided to seek out additional manpower to augment the Moretti clan. During his time in the central Pyrenees, Pelfort had come into contact with a crew of young cable operators from the Italian Swiss Alps who were working on installations in the area. Pelfort was able to lure to Mendive Monsieur Italo and a handful of other daredevils ranging in age from eighteen to twenty-six years old, as well as two men who had worked under his direction at the Chantier de Jeunesse: Jean Bouleux, a twenty-two-year-old hired to be a jack-of-all-trades for the company, and Pierre Faubert, engaged as the new marketing director. With the assistance of forest service officials, Pelfort recruited several employees who had experience in the lumber business, some of whom came from the Free Zone and others who somehow managed to get across the Line of Demarcation. Pelfort hired the company's five master sawyers who, like their predecessors at the factory, were originally from the Landes. Through the forest service as well he found Señor Perez, a charcoal-maker (and Spanish Civil War refugee) living in Bordeaux. Perez's wife Modesta had stayed behind in Spain and risked arrest by the Spanish border guards to join her husband in the Forêt d'Iraty late in the fall of 1942, initially working as his assistant and later as the cook at the company's canteen at the Plateau d'Iraty.

By the fall word-of-mouth advertising had enabled Pérot and Pelfort to fill the ranks of the company's workforce. Only a small percentage of the mill's employees needed to be professional tradesmen such as carpenters, blacksmiths, electricians, or metalworkers; what they needed most was manual labor. The company attracted a mix of Basque shepherds from the surrounding villages, their cousins and in-laws from neighboring valleys, and many other young Frenchmen who had left the Occupied Zone during the invasion and who were now trying to avoid service in the German war factories.

Although Madame Pédelucq regretted the low price that her brother-in-law had negotiated for the sawmill, she and her family proved to be another source of assistance during the company's start-up period. When they arrived for their summer visit in July 1942, Madame Pédelucq, knowing well the shady reputation of Pedro Hernandez, voiced concerns already expressed by Thérèse Esponda and others about the security of the company's files when left unattended in Pérot's room at Auberge Pedro. Pérot readily took up Madame Pédelucq's offer to relocate the office to her house across from the factory until one could be set up on the grounds.

During their summer holidays Madame Pédelucq's two teenaged sons, Léon and Henri, often spent time at the family's mountain chalet in the Forêt d'Iraty. Not far from the cottage and just over the Spanish border was the Casa del Rei, a large rustic hunting lodge built in the seventeenth century for the Spanish monarchy that was now operated as a mountain inn. Because of its strategic location, even before the war the innkeepers were adept at serving clientele who were enemies — most notably the Basque shepherds and smugglers from both sides of the Pyrenees and the French and Spanish border guards — by simply segregating them. Now, with more Carabineros present in order to capture people fleeing through the Forêt d'Iraty, the owners had to be even more vigilant about the timing of their guests' visits. During one of his midsummer mountain excursions Léon got a "clear" signal and entered the inn, where he told the innkeepers the news about the revival of the sawmill and the immediate need for a logging crew. The wife of the innkeeper sent word to her brother, a Spanish Basque farmer from the mountain village of Orbaiceta (in the Rio Iraty Valley). Within a week Monsieur Pérot met Señor Compains at the Casa del Rei. Together they walked the parcel of land the forest service had designated for cutting. Since Pérot did not speak Spanish and Compains did not speak French, the Spaniard who hoped to be the company's new *contratista* (boss) simply wrote down a figure for his services, a sum that seemed acceptable to the novice lumberman.

Before Pérot met Compains the Pédelucqs had described to him the long-standing tradition of employing Spanish woodcutters and the customary payments for their work. At the end of the fall when the work was completed the crew would be paid for harvesting the trees and constructing the barracks for the workers in the logging camp and on the plateau. Pérot was aware that during the work period the company would provide draft animals to the *contratista*'s crew, as well as provisions to feed both men and animals. Thus, instead of being a first exercise in labor relations, Pérot's encounter with Compains was rather an initiation into Basque politics. The risk associated with a team of Spanish Basque loggers coming to work illegally in Vichy France was not addressed. Pérot quickly realized that "to Compains, the opportunity to make money outweighed the potential problems of being caught by the immigration service. The border between the countries represented to him an arbitrary division of the Basque people, and was thus justifiably ignored." Pérot did not see any difficulties with the arrangement as long as the lumberjacks stayed high up in the mountains and did not descend to the valley — an informal but well-established rule in the area.

With the impending arrival of Compains and his crew Pérot needed to hire a herdsman to tend the company's mules and oxen. The Pédelucqs had a ready solution in the person of Raymond Sarochar, a Basque neighbor whom they claimed had a special rapport with animals. Madame Pédelucq explained the dysfunctional relationship within the Sarochar family and the attachment of her own children to Raymond and to Jean, Raymond's older brother, an aging bachelor shepherd who lived alone high in the mountains above. Raymond's service to the family was a selling point to Pérot, and the Pédelucqs' introduction of Pérot as the new *maketo* plant manager was an equally strong endorsement to Raymond.

Once hired, Raymond's first assignment was to acquire the necessary draft livestock, most of which he purchased from farmers within a thirty-kilometer radius of Mendive. Special wooden yokes and leather harnesses needed to be made or purchased, which Raymond suggested they acquire from artisans in Mauléon, a town thirty kilometers to the northeast. Raymond and Pérot traveled on the back road to Mauléon (along the same route he and Vernieuwe had walked on their scouting mission) aboard the company's newly purchased *gazogène*, a World War II adaptation of an existing truck or car that burned charcoal instead of gas in a stove mounted on the side or rear exterior of the car. The weight of the mini-furnace was particularly hard on the vehicle's springs and brakes, and a coating of soot was an unhappy souvenir of a *gazogène* ride. But the *gazogène* was an indispensable unit for transporting goods across long distances in the mountainous terrain.

After less than an hour's ride in the converted Model T Ford, Pérot and Raymond were at the shop of the Darracq brothers selecting the necessary pieces of equipment. Raymond introduced Monsieur Pérot to the harness-makers but the boss chose to only observe as Raymond negotiated in Basque for the items. The artisans' workshop reminded Pérot of the plea-sure he had known as a boy in Mouscron, wandering across the street to stand in the doorways of the local blacksmith and the wheelwright, watching their deft hands at work. Although the language and people were completely foreign, the shop's interior had a familiar quality he had rarely experienced since his arrival in the Laurhibar Valley.

Soon after Pelfort arrived in Mendive one of the first small projects to be undertaken on the mill site was the conversion of a barn, situated near the road and just above the structure that housed the cable terminal, into the new company office. With the help of local carpenters a wraparound porch with a set of stairs that led down to the yard was added, as well as another set of stairs that provided access out to the road. The building's interior was divided into three rooms: a large outer reception and secre-tarial space and two adjacent smaller managerial offices. Pérot purchased a set of crude desks and chairs, three typewriters, a filing cabinet, and a safe from suppliers in Bayonne. A telephone on the director's desk was the office's only modern amenity and a calendar the only decorative item on the bare walls.

To complete his office staff Pérot hired two additional secretaries and an unemployed bookkeeper named Werner, a man of Huguenot descent who had left Normandy and relocated to the area during the 1940 exodus. Once the renovation was under way Pérot also decided to establish a small office in St.-Jean-Pied-de-Port for both practical and precautionary rea-sons: for company banking and shipping, as well as providing a more private environment to telephone Cyrille to confer about the renovation project (although the call went through an operator in Bayonne, who had to relay the conversation back and forth). Furthermore, Pérot thought it would be prudent to have a location outside Mendive where he could receive personal correspondence.

Again, it was through a Pédelucq family connection that he found a secretary for his satellite office: a vivacious young woman named Marie Esponda whose older brother was a friend of Léon. The Esponda family house was located on the same block as the Etchendys' inn on the main square, and the family agreed to let Pérot use a spare room at the back of the first floor for the company's auxiliary office. Every week Monsieur Pérot would bicycle to St.-Jean-Pied-de-Port to pick up his mail and dictate a few letters. Marie also cared for the paperwork related to delivery and eventually shipment of items from the local railroad station.

The pressure to assemble the workforce, to restart logging in the Forêt d'Iraty, and to renovate the structures as quickly as possible consumed Monsieur Pérot for his first four months in the Laurhibar Valley. Through his daily encounters with people in Lecumberry and Mendive, his attendance at Sunday Mass, and his weekly excursions up to the Forêt d'Iraty and to St.-Jean-Pied-de-Port, Pérot began to gain insights about local traditions, habits, and attitudes. He admits knowing almost nothing about the Basques on his arrival. From pro-German newspaper articles that he had read while still in occupied Brussels he knew that their identity as an ancient European people had attracted the racist interests of the Nazis; the Basques, much like the Flemish in Belgium and northern France, were an ethnic minority seeking political recognition for their language and culture. During the first weeks he was in Mendive, however, Pérot mistakenly identified their lifestyle with that of the gypsies because of the active and even open traffic in contraband that seemed to be such an accepted part of community life. That incorrect notion was gradually replaced by a more complex profile of the local mountain people: "What struck me most was that they were very reliable, and they did not talk much — they only spoke when it was absolutely necessary. They seemed very religious and stoic."

Never before had Pérot seen men with the superhuman strength and stamina of Compains and his burly crew of Spanish Basque farmer-loggers, most of whom were under twenty years old. They worked seventeen-hour days, from four in the morning until nine at night; the muledrivers arose an hour earlier to feed and harness the animals, and the oxen drivers got up two hours earlier to give their slow animals ample time to feed. Pérot recalls that within a matter of days, to his amazement they had built a temporary colony of timber-frame structures at the lumber camp without any nails.

Watching the head lumberjack make a few strategic cuts with his ax to fell a giant beech tree reminded him that in "tree chopping, like surgery, it is not force, but accuracy that counts."

With its cooing, guttural sounds the Basque language seemed completely mysterious and indecipherable to Pérot. What he did come to understand during these initial months, however, was the prevalent mix of attitudes among the Basques toward the Vichy government and a general resentment of the Germans.[3] Their bitterness was due to the widespread loss of relatives in World War I coupled with the bombing of Guernica during the Spanish Civil War and, most recently, to the invasion and division of France — which for many valley residents meant separation from their families in the Occupied Zone. Pérot's experience in Mendive made it clear that the local population regarded German interest in Basque nationalism purely as a ploy for collaborationism, and that despite their eagerness to have their language taught in the schools they saw themselves as loyal French citizens.[4] Pérot remembers overhearing discussions in French about incidents involving the Germans among Basques and other company workers in the office, within the mill, and at the cafes. "Any news about the Germans spread like wildfire throughout the valley. The Basques were always gladdened by successful mountain escapes, and angered by arrests."

Pérot's eavesdropping allowed him to hear a variety of tales of how local inhabitants had outsmarted the Germans at the checkpoint of St.-Jean-le-Vieux to get into the Occupied Zone. The Basques in the valley particularly resented the disruption of the cherished ritual of the Thursday market in St.-Jean-Pied-de-Port. The daylong gathering was far more than a weekly bazaar in the lives of the residents of the region — the event mingled commerce, socializing, and festivity for all ages and provided respite from the demanding chores of farm life. The men's market, where livestock was traded, took place in the morning, after which the farmers spent long hours eating, drinking, singing, and playing cards in the cafes while the women sold farm produce around the main square, then shopped and gossiped over cups of hot chocolate as the children played in the surrounding streets. After dark young people assembled in the square to perform Basque folk dances and to serenade their peers. Lively *pelota* or *chistera* matches (similar to handball) that brought together the best players of the region provided an alternative finale for other family members.

The Germans had attempted to restrict this time-honored tradition by requiring that only people with official business or vendors with provisions would be issued an *ausweis* for travel to the St.-Jean market. Long used to cat-and-mouse games, Basque farm families simply shared their livestock or baskets laden with produce with those who needed something to sell, and thus the caravan of people coming from the valley was only minimally diminished. The rationing of wine plus the eight o'clock curfew in effect also served to curtail the customary evening activities, although before returning to their farms some men resumed their merrymaking back at the local valley cafes.

While his discovery of the locals' anti-German sentiment was reassuring, an incident during the renovation period also alerted Pérot to the unexpected dangers of being an influential but mysterious foreigner in a Basque village. In the early fall of 1942 the wife of an employee of the Compagnie d'Iraty had an abortion, a criminal offense that someone in the community reported to the local gendarmerie. Pérot had no idea about the situation until the police came to question him. He had learned from his previous arrest by the Vichy police that when being interrogated it was important to be casual rather than defensive, so when asked about his background, in his soft-spoken, lilting voice he matter-of-factly informed them that he had "worked as a pharmacist briefly when he got out of school at a town in eastern France, but then had decided to go into business." Luckily his answers satisfied the French gendarmes, and they did not notice Monsieur Pérot's hands with their fine, elongated digits.

Chapter 8

The discovery of a vacant sawmill linked to an aerial tramway on the border between France and Spain was surely a serendipitous development for the Belgian underground. Yet success in reactivating the logging and milling operation was far from assured—the company needed to locate and purchase steel cable to restring both the primary and feeder cable lines (demanding three different weights and textures of cable), as well as lengths of steel for the pylons and tallest posts. These goods then somehow had to be transported to southwestern France. When Cyrille returned to Paris in June he sent to Cette Schepens, via an employee who was traveling on business in Belgium, news about her husband's successful resettlement in the unoccupied section of France and of the new enterprise in Mendive. At Pérot's urging he also contacted Cette's father to enlist his help in acquiring the quantities of (rationed) steel they were seeking. Monsieur Vander Eecken had a friend, Marcel Cock, who owned a rope factory and who agreed to serve as the go-between to buy spools of cable through the Brussels black market.

With little difficulty and an exorbitant sum of money from Trait D'Union (an amount never revealed to Monsieur Pérot), Monsieur Cock obtained the cables for the three different lines in the late summer of 1942. To get them exported from Belgium, together Cyrille and Nicolas Rosenschild bribed a German general to authorize the train transport of the cables to the railway station in St.-Jean-Pied-de-Port. In addition, Cyrille procured the steel for the pylons through the French black market and, again through a bribe, obtained its delivery to the train depot in St.-Jean-Pied-de-Port. To expedite the purchase of other kinds of rationed commodities that Pérot needed for the reconstruction and future operation of the mill, Cyrille obtained from the Reich a false commission for lumber for the Atlantic wall that was under construction along the coast of France, a copy of which he sent to Mendive.

Pelfort engineered the delivery of the materiel from St.-Jean-Pied-de-Port to Mendive after the shipments arrived in late August and early September. Since the company no longer operated a private railroad line to the main depot they used a tractor as well as teams of oxen to tow the giant spools and sections of steel on flatbed trailers. To the inhabitants of the valley the size of the procession was less impressive than the sheer quantity of material being transported — it was not contraband from Spain but rather industrial components virtually unavailable in the region, even through the black market. Monsieur Pérot was quickly gaining legendary status among residents of the region. For the first time some even speculated whether he might be working for the Germans.

With the war raging and cash in shorter supply than during the depression in the thirties, Pérot had little trouble finding farmers willing to sell oak and pine so that the company could replace the damaged posts for the cable. Over the summer the Morettis and other company employees had been at work erecting and re-erecting the support structures, as well as attempting to salvage existing sections of the cable system. Pelfort assigned the more high-flying tasks required for the reinstallation to the younger team of cable operators who arrived late in the summer. The tallest structure in the system was a twenty-three-meter (seventy-five-foot) pylon, the last post in the valley located near the end of the paved road on the hillside not far from the Irigoin family farm. Because of its height the post had to be constructed of metal rather than wood. Steel from the Bordeaux shipment was used to fabricate the pylon at the mill, but when Italo and his men attempted to position it in place they ran into problems. As Pérot vividly recalls the scene, he, Pelfort, and a group of factory workers looked on in disappointment as the pylon torqued: "The cross pieces didn't fit, so Italo, who was absolutely fearless, climbed the pole to hammer on the I-beam. When he was at twenty meters, he fell off and landed on some bushes below." To Pérot's amazement not only did he "get up and walk away unfazed by the accident, but the next day he climbed back up and fixed it!" Italo's display of physical courage rivaled the endurance of Compains and his crew in the mind of the surgeon-turned-manager, and it is a story he tells and retells.

Restringing the cable lines was an extended process that involved the participation of all 120 company employees and their accompanying menagerie of animals. For several days a swaying, serpentine procession of teams of yoked oxen and men in berets hauled the three sets of cable up the eighteen-kilometer course to the Plateau d'Iraty as Monsieur Pérot watched and photographed in silent wonder. At the suggestion of the cable technicians, Pérot and Pelfort decided to initially only reinstall the main system and wait until the following spring to do the auxiliary lines. Even so, and considering the vicious southern winds from Africa that added further drama to the already daring undertaking, it took several weeks for the cable crew to complete the rigging. Pérot remembers that the mules balked during several hailstorms, in effect shutting down all work in progress.

By late October the first felled log made its descent to the valley. Unlike twenty years earlier when Angèle Moretti had taken a test ride down the length of the cable, no one repeated his acrobatic performance nor was there any public celebration in the village. For Pérot successful completion of the mill's renovation meant that he could now relax enough to plan for his next project: the arrival of his wife and children. His experience over the previous months living in the Basses-Pyrénées convinced him that "life was so much easier in Mendive than in Belgium. The weather was milder, and finding enough to eat was not the problem it was there. I felt like a tracked animal in Brussels and Paris. In Mendive, I felt a tremendous sense of freedom with my new identity. I thought Cette and the children would also be less exposed in southwest France."

Through Madame Chateauneuf, Monsieur Pérot learned about the possibility of leasing a house in Lecumberry owned by Monsieur Argain, who was among the valley residents referred to as *Amerikanoak*: young, landless Basque shepherds who had emigrated to the Americas at the turn of the century but returned to their homeland some years later as prosperous men. Upon his return to his native village Argain married the daughter of a local family, bought an existing farmstead that fronted the main valley road, and erected a second house next door. He then bought a bus and introduced travel service between the valley and St.-Jean-Pied-de-Port for the weekly market. Well-settled into the new dwelling with his wife and daughter, Argain willingly rented the old vacant farmhouse to the new director of the factory.

Pérot's valley residence was an eighteenth-century four-square stone dwelling originally built to store agricultural equipment and harvested crops on the ground floor and to provide family living quarters on the upper levels. Behind its whitewashed facade and wide decorative entry portal lay a cavernous foyer that led to a wooden stairway at the rear. On one side of the central vestibule was a primitive kitchen with a wood stove, while the dining room on the other side had a large hearth. The upstairs consisted of three bedrooms; an outhouse was attached to the back of the building. A few crude tables and chairs were its spare furnishings, and the only natural light that penetrated the cool, dark interior came through several windows on the main facade and a single second-story window on each of the side and back walls of the house. Though it had no running water the farmhouse had undergone a few improvements during its two hundred years: a tiled floor had been installed when the downstairs was converted into living space, and low-wattage electric lights dangled in several of the rooms. The home was a far cry from the Schepenses' well-appointed townhouse in Brussels, but Monsieur Pérot was certain that his artistic wife could transform it into an attractive and welcoming homestead and that the presence of young children would surely dissolve its pervading gloom.

On a shopping expedition to Bayonne to purchase a collection of furniture in advance of his family's arrival Pérot acquired an assortment of Basque furniture, including tables, chairs, beds, armoires, and a buffet which, like the dwelling, were all striking in their massiveness (transported home in the *gazogène*). He also bought cooking utensils, bedding, and a variety of linens woven with the traditional striped patterns. He remembers being very proud of his purchases, and certain that his attempt at interior decorating would please and even impress his exacting wife.

Over the summer and early fall Monsieur Pérot made a few trips to Paris to privately discuss matters away from the ears of the telephone operator in Bayonne. During these conferences in Paris he reviewed with Cyrille the progress of the renovation and the company's finances, as well as previewed needs for additional materials from the black market. They also used the time together at St.-Brice to plot how to accomplish his family's escape from Belgium and relocation to Lecumberry. Pérot's memories of these visits inspire stories of his re-immersion into Russian culture — a dramatic contrast to the reticent world of the Basques to which he was becoming accustomed — and some curious details of his travel experiences. Occasionally if he had business in Pau or Toulouse he would take the longer eastern route to Paris via Lyon, laying over at various establishments that had been identified as safe houses. His most unusual encounter was at a shelter in Toulouse where the landlord of an apartment building scheduled for renovation rented out space in the tenants' suites when they were not on the premises. Pérot was assigned the apartment of "an old man who was working at night, sleeping during the day, and taking fifteen different kinds of medication."

It was evident that the most direct route to southern France, the overnight train to Bayonne, would be the preferred itinerary to transport his family to southwestern France. Thus, as Pérot made ready their new living quarters, Cyrille journeyed to Ghent to relay to Cette her husband's plans for their reunion: she and the children would travel by train to Paris in late October, where Charles would meet them at the Gare du Nord. Together they would continue on to Bayonne. To expedite their passage out of the country Cyrille would arrange for Gustave Schepens (Charles's eldest brother) to meet them at the station in Mouscron, then drive them across the border and put them on the train to Paris, a scheme that seemed safe because the Germans were used to Gustave's frequent trips for medical calls back and forth between the two occupied territories.

On the appointed day the Schepens family arrived at the train station in Ghent to begin their expedition. The one family souvenir that Cette had packed, beyond a few suitcases of clothes and a small collection of toys, was a missal interlaced with photos, letters, and memorabilia. She remembers that an unexpected encounter with a cousin in the station flustered her "because I did not want to reveal my itinerary to my relative." Cette was aware that she did not have her husband's facility in adopting an alias or providing an alibi, and she worried greatly how she would fare if anything did not go according to the plan.

Cette was leaving Belgium with great trepidation, knowing that she would be far from her parents and all that was familiar. When she and Charles previously had traveled or lived abroad their adjustment to new circumstances had been eased by family ties and the welcome of friends. For instance, when Charles worked at his internship in England in 1936, two women—a British classmate whom Cette had known during her boarding school days in Italy, and a Belgian friend of her family now living in London—provided much-appreciated hospitality, since they felt excluded from the tight social circle of the hospital staff. Similarly, when the young couple needed housing in Brussels after their marriage Cette's father's connections as a *notaire* had helped them find a townhouse to rent. Now, in contrast, she knew that moving to southwestern France meant an indefinite stay abroad surrounded by a completely unknown culture.

Cette had known her husband long enough to realize, as well, that life with him was "une grande aventure." Indeed, their honeymoon had been an initiation into her husband's maverick style. Since he did not have the means to afford a trip to the French Riviera or to the Lake District in Italy (the most fashionable destinations of the time), Charles had convinced the editor of *Le Bien Public*, one of Ghent's daily newspapers, to pay for plane tickets to several European cities in return for his writing a series of travel articles. Their most memorable plane trip was aboard the maiden flight of Air Yugoslav, a plane flying from Belgrade to Sarajevo. The only other passengers on the ten-seat airplane were the Yugoslav prime minister and his wife and daughter. According to Cette, when they encountered a violent thunderstorm en route, "these three got down on their knees and began praying for their lives." On their final descent into Sarajevo she was first awestruck by the panorama of gleaming white minarets, and then dismayed to see that the landing system consisted of a man sitting in a wicker basket atop a pole on the airfield waving red and white flags to signal instructions.

Through the years of their courtship and marriage Cette had gained deep admiration for her husband's passion for scientific research and his overarching ambition to conquer blinding eye diseases. And, although she greatly respected his current patriotic acts of bravery and sacrifice, it was clear that relocating her family to a Basque mountain village would truly test her devotion as a camp follower. Her departure was so stressful that today she retains only blurred recollections of her reunion in Paris with her husband after his six-month absence: being distracted by seeing someone having a piece of luggage stolen in the Gare du Nord, hurriedly collecting their bags to transfer stations to catch the overnight train to Bayonne, and feeling, most of all, the need to suppress strong emotions in such public places. For his part the admiring Monsieur Pérot was quite impressed by his wife's professional performance in her first hours as "Madame Nathalie Pérot."

Attending to the needs of a two-year-old and an overstimulated four-year-old preoccupied both Monsieur and Madame Pérot during their overnight train journey to the south of France. A trip to Lecumberry aboard the *gazogène* awaited them the next morning when they finally reached Bayonne. Monsieur Pérot had seen no need or purpose in having them travel with false identity cards since, by then, "I was familiar enough to the Germans at the Line of Demarcation in St.-Jean-le-Vieux, and I knew they would like the blond hair of my wife and children. As I expected, they waved us through."

The autumn scenery that would have enchanted the painterly eye of Cette Schepens — a collage of rich color patches resembling the contents of a set of spice jars — was hardly even noticed by Nathalie Pérot during her first ride through the Basque countryside. Even the panorama of the majestic silhouette of the Pic de Behorleguy as they approached the Laurhibar Valley made only a brief impression. She talks, instead, about the maternal anxiety that gripped her, particularly about "the kind of shelter and refuge I would find for my children." The relief she felt in finally arriving at their destination was deepened by the warm welcome of Madame Argain, who almost instantly assumed the role of mentor and surrogate grandmother. Although charmed by the craftsmanship and rich dark tones of the cherry and oak furniture that Madame Pérot's husband had purchased for their rustic dwelling, more than anything else it was her neighbor's presence that "lessened my feeling of abandonment and exile."

In final preparation for their arrival Monsieur Pérot had lined up the services of a nanny-housekeeper, eighteen-year-old Beppina Moretti, the youngest daughter of François Moretti. Beppina quickly bonded with the children and occasionally brought along her nephews, Jean and Charles Moretti, as playmates for her charges. In addition to cleaning and cooking, her daily tasks included excursions to buy food from the local butcher and baker. Once or twice a week she also would do the family's laundry, which involved soaping up the clothes and then rinsing them in the river behind the house. The only tasks that she did not enjoy were hauling water from the Laurhibar River for household needs — "twenty-six steps!" back to the house — and collecting drinking water from a spring that was located a kilometer away.

The Argains' farm menagerie provided endless hours of distraction for the children, who relished Madame Argain's affection as well. Once the new Madame Pérot settled into their house, however, Cette rarely ventured forth by herself. The one daily ritual that took her away from the children was attendance with her husband at morning Mass. Their presence was a curiosity to the local people, both because Monsieur Pérot brought along a missal and also because he sat with his wife on the ground floor rather than up in the balcony with the men. Among French Basques married men and women did not associate in public, whether in church, at the weekly market, or at a village celebration. Indeed, never would a man call his wife by her first name or show any sign of affection outside of the home. Thus the Pérots' practice of sitting together was almost as strange to the villagers and as permanently etched in their memories as seeing the Spanish Basque lumberjacks in the forest eating out of a communal pot had been decades earlier. Monsieur Mendury, the parish priest in Lecumberry, was less reticent in his disapproval of Monsieur Pérot's habit of wearing his hiking shorts to the service. Consequently, the factory director and his wife preferred going to church in Mendive where they knew Monsieur Goyenetche was far more accommodating.

Monsieur Pérot realized that despite their conscientious efforts to project a new identity as a French family, an unexpected question or comment by their children about their Belgian past could be disastrous. Charles's misgiving about a potential information leak proved to be well founded when "out of the blue, in the presence of Beppina and the Argains, my daughter piped up in a loud voice, 'It is funny, but each time we move, Daddy gives us a new family name.' We said nothing, and fortunately she never repeated the comment."

In just over four months the Laurhibar Valley had thus witnessed another chapter in its long history of miraculous constructions. However, though Monsieur Pérot's Basque neighbors did not yet know it, the real stuff of legend was yet to come. The sawmill's revival was complete and the Pérot family was resettled, which meant that the manager of the Compagnie d'Iraty could now tackle his ultimate mission: stage-managing the secret work of the entire enterprise.

Chapter 9

Within a few weeks of the Pérot family's arrival to the Laurhibar Valley the Germans broke the Armistice and occupied all of France in retaliation for the Allied invasion of North Africa. Indeed, the event complicated the original plans that Pérot and Vernieuwe had concocted for an underground operation in Mendive but also made the effort more urgent.

Since the establishment of the Line of Demarcation in late June 1940 the Germans had not patrolled the mountain border area separating France and Spain in the Free Zone. Until 11 November 1942 only the French customs officers and Vichy military police were in evidence in the region, and their numbers were insufficient to effectively monitor the passage of goods and people out of the country.[1] Thus in the first two years of the war, aside from the inherent dangers of travel in the Basses-Pyrénées — the winds, violent rainstorms or sudden snowfall, dense mist, and slippery footing throughout a hike of six to sixteen hours — the major obstacle confronting those seeking escape was the possibility of capture by the Spanish guards swarming the far side of the border. The Carabineros maintained an almost constant vigil in the environs of the Casa del Rei.

Arrested fugitives would be marched another several hours to a local jail or regional military prison and eventually sent to one of the Spanish detention camps, where they would be housed for several weeks or months until release was somehow arranged by a foreign consul, a relief organization, an intelligence service, or through private connections.[2] The infamous camp at Miranda (in the province of Castille) was one of the largest of such facilities.[3] Originally built for Franco by the Germans during the Spanish Civil War as an internment center to house Republican rebels, early in World War II the camp gained a reputation among resistance networks throughout the occupied territories for its overcrowded, filthy conditions and severe privations, especially the lack of water. It was not uncommon for a prisoner to lose thirty pounds during a miserable forced stay at the prison.[4]

Vigilance along the frontier was ostensibly a way to insure that Civil War refugees did not return to their homeland and pose a threat to Franco's dictatorship.[5] In effect the operation of Miranda and other similar camps was a profit-making enterprise for the Spanish, who demanded remuneration from the Allied governments for both the maintenance and release of the internees. The poorly paid Carabineros, Guardia Civils, and local town officials also benefited from the border area's intensive ambush effort as they helped themselves to the valuables confiscated from refugees.[6]

To tighten the net on the French side of the border the Germans redoubled patrol of the frontier area and negotiated an agreement with Spanish authorities that fugitives caught by the Carabineros within ten kilometers of the border be turned over to them.[7] The Germans dispatched regiments of Schutz Stauffel (ss) and replaced French customs agents with a much greater force of their own, the Grenzschutz.[8] The majority of these soldiers were Bavarian reservists who were too old to fight in Russia but whose alpine experience made them ideal for the assignment.[9] Grenzschutz troops were billeted in the valleys that served as gateways to the mountain passes. Beginning in mid-November 1942 a contingent of two dozen Grenzschutz and their German shepherd dogs took up residence in the Laurhibar Valley, confiscating the medieval Chateau of Lecumberry for their headquarters and using one of the huts belonging to the French forest service for their mountain outpost.

The presence of the Germans in the former Free Zone in turn precipitated a dramatic rise in the number of people attempting to flee through the Pyrenees, even though the onset of winter made the passage more difficult.[10] Of these political refugees the largest percentage were former military personnel and young French men and women determined to avoid conscription. In early September the Germans had instituted a pol-

icy that superceded their former voluntary prisoners-for-workers arrangement with the Vichy government. Thereafter, French citizens from designated diverse industries (men aged eighteen to fifty and unmarried women
aged twenty-one to thirty-five) would be *required* to work in German war
factories.

Statistics indicate the failure of the new conscription program, known
as La 2e Relève: only one-third of those from the Basses-Pyrénées drafted
for service to Germany actually reported for duty.[11] The entry of American forces into the war brought new hope to occupied France and new
interest in joining the fight in either Africa or England. With escape by sea
virtually impossible because of the German blockade, however, the mountain passes of the Pyrenees represented the only realistic means of exit. The
only choice was whether to attempt the more challenging climb through
the high peaks or endure the longer but less steep passage through the
western or eastern end of the chain. Thus another element was grafted
onto the original concept of using the sawmill as a secret site for the Zéro
resistance network's efforts to ferry documents and high-level officials,
downed pilots, and undercover agents out of France: providing a final
relay station for young labor draft dodgers.

During the sawmill's renovation process Pérot periodically met Vernieuwe
either in Mauléon, Oloron, or Paris, to keep him apprised of the progress
of the reconstruction effort and to share other information. Through these
encounters Pérot discovered that Vernieuwe and his wife had decamped
Brussels in August, barely ahead of the Gestapo, to Villard-de-Lans to be
near Ugeux, who was now functioning under the alias of "Monsieur
Berthier." Pérot also learned that a large factory in Grenoble was serving
as a bank for the Zéro network and for Ugeux's coordinating organization
(Poste du Commandement Belge), and that a young Frenchman named
Vallier, whose family owned another factory in Grenoble, had become a
part-time courier for the Belgian information and evacuation service.
Pérot and Vernieuwe's discussions provided the opportunity for Pérot to
cue his colleague into the web of people in the Basque country whom he
had recruited to assist in their resistance work.

Pérot had used his business travels during the start-up period to recon-
noiter what were referred to in the underground as *"bonnes addresses"* —
local establishments that would harbor refugees or in some way be helpful

to the secret operation. In addition to the Etchendy hotel in St.-Jean-Pied-de-Port, Pérot had lined up several other inns in the region. On his excursions to Oloron he had made a point of frequenting the tiny country hotel-restaurant in Hosta to cultivate the goodwill of the owner, and had made connections with two other larger inns in the neighboring valleys that were already serving as safe houses. Pérot followed up on a rumor that he had overheard about the Hotel Bidegain in Mauléon, a place that was "located strategically above a stream, and that the owners would use to help people escape if the Germans appeared at the hotel." On one of his bicycle trips to Mauléon he stopped in for dinner to observe it for himself. While en route he had gotten caught in a rainstorm and arrived drenched. He introduced himself to the owner's wife as she sat knitting in the hotel parlor; the woman offered to help dry his clothes. But Maitena, the inn-keeper's teenage daughter, impressed him most. In her position at the reception desk she was strategically positioned to view anyone coming through the front door, anyone sitting in the parlor and dining room, and anyone descending from the rooms upstairs — all at once. Pérot realized that the young woman was expertly directing the hotel's internal traffic. Subsequent visits during which he observed Maitena ushering people to the kitchen, where her father presided as chef, confirmed his initial impressions that the Hotel Bidegain was a reliable site for cover.

A chance encounter with a Spaniard doing business in St.-Jean-Pied-de-Port gave Pérot the other lead in recruiting a sympathetic innkeeper. The man owned a cafe-hotel and cinema complex in Elizondo, a Spanish village located in a neighboring valley to the west. In passing the Spaniard mentioned that he often frequented the Hotel Baillea in Les Aldudes where Madame Erreca, the female proprietress, was "very hospitable," and that many of his "guests" had been accommodated there on their way to Spain. One day Pérot extended a bicycle trip to St.-Jean-Pied-de-Port and journeyed down the narrow Vallée des Aldudes to the remote mountain village, which was a kilometer from the Spanish border. In the center of the village was a huge four-story hotel, most likely built originally as a pension to house the transient workers who came to the valley to work in either the forest or the iron industries. Especially appealing to Pérot was the size of the hotel, surely a place where it would be easy for refugees to be concealed. He introduced himself as the director of the sawmill of Mendive and mentioned the Spaniard who had recommended her establishment. Pérot remembers that with a knowing smile "she indicated that she would be glad to help me in any way she could."

The combination of the Etchendy inn in St.-Jean-Pied-de-Port, the hotel in Hosta, the Hotel Bidegain in Mauléon, the Hotel Baillea in Les Aldudes, the Casa del Rei high in the mountains, and the cafe-hotel in Elizondo gave Pérot a support network for Zéro's evacuation efforts. Equally important was a garage in Oloron that agreed to serve as a depot for secret shipments of packages destined for the sawmill from Zéro headquarters in Brussels. The Compagnie d'Iraty already was actively using his services as a mechanic and, banking on his eagerness to do a favor for a steady customer, Pérot proposed the idea of his receiving deliveries and holding them for pickup. Unlike all the other individuals in the region whom he had approached, however, Monsieur Haurat was the chief of the local Légion des Anciens Combattants and very pro-Pétain.[12] (The legion had been created by Pétain in August 1940 to consolidate all the existing veterans groups into one organization and to enlist its members to perform a mix of civic and surveillance services in their communities). In order to court him Pérot waxed eloquent on the virtues of the Vichy regime, his appreciation of his colleague's patriotism, and his own sense of honor in being able to provide service to his government. The garage owner was easily taken in by Pérot's chameleon-like persona.

The last—and most critical—role to be cast by Monsieur Pérot was the *passeur*, or escort, to lead the escapees over the mountains into Spain. For the first two years of the war (before the Germans took over all of France) it was possible, but inadvisable, to make an escape attempt without the assistance of a local guide. Indeed, in the early summer of 1940 Basque border villages like Mendive witnessed the passage of a new breed of mountain pilgrim who came alone, in pairs, in families, or, on occasion, even in small parties. Monsieur and Madame Irigoin, whose farm lay at the end of the main road through the valley, were among those who from the beginning of the war had generously harbored people in flight. Inns like Auberge Pedro's were well-established information centers and often the first stop for clueless fugitives seeking directions out of France. Quickly profit-minded innkeepers like Pedro Hernandez—who had already developed a smuggling operation as a sideline—realized the potential of a clandestine escort service that would serve these unfortunate *maketoak*. However, only the wealthiest could afford Pedro's exorbitant rates; most of the younger refugees ventured off on their difficult ascent armed only with general instructions and a few provisions from local farmers.

Basque shepherds and professional smugglers were the natural candidates to act as *passeurs* since they knew the most direct and the most circuitous routes through the Forêt d'Iraty, the hiding places afforded by the mountain terrain, and the patterns of the French and Spanish border guards.[13] (Refugees from the Spanish Civil War living in the French mountain valleys were another smaller pool of people who had made their services available.) The majority of the Basque *passeurs* saw their work as a form of patriotic service and as a business. They charged varying sums depending on the nationality, the age and size of the group, and the destination in Spain, with fees commensurate with the fines or punishments they themselves could face if arrested.[14] Jewish refugees paid the highest prices. In the fall of 1942 four to five thousand French francs per person was the commonly paid rate, usually in French paper currency although gold pieces and jewelry were also used in negotiations.

Once the Germans occupied all of France, in order to make it over the mountains and across the border it became a virtual necessity to enlist the services of a *passeur*, but the prices increased. By 1943 four thousand francs per person was a cheap fare.[15] As the argument went, the *passeurs* incurred greater risk if they were denounced or apprehended en route since they could be shot or sent to a German concentration camp.

Through his daily routine during the early months of his residency Pérot had become aware of the illegal guiding activities taking place in the surrounding mountains. He also had heard several tales of "*mauvais passeurs*," the dishonest Basques who had been paid by their clients only to abandon them short of the border. With the Germans now ensconced in the valley he realized the added danger of denunciations by people seeking to settle personal vendettas and to collect a bounty in the process. He came to understand how critical it was to find someone who was reliable, knowledgeable, and nearly invisible to the community in order to minimize the possibility of word circulating about the evacuation activities. That person was Jean Sarochar.

Sometime in the late 1930s Sarochar had ended his services as the area's substitute postman and once again retreated full-time to his mountain den. His only regular contacts were his brother Raymond, who regarded Jean as his ally in the family; other shepherds, whose mountain properties

(*Left*) Abbé Erdozaincy at the Chapelle St.-Sauveur, 1983. (photo courtesy Del K. Sheldon)

(*Below*) Aerial transport of a log from the Forêt d'Iraty to the valley, c. 1928. Three different steel wires formed the aerial transport system from the mountain to the valley: a thick and heavy stationary cable from which the loaded chariot was suspended; a parallel cable of smaller diameter, also nonmoving, to relay the carrying apparatus back to the loading point; and the smallest and only moving cable running below and attached to the two others. (photo courtesy Jean Moretti)

Valley terminus of the cable system. The arrival of a log at the valley station is pictured in this postcard, c. 1930. The moving cable was fed in a figure-eight configuration between the gargantuan pulley wheels positioned in the sending and receiving stations. The system was powered by a steam-driven electric motor located in the lower station. (photo courtesy Jean Moretti)

The 370-square-meter (4,000-square-foot) open-span cutting shed at the Mendive sawmill. Several different sizes of circular saws, a twelve-section sash gang saw, and a massive band saw were purchased from Panhard, a famous French industrial firm. (photo courtesy Jean Moretti)

A panoramic view of the Mendive sawmill, looking southeast. In addition to the cutting shed, the roughly four-acre site included a long, double-sided block of open-air sheds, a forced-air drying kiln, an electric generating plant, and an assortment of small workshops. (photo courtesy Jean Moretti)

Paul Pédelucq's custom-made half-track vehicle. (photo courtesy Jean Moretti)

(*Left*) Painting by Cette Schepens of the salon of 72 chaussée de Haecht, 1942. (courtesy Mrs. Charles Schepens)

(*Below*) Charles Schepens, age 18, performing morning medical inspection during his Boy Scout troop's annual camping trip c. 1930. (photo courtesy Dr. Charles Schepens)

Charles Schepens and Oleg Pomerantzeff during their university days. (photo courtesy Dr. Charles Schepens)

Cyrille Pomerantzeff in French army uniform, 1939. (photo courtesy Dr. Charles Schepens)

Charles and Cette Schepens' June 1936 wedding procession. (photo courtesy Dr. Charles Schepens)

The Chateau de Gavergracht, Cette's parents' country estate and the site of Cette and Charles's wedding reception. (photo courtesy Mrs. Charles Schepens)

(*Above*) The work procession to haul the cable lines up to the Plateau d'Iraty in 1942, that Jacques Pérot photographed with his Leica camera. (photo courtesy Dr. Charles Schepens)

(*Left*) A barn (above the plant yard) that Monsieur Pérot converted into the sawmill's office. (collection of the author)

Jacques Pérot with his children, Luc and Claire, behind their house in Lecumberry, 1943. (photo courtesy Dr. Charles Schepens)

Marius Pelfort on an outing in the mountains with the Pérot family, 1943. (photo courtesy Dr. Charles Schepens)

The Casa del Rei, the mountain inn just over the Spanish border (author's photo).

The Chapelle St.-Sauveur. (photo courtesy Del K. Sheldon)

(*Above*) The August 1970 dedication ceremony of the plaque at the chapel. (*From left*) Jean Sarochar, Abbé Erdozaincy, William Ugeux, Charles Schepens, Bernard Ardohain, Oleg Pomerantzeff, and Anselme Vernieuwe. (photo courtesy Dr. Charles Schepens)

(*Opposite*) The commemorative plaque placed outside the western entry of the Chapelle St-Sauveur. (author's photo)

DE 1942 A 1944
POUR DE NOMBREUX PATRIOTES
BELGES REJOIGNANT LES FORCES
ALLIEES L'IRATY FUT UNE HALTE
SUR LE LONG CHEMIN DE LA LIBERTE
LES SURVIVANTS ONT CHOISI
CE SANCTUAIRE DE PAIX
POUR REDIRE LEUR GRATITUDE
A DIEU QUI LES PROTEGEA
ET A CEUX QUI EN PAYS BASQUE
LEUR FURENT FRATERNELS.

1942-TIK 1944-RAINO
INDAR BATERATUERI BURUZ ZOATZIN
HERRIZALE AINITZ BELGIKANO
IRATI-N
DOI BAT HATS HARTUZ DIRE IRAGAN
LIBERTATERAKO BIDE LUZEAN.
BAKEZKO KAPERA HAU DUGU
BIZIRIK GAUDENEK HAUTATU
ESKERRAK NAHIZ EMAN
ZAINDU GAITUEN JAINKOARI
BAI ETA ESKUAL-HERRIAN
ANAI AGERTU ZAIZKIGUNERI

Jean Sarochar, age 78, and
Charles Schepens on a walk in
the mountains. (photo courtesy
Dr. Charles Schepens)

lay in close proximity to his family's and encountered Jean during the summer months; and members of the Pédelucq family, especially Léon and Henri, who made periodic visits up to his hut and joined him on foraging expeditions during their summer holidays. To the other residents of Mendive and Lecumberry the figure of Manech was spotted only rarely in the valley. What people remember most about him, aside from his continued role as *le grand menteur* of the village, was the man's little gray dog whose intelligence was remarkable. A favorite anecdote told about the animal is that even *he* could grow impatient with Jean's endless capacity for storytelling, and would tug on his master's pant leg to remind him that it was time to be on their way.

Manech, ever proud of his patriotic record, did not subscribe to the new Vichy ideology (unlike the majority of *anciens combattants*, whose dislike of the Germans often coexisted with admiration for Maréchal Pétain until the fall of 1942).[16] Nor was Manech among the enterprising Basque shepherds in the region who were providing guiding services to fugitives. Indeed, one night as he returned to his mountain hut he sensed danger when he saw the path to his door littered with unfamiliar small footprints. When he charged in to attack the intruders, to his surprise he discovered a troop of twenty young female draft dodgers camped inside. With them was a shepherd from Behorleguy, an escaped prisoner of war turned *passeur* who had attempted to lead the large party of women over the Pic des Escaliers but had turned back when they couldn't ford an icy stream. Manech allowed them to stay and grudgingly agreed to help them re-attempt the passage. Before the caravan set out the next morning he watched first in shock and then in amusement as "the women powdered their faces, applied lipstick, and put on fancy shoes as if they were going off to work." He helped them as he had promised, but was not an eager guide for a group so large or ill-prepared — something Pérot later learned for himself.

Until the fall of 1942 neither the war nor the revival of the Compagnie d'Iraty had much impact on Manech's simple and solitary existence. Only through Raymond's work for the sawmill did Jean come to develop an interest in and involvement with the company's operation or its clandestine mission. As part of the food rationing system meat could only be purchased from an authorized butcher, and quantities were severely restricted. The regulation caused great concern for Pérot and Pelfort because they needed to feed both the lumberjacks and the employees housed up on the plateau. According to the former Pérot, the Spanish loggers each consumed six to seven thousand calories per day. To augment the provisions purchased from local purveyors they decided that the company's older livestock should be slaughtered for food; they charged Raymond, as the herdsman, to carry out this illegal activity. Pérot remembers that Raymond was "someone who, if he had confidence in you, became very attached. He asked no questions." Raymond enlisted Jean's help, and together they secretly butchered the animals somewhere up in the mountains.

No questions asked beforehand, no repercussions afterward—their fulfillment of the assignment was a promising sign to Monsieur Pérot. Using Raymond as a go-between, Pérot several times during the fall again enlisted Jean's services for other covert food-related errands in the mountains to further test his reliability. "He performed perfectly," remembers Pérot. Convinced that he had found the right candidate, late that fall Monsieur Pérot finally ventured up to Jean's hut to meet him alone, face to face, to personally engage him as the *passeur* for the network. What Pérot did not know at the time was Jean's reputation in the village as the local blowhard, a trait that once he discovered it further confirmed the wisdom of his choice: even if Jean did brag about his activities no one would believe him anyway. His reputation would allow him to hide in plain sight.

By then the despised German "wolves" were very much in evidence in "his" forest and mountains, and Jean was ready to participate more actively in resistance activity. Raymond had arranged the visit but did not know its exact purpose. Pérot was not concerned about being spotted at Jean's property because he often was seen stopping at local farms to purchase food or request some service for the revived factory. Indeed, the brevity of the encounter rather than the actual experience is what Pérot now recalls. The two men sat across from each other at the table in the smoky darkness as the Belgian indicated in simple terms what he wanted: "To be able to send to him people who needed a guide through the Forêt d'Iraty into Spain." Sarochar nodded in agreement, but conveyed his desire "only to take very small groups of people." The two men did not discuss their political sympathies during the visit, nor did Jean demand any payment. Monsieur Pérot descended back to the valley extremely satisfied but also curious about this "unusual man of nature."

Sometime in December 1942 Vernieuwe secretly came to visit Monsieur and Madame Pérot at their home in Lecumberry to confirm the readiness of the factory and the cable, and to review the sequence of activities required to relay both packages of confidential materials and the refugees out of France. Because of previous security breaches in Zéro's other principal evacuation route through Perpignan, Vernieuwe also wanted to personally insure that adequate safeguards and contingencies were in place. In actuality Monsieur Pérot had already initiated the parallel work of the plant.

After the German takeover of the area Pérot had decided to issue a special identification card to all of his employees. This company pass, written in German, would ensure their free circulation in the Forêt d'Iraty and the surrounding mountains. He informed the Germans of the cards so that they would not question the comings and goings of his workers, be they permanent or transient. Almost concurrently Pérot used the local grapevine to let it be known that even though the factory was back in operation, the company was always looking for additional laborers. In anticipation of their appearance he told Pelfort that "any new jobseekers should be interviewed, then issued an identity card and assigned to work up at the Plateau d'Iraty." Thus, starting in mid-November a trickle of young men started appearing at the factory to seek employment. After a few weeks of service — enough time to collect several hundred francs and to find a *passeur* — they would desert their jobs and head for the Spanish border. For these fugitives, almost all of whom were young labor draft dodgers or escaped prisoners of war, engineering an escape had to be a do-it-yourself proposition since Pérot wanted to reserve Sarochar's services only for the Allied military officers, Belgian government officials, and *résistants* being relayed by the Zéro couriers. By the end of 1942 Pérot's plan had taken effect and ten recently hired French workers had disappeared.

Pérot's open hiring policy and his lack of concern for turnover were intended to reveal to Pelfort the covert purpose of the enterprise, if he had not already understood it. Monsieur Pérot never was sure at what moment his assistant actually realized the nature of their work, but "we never openly discussed it. It was clear Pelfort observed, knew, and played along."

When Vernieuwe came for his debriefing Pérot thus was assured of key alliances as well as the feasibility of using the company's logging activities in the Forêt d'Iraty as a smokescreen. Paramount in Pérot's mind was his belief that Mendive should not become a recognized destination for the

Belgian resistance like the Basque coastal town of St.-Jean-de-Luz had become, that his operation be reserved for emergencies, and that he have as little contact as possible with any individuals or parties in passage. He preferred Vernieuwe escort his own charges (arriving either from Pau or Oloron) to the little hotel in Hosta, where Pérot would arrange for Jean Sarochar to meet and then accompany them by night to the border, thus alleviating any need for them to come into the Laurhibar Valley at all. Alternatively, were someone to need time to regain strength before attempting the strenuous expedition through the mountains or if a problem occurred while en route, an escapee was to be informed about the possibility of temporary employment at the factory. Were this to be the case, Pérot would use the same procedure as for the other fugitives arriving at the factory (that is, issuing company work cards), but would dispatch them to the mountain work zone via Jean's hut.

Pérot had prearranged a meeting with Jean during the visit so that his Belgian colleague could meet their *passeur*. Since Vernieuwe was not an enthusiastic hiker, Jean and his canine sidekick came down to the village and made his first clandestine appearance at the Pérot house in Lecumberry. In the presence of the two men Jean was quite shy and Monsieur Pérot spoke on his behalf, emphasizing his preference for only conducting a few people at a time through the mountains. Again, Jean's reserve made an impression on Monsieur Pérot.

As Pérot and Vernieuwe reviewed the scope of the plans it became apparent that the principal function of the lumbermill would be to relay clandestine cargo to Spain; such deliveries would occur far more frequently than the evacuations. Some of the material was to be sent immediately via the cable, while other packages — containing funds to be allocated to Zéro's agents and clients for expenses incurred in transit — were to be stored temporarily in the company safe. Most of the brown bundles would come via Oloron and the sensitive contents would be concealed by an outer layer of innocuous material in case the customs agents or other officials wanted to inspect. Pérot also could expect some small parcels from Spain, which would need to be retrieved at the Casa del Rei.

Vernieuwe's mission concluded with a visit to Monsieur Haurat's garage in Oloron. Pérot introduced the Zéro courier to the garage owner as a "fellow Vichyist" and one of the Compagnie d'Iraty's associates who would be dropping off packages for later pickup. Vernieuwe then returned to Grenoble to inform Berthier (the former William Ugeux) of Pérot's masterful arrangements and his conditions for participation.

In early January 1943, just eight months after the initial scouting mission, the first delivery took place but it was Berthier, not Vernieuwe, who transported the two bundles of material (each weighing about fifteen pounds). As the chief of the network Berthier wanted to test the efficacy of the relay operation as well as confer with Monsieur Pérot in Oloron. In fact, when he changed trains in Toulouse the Vichy police ripped the outside wrapping of one of the parcels Berthier was carrying but luckily what they discovered inside was a newspaper article in French about the size of eggs for export. He was not interrogated. Pérot had arranged to meet him at the garage, where he loaded the packages into the *gazogène* and made sure to introduce Monsieur Haurat to "another of the company's eminent Vichy associates." After their meeting Pérot returned to the sawmill and activated the system he had planned. To Berthier's delight, within a few weeks the packages had reached London.

Thereafter Pérot was never directly involved with the material in transit—and from then on Vernieuwe carried the parcels in suitcases during the train trips and unloaded them at the Oloron garage. There Bouleux and Pelfort picked up the parcels and loaded them into burlap bags as part of the normal weekly course of company errands in the region. After the sacks were delivered to the plant other company workers loaded the parcels into the trunks, camouflaged among the bags of provisions and tools for the company's mountain workers, eventually to be carried via the cable up to the plateau. The last leg of the relay was accomplished by Compains (or one of his loggers), who retrieved and conveyed the contraband either by man or animal to Orbaiceta, his native village. Once the goods reached Spain a courier affiliated with Zéro took charge of getting them to San Sebastian, and then forwarded them to London.

Thus Monsieur Pérot anonymously joined the brotherhood of mountain smugglers. Just as he never opened the small parcels that had been delivered to his office in Brussels, not until long after his stay in Mendive did he learn the actual nature of the cargo: in addition to microfilm, secret documents, and communiqués, the bulk of the material was copies of *Le Moniteur Belge* and other resistance propaganda intended to encourage the continued engagement of Belgian expatriates all over western Europe in the clandestine war against the Nazis.

Chapter 10

"They did not know what to make of me," recalls Monsieur Pérot. The director of the sawmill was indeed quite a puzzle to his employees and to the other residents of the valley, a perception that could not have pleased him more. Once the Germans took up residence in the local chateau, Pérot deliberately adopted the guise of a double agent in order to further protect his family and himself.

On one hand Pérot's physical vigor impressed people in the region. He was constantly seen riding his bicycle on errands when he easily could have used the company's *gazogène*. Once the cable was in operation either he or Pelfort would make a daily visit up in the mountains. Unlike Paul Pédelucq he did not have a half-track vehicle to make the journey, nor did he choose to go by mule. Instead the graduate of the Verberie outdoor fitness training program would rise at four o'clock in the morning, ride his bicycle to the end of the main road and leave it at the Irigoin farm, then climb for two to three hours to reach the Forêt d'Iraty. Unlike the Basque shepherds, Pérot hiked without a walking stick. During his ascent and while it was still dark he would on occasion encounter local Basque smugglers and their mules returning with various forms of contraband: alcohol, coffee, cloth, chocolate, cigarettes, soap, saccharine, and sometimes even livestock. As the day grew lighter Pérot would see members of the cable crew descending to inspect the upper portions of the cables that stretched from the plateau to the relay station at St.-Sauveur, where they would meet a team who had walked up from the valley on similar duty. He usually spent six or seven hours in the mountains visiting both work zones. He would stop for lunch either at Modesta's canteen or at Chalet Pedro, a satellite restaurant that Pedro Hernandez had established to capitalize on the increased activity in the mountains and to serve as a convenient delivery station for his own smuggling network. Toward the end of the workday Monsieur Pérot would then head back to the village, along the way encountering shepherds from Mendive and Lecumberry who were guiding their flocks to their night pastures. Of course his mountain forays also familiarized Pérot with the patrol schedule and circuits the Grenzschutz took around Ahusky and between the Plateau d'Iraty and the Casa del Rei.

Monsieur Pérot worked deliberately to establish the impression of a hardworking and hard-nosed manager. For instance, although it was strictly forbidden for employees to ride the cable, on a few occasions he observed a handful of the more audacious young men using the aerial system to get down from the mountains. He remembers one time seeing a man suspended a few hundred meters in the air when the cables stopped moving, and fearing what could happen if the worker fell. Pérot learned the names of the culprits and called them to his office, where he reprimanded and warned them not to do it again, reasoning that the fright of being suspended was the best punishment for foolhardy behavior. He did assert his authority more aggressively, however, when a section of cable intended for installation as part of the auxiliary network was stolen in early 1943. In order to recover the cable he announced to his employees that "he would have to report the theft to the police if the cable could not be found or replaced." The threat proved effective: the cable had been sold to the mayor of another village but reappeared several days later. He fired the guilty employee.

Monsieur Pérot's public relations in the community proved to be especially effective in his efforts as a double agent. Before his family arrived he made it a practice to attend Sunday Mass at the church in Mendive. He remembers "often being invited for breakfast afterward by the priest, Monsieur Goyenetche. We drank schnapps and a little coffee, and ate some bread together. But the schnapps was the main offering." Not only was this association helpful during the start-up process, but even more important it signaled approval by one of the community's leaders. Pérot also made a point of visiting with his neighbors the Argains, the innkeepers at Hotel Chateauneuf, and other local residents such as Monsieur and Madame Irigoin, who would invite him in for wine or bread and cheese when he picked up his bicycle at the end of the workday.

What perplexed the Basques, therefore, was Monsieur Pérot's camaraderie with the Germans. "We thought we were working for a collaborationist," remembered Arnaud Harguindeguy, then one of the young men from Mendive who worked in the factory. The presence of the Germans in the valley was very definitely an unwelcome development for those living in the nearby villages. The Grenzschutz, an older contingent of military men who had left their families behind, were much less intimidating than the younger border guards or the Gestapo agents in St.-Jean-Pied-de-Port (whose rigid posture was likened by Arnaud Harguindeguy's younger brother Pierre to "green wine bottles"). Some of the Grenzschutz tried to gain the goodwill of the inhabitants by giving candy to the children and cigarettes to the men, offerings that were gladly accepted but which did not change the reigning negative sentiments of the population.

Indeed, the inhabitants resented and feared the increased scrutiny of these outsiders with high-powered binoculars and attack dogs. Madame Irigoin vividly remembers one tragic incident that happened near their farmhouse on a January night, when two men from Mendive went fishing illegally in the Laurhibar River to catch trout for a wedding banquet. The lantern they were carrying attracted the attention of the Germans, who arrived in a fleet of sidecars ready to arrest what they thought were fugitives. The two locals fled; one successfully found a hiding place and the other escaped up the mountains but died of pneumonia. Another well-remembered event occurred when the Germans attempted to confiscate all of the firearms in private possession, a story that illustrates not only the defiance of the local civilian population but of the unexpected solidarity of the French police. One day someone from the village shot off a rifle and in retaliation the Germans demanded eighty hostages from the surrounding villages until the culprit was found. Fortunately, the local chief of the gendarmerie came to the rescue by explaining that the shot was fired as part of a training session with his men.

But the Germans' physical presence wasn't the only thing that offended and angered the Basques. Nazi occupation of the region meant the forced requisition of services and food from their farms as well as the imposition of a series of new restrictions, including an eight o'clock nightly curfew and a ban on listening to the nightly BBC radio broadcasts. Not every home had a radio, and neighbors would thus invite others to visit them in the evening to hear the program "Les Français parlent aux Français." Since the tightly closed shutters of the farmhouses provided a relative measure of security, being seen circulating outside after dark posed the greater danger. Among the interdictions most resented by the local farmers, however, was the prohibition against having brush fires beyond early afternoon. Burning the hillsides was an annual fall ritual that dated back centuries and accounted for the harsh, denuded appearance of the landscape, and provided a way both to fertilize the terrain and to insure that unwanted growth (such as gorse and brambles) was eliminated from the pastures. These fires typically burned for several days and were timed to take advantage of active winds from Africa. Unlike many other interdictions that could be subverted, there was no way to camouflage a burning fire.

During the first six months of 1943 the Germans announced other decrees that adversely affected the local population. In February the Vichy government, under instructions from the German High Command, created the Zone Réservée Pyrénéenne which encompassed all of the land within thirty kilometers of the border and where only residents of the local communes who held identity cards and others in possession of an *ausweis* would be permitted to circulate. When the Basques took their flocks up to the high pastures for the summer months it was common for male members of a household to rotate on a weekly basis between the valley farm and the mountain dwelling, a situation that the Germans did not like but could not control. A shepherd whose family hut was situated on the Plateau d'Iraty remembers almost being arrested by a guard one day because the German did not recognize the other young shepherd with him. Furthermore, the occupier's solution to regulating and reducing the activity in the mountains was to conduct a census in 1943 of all the shepherds, livestock, and domestic animals within a commune's jurisdiction.[1] Thereafter only a limited percentage of flock owners would be granted mountain pasturing rights, and only by permission obtained from the regional German office in Oloron. The action violated a centuries-old tradition and severely hampered a population dependent on the pastoral economy.[2]

However, by far the most serious economic threat to the labor-dependent farm families living in the valley was the imposition of the Service du Travail Obligatoire (STO).[3] Under this new regulation, which replaced the failed 2e Relève, all those born from 1920 to 1922 were required to work for two years in Germany; draft dodgers, if caught, could face three to five years in prison and fines up to one hundred thousand francs. The prefect of Pau was charged with conducting a census to determine eligibility and exemptions. Among the first convoy of conscripts scheduled for departure in March were ten young men from Mendive, including Pierre Harguindeguy, who attempted to escape en masse to Spain but were arrested and eventually sent to the prison at Totana. The March departure was the first of thirteen convoys that departed for Germany over a six-month period; statistics indicate that only one-third the number of draftees actually showed up, and the other two-thirds either went into hiding or fled the country.[4]

Moreover, for the Basques of Mendive and Lecumberry the German occupation increased the worry about informants circulating within their midst. Monsieur Etcharren remembers his parents' concern about whether they had been entrapped by an undercover German agent when they fed or gave directions to a *maketo*. Local inhabitants looked with particular suspicion on people who associated with or worked for the Germans on a regular basis. Among those still remembered as collaborationists were the daughters of one of the company's foremen who came from the Landes. Even today the daughters are regarded with disdain by people from the area because they worked as housekeepers at the chateau in Lecumberry; many still believe they were traitors. At the end of the war the two young women had their heads shaved in public as a form of humiliation for their perceived treachery.

Given such prevailing sentiments, Monsieur Pérot's demonstrative friendliness to the Germans was quite baffling to those in the community. He first ingratiated himself to the teams of German border guards by inviting them to use the cable to transport their rifles and knapsacks to and from the Forêt d'Iraty, an offer the guards gladly accepted. On a daily basis their personal effects were loaded by company workers into empty trunks and delivered to one of the relay stations. Even more galling to the Basques was seeing their boss dining in the company of Herr Müller, the deputy chief of the local guards' brigade. Monsieur Pérot sometimes invited Müller and other members of the Grenzschutz to join him for lunch at either of Pedro's restaurants, and would make a point of speaking German in their presence. In full view of his workers Pérot would pass around a gourd of wine to the officers at his table. It was rumored (but untrue) that on occasion he even hosted Müller and other German officers at his house for dinner. In fact, he did sometimes send over luxuries such as ham and cheese for the enjoyment of the German guards at the chateau, and willingly gave them provisions when they came to requisition food.

Thérèse Esponda was one of the company's employees who had daily contact with Monsieur Pérot and who picked up on some of the discrepancies in the operation of the business. Pérot admits, "I was sure that she had seen my own false identity cards when the office was first at the Pédelucq's house and she was working alone there. But she never asked any questions." One day during a conversation she did let slip a comment to him about the fact that "the employees were talking a great deal about his being with the Germans so often," to which he replied, "tant mieux" (all the better). At the same time Pérot knew that he should not overplay his part as collaborationist if he was going to sustain the cooperation of his workers so, as Arnaud Harguindeguy also recalled, "he assembled all of the plant's employees and announced that he was not working for the Germans. As proof, he reminded us that if he were he would have been able to get gas and would not have to use the *gazogène*." According to Pérot, "they still did not know what to make of me."

Monsieur Pérot worked conscientiously to fool both the Basques and the Germans. Meanwhile, Berthier's camouflage effort allowed Pérot to successfully remain completely invisible to British and Belgian intelligence operations in London as well. Since Pomerantzeff was already subsidizing the plant's operation, Berthier saw no need to appeal to the secret service for financial support of the sawmill. Moreover, were he to reveal the secret of Mendive, operatives in London would demand more information and accounting. As he confessed later, "It was better that they not intervene in this risky undertaking." Thus, only the money being delivered by the couriers and deposited in the company's safe came from London, and 90 percent of it was from the treasury of the Belgian government. Berthier simply disguised these funds as part of Zéro's general travel expenditures.[5] Monsieur Pérot nonchalantly put in the vault, as his office staff looked on, the brown packages containing a mix of hard currencies worth great sums — French francs, British pounds, and American dollars — alongside the company's own cash reserves.

Jacques Pérot, for his part, regarded the operation of the sawmill in Mendive as an autonomous service to the resistance, something affiliated with but not under the direction of Berthier. By playing the role of double agent, by insulating himself from the actual relay of people and parcels, and by guarding the secret as closely as possible Pérot was confident that "I would never be caught." For his own security as well as for those who were directly or indirectly serving as accomplices he attempted to limit their knowledge of the scope of the operation. Only Vernieuwe comprehended all of the details of the complex scheme. (As an escort for the Zéro network the Belgian courier was in a way even more informed than Pérot because he knew the identities of those in flight.) As for Berthier, Pelfort, Pomerantzeff, and Sarochar, each had a somewhat more generalized awareness of the clandestine activities and the other personnel contributing to the effort. The plant workers who were providing services as errand-runners — Faubert, Bouleux, Murillo, and Compains — had only fragmentary information about the company's covert business. And those operating in an indirect supporting role — Vernieuwe's wife Loulou, Nicolas Rosenschild, and Cette — were privy to as little as possible of what was going on behind the scenes.

Monsieur Pérot did undertake one small precaution, just in case: at night he suspended a rope from the second story window at the back of the house. Madame Alchouroun (née Argain), a teenager during the war years, recalls her parents commenting on the Pérots' unusual practice but never attributing it to devious activity. In fact, Jacques Pérot was so adept at covering his tracks that Beppina Moretti, who on occasion slept in the extra bedroom in the Pérot house, never remembered seeing the rope nor ever having had the least suspicion that her employers were anything but proper and kind.

Two private and spontaneous acts of conscience demonstrate the level of confidence and security that Pérot felt, even with the Germans living in such close proximity. On one occasion an outside team of plainclothes Vichy police came to investigate a crime in the area. Once they had concluded their work the local police chief solicited a ride for them to Mauléon from Monsieur Pérot. Conscious to court the favor of this particular Vichy authority, the factory director willingly volunteered to take them in the *gazogène*. As he tells it, "When we reached the top of the Col d'Osquich I stopped to check the tires. I knew it was a very windy spot, and when I got out of the vehicle I opened up the case containing their dossiers that was strapped to the roof. The papers went flying! They lost some of the documents, and of course I apologized profusely." The other incident was far more risky and struck at the heart of his ethical underpinnings: "One day in the spring of 1943 a carpenter working for the factory came into my office with a metal splinter in his eye. He was a Parisian who had killed a German and then had fled to the south of France. He refused to go to the hospital in St.-Jean-Pied-de-Port to be treated because there was a reward that had been advertised for his arrest. Seeing the serious-ness of the injury I told him I had once had first aid training and perhaps could remove it." The man agreed to let the boss try his hand. Using only a safety pin and without any local anesthesia Monsieur Pérot masterfully extracted the piece of metal. The carpenter went back to work and the fac-tory floor was abuzz with praise for Monsieur Pérot's handiwork. Luckily the news of this makeshift eye surgery did not go any farther.

The former physician, however, chose not to use his medical skills when it came to treating himself or his family. Monsieur Argain, their neighbor, was regarded as one of the local healers and would often suggest herbal remedies for dealing with the children's common woes. As it turned out, it was not the Pérot youngsters who required medical attention during their stay. When Cette contracted pneumonia early in 1943 her husband de-cided to send for the doctor from St.-Jean-Pied-de-Port. The doctor di-agnosed her condition and administered a nineteenth-century treatment known as "cupping," whereby heated glass containers are applied on the patient's back to bring blood to the surface. Also during their tenure in the Basque country Pérot developed a painful condition in his right knee that he knew was due to loose cartilage. He paid a visit to the same doctor, who correctly diagnosed it and then treated it by "creating little burns around the affected area" — exactly what Dr. Charles Schepens would have done.

Though for the Basques the presence of the Germans represented a threat to their traditions and to their sense of independence, for Monsieur Pérot it was more of a nuisance to be managed and was far preferable to the claustrophobic feeling he had experienced living in Brussels. Even now he admits to enjoying his new life. "Things were going so smoothly, and I had so little financial responsibility. I remember singing for joy to myself as I would bicycle through the countryside. At the time I even had the idea that I could spend the balance of my life there, give up medicine, and get a diploma from some forestry department."

Chapter 11

Charles Schepens felt secure and at ease living life as Monsieur Pérot. His wife, in contrast, remained remote and fearful. Cette was well aware that her husband had gained a reputation as a collaborationist, which made her feel self-conscious and uncomfortable. As she recalls, "I was not in contact with the population of the valley, only [with] Beppina and the Argains. And I was not intimate with anyone, apart from Madame Argain, who was a wonderful 'mother hen.'" Cette's world revolved almost entirely around her children and the house, and they are the basis of her memories of their time living in Lecumberry. Sporadic family weekend expeditions via the company's mules up to the mountains to spend the night at the Pédelucq's chalet, occasional pilgrimages to the market in St.-Jean-Pied-de-Port, and her attendance at church were the only outings that took her away from the sanctuary of the Pérot home. Cette now readily admits that she has blocked out as much as possible from her memory of this traumatic chapter of her life.

Cette was, nevertheless, determined to adapt to the difficulties that her situation posed. As she asserts, "I am an optimist by nature. I'm not someone who reflects on options or agonizes. I like to do physical things to keep myself going." One of the more rewarding chores she found to occupy herself was cultivating large flower and vegetable gardens around the house. With the help of Madame Argain, Cette discovered the time-tested benefits of using the contents of the outhouse as fertilizer for the plants. Her exquisite bouquets of flowers from the garden and local wildflowers are a detail commonly remembered by those who gained entrée into the Pérot home. A family photograph taken in the garden, one of the few dozen that survive from this period, provides silent testimony to her horticultural success.

A gift brought by Cyrille Pomerantzeff on one of his business trips to Mendive also helped to perk up Cette's spirits. After Cyrille surprised her with a set of paints and brushes from Paris, she commissioned her husband to purchase an easel and canvas, which he found in Bayonne. Since their Basque farmhouse was so dark she became an open-air painter, using the garden as her studio. As much as this artistic activity was a connection to her past, ultimately it provided a form of distraction and today Cette has only vague recollections of the paintings she produced during their residence in Lecumberry or what eventually became of them. In fact, two of the paintings have more than survived: the portraits of young Jean and Charles Moretti have occupied a place of prominence in the Moretti home in Mendive since she presented them to the family more than half a century ago.

Much more vivid to Cette are memories of Cyrille's visits and the joyous energy he brought into their lives. At least once a month he spent a few days with them, always bringing toys and books for the children and tidings about their families and friends. Because the family felt so isolated they appreciated hearing news of any kind. For both Cette and her husband the most disturbing news Cyrille bore on one of his trips was the discovery that Oleg had been imprisoned in Yugoslavia by the Germans. Cyrille, who had not heard from his brother since the outbreak of the war and had learned of his plight through a German contact in Paris, also told them that he hoped that a bribe would facilitate Oleg's release.

Occasionally Cyrille brought along Madame Monmerle, his elegant secretary who Cette remembers as "temporarily transplanting Paris into our house." These eagerly awaited visits re-inspired all of Cette's hostessing talents, which made a strong impression on both Beppina and the Argains' daughter, who were often engaged as "waitresses" at what they remember as very fancy dinner parties. Monsieur Pelfort was a frequent participant in these sophisticated soirees and Cette remembers the delight her husband's assistant showed on being included. She knew that the Toulousain bachelor greatly enjoyed Beppina's spicy cooking, a cuisine filled with pimentos, garlic, and peppers that Cette's Northern European palate only gradually learned to appreciate.

Another favored though infrequent overnight guest was "Selmo" Vernieuwe, whose presence also helped to recall their former lives. It amused Pérot that this "230-pound, blond-haired giant, when asked how he had managed to make it through all the checkpoints, would say that he just melted into the crowd." Of course Pérot knew from his own experiences traveling with Vernieuwe that the Belgian's connection to de Saule gave him a high level of protection. The courier's visits were an opportunity to catch up on the progress of the war, since Pérot did not read the underground newspapers being relayed via the cable nor did the family have a radio in their house. Pérot also learned from Vernieuwe what was happening in Belgium and some anecdotes about other resistance initiatives. Often Vernieuwe's stories of their colleagues were tragic tales that ended in arrests and deportations to the German concentration camps. Indeed, Vernieuwe's own fear of being caught and tortured was so strong that he and the other Zéro courier, "Halloy" (formerly de Hepcée), had made a pact to take care of the other's family if something terrible happened to either one.

An unexpected and surprising group of visitors — Belgian friends and associates who were now fugitives seeking passage out of France via the Pyrenees — soon reminded Jacques Pérot and his wife of the vulnerability of even the most tightly run resistance network and the dangers that threatened the undercover agent and his dependents as well. In early March 1943 it was not Allied military personnel or government ministers whom Vernieuwe was escorting through the area, but his own wife Loulou and three operatives affiliated with Zéro, all of whom the Germans were actively pursuing. In February Berthier had received formal orders from London to liquidate his command post in Grenoble because the Gestapo had made a rash of arrests of Belgian and French underground agents. A manhunt for Vernieuwe and de Hepcée by both the Germans and the Vichy police had also begun in the region after the two Zéro couriers had helped a group of former Belgian ministers (living in exile in France) gain passage to Spain but somehow had been discovered by the enemy.

One of the traveling quartet who arrived that March was "Roll," a man who had distinguished himself while working under Berthier both for his expertise as the radio transmitter and for his irrepressible cursing. Roll reluctantly accepted the order to return to London, and even more reluctantly departed within a party that included two women. Before sending off Vernieuwe with this first contingent Berthier decided to take one further precaution: he created false passports for two married couples, which he knew would prevent them from being sent to one of the internment camps if they were arrested on the far side of the border (the Spaniards would not separate people who were legally married).

Berthier had been so diligent about not revealing the secret work of the sawmill of Mendive that only Loulou Vernieuwe knew in advance that it was her husband's colleague Monsieur Pérot who would engineer their escape. The group arrived in the Basque country without any problems, then spent three days resting before their mountain passage. As Pérot remembers it, "Roll," "Marius," and "Simone" lodged at Auberge Pedro, while Vernieuwe and his wife stayed at their friends' Basque farmhouse in Lecumberry. The event was a welcome reunion for Cette and Loulou, who had not seen each other in more than a year, but it offered little opportunity for time alone to exchange personal feelings about the trials they had both faced. Loulou's enduring memory of the stopover is time spent sitting for a portrait by Cette, a moment of calm that she appreciated even more after the events that followed during their escape. Her visit, however, was too short for Cette to finish the painting, and after the war Loulou somehow retrieved the small unfinished canvas. Many years later Loulou's daughter completed the painting, and the portrait still hangs on the walls of the Vernieuwe family house in Brussels as a memento of a harrowing pilgrimage.

Until the convoy's arrival Monsieur Pérot had stayed very much in the background in relation to Zéro's evacuation efforts. During the previous four months whenever Vernieuwe arrived in the region he would send a messenger to Mendive, usually a factory employee from Mauléon named Murillo who regularly went back and forth to his hometown. In response Pérot would alert Jean Sarochar of an upcoming rendezvous. The sawmill director never knew what became of the refugees once they reached Spain. The shepherd simply relayed the message via his brother Raymond that he had successfully accomplished his mission, which Pérot understood to mean that he had delivered his charges to the Casa del Rei. This time Vernieuwe was accompanying Jean on the mountain passage, and as a result of the escape plans going awry Monsieur Pérot gained new insight into the true worth of his extraordinary Basque *passeur*.

The group assembled at midnight beyond the village of Behorleguy to begin their journey with Jean and his renowned dog. Pérot knew that Jean had picked the location and the roundabout course they would follow based on the shepherd's reconnaissance of the patrol patterns of the Grenzschutz. Loulou Vernieuwe recalls "being dressed in a fur coat and hiking boots, and walking for twenty-seven hours straight. During our ascent of the Pic des Escaliers I gripped trees and branches." She also remembers witnessing the keen tracking abilities of Sarochar's dog, who had developed a radarlike nose for the scent of the Germans' leather boots. "At one point Sarochar sent his dog off, and when he returned he was acting strangely. Sarochar went off to investigate and found two Germans sleeping by the path, so we had to change our course. To keep us going on this difficult climb Sarochar would remind us over and over how many more peaks and valleys until we reached Spain. When we approached the Casa del Rei a young Frenchman, who had already been caught by the Carabineros, attempted to warn us, but it was too late and we were all arrested and detained in a barn adjacent to the inn."

During the night Vernieuwe and Sarochar managed to escape through the Forêt d'Iraty, and sent word of the capture of the convoy to Zéro affiliates in Spain via contacts at the Casa del Rei. At this point Berthier's scheme of giving the escapees the identities of married couples proved prescient, and the group was taken to a residence in Pamplona being used as a detention center. For the next six weeks genteel, convent-educated Loulou Vernieuwe and Roll shared a room with one bed, an ordeal she remembers as being nearly as trying as their escape through the mountains.

For the unscheduled return trip Sarochar led Vernieuwe on a course that circumnavigated the Plateau d'Iraty. When daylight broke he parked him in a natural secluded site. Later that day the shepherd returned with Monsieur Pérot for a conference. During their ascent through the mountains Pérot was introduced to his *passeur*'s storytelling abilities and talents for mimicry as he heard the story of the group's passage and the fate of Loulou and the others. Pérot learned that the trek over the snowy terrain had been so arduous that Vernieuwe had collapsed, and the group had had to stop and help him revive using the women's coats for blankets to keep him warm. When they reached their destination Pérot heard a second version of the experience from his Belgian colleague, including how the fortitude of the women had outshone their male counterparts through the entire exhausting expedition.

Vernieuwe also described in depth Jean's (and his dog's) heroic performance in shepherding them through the ordeal. For the first time Monsieur Pérot heard an account of the remarkable physical stamina of this wiry Basque who, according to Vernieuwe, had the unusual habit of eating only small doses of salt for sustenance and constantly jabbering to himself. Throughout their grueling journey through the forest, especially when Vernieuwe was on the verge of collapse, he had urged Sarochar to go on without him but Sarochar refused and moved him along by poking him with his walking stick.

During their second unexpected encounter the two Belgians formulated a strategy for Berthier's projected escape via Mendive that had been planned to occur sometime within the forthcoming few weeks. Berthier had organized the recent mission with the expectation that Vernieuwe's passage with the four-person convoy would be his final assignment as a courier for Zéro, and that from Spain he would at last be sent to England to join the RAF. Now that Vernieuwe had personally endured the hardship of the journey, however, he realized that Berthier, an intellectual of portly bearing and sedentary habits, could not make the trip through the mountains without Vernieuwe's assistance, nor was Berthier in any condition to make the entire ascent on foot. Vernieuwe departed for eastern France and Pérot was left to devise a scheme that would enable them to travel together up to the mountains by day and follow a much more direct route to the border.

Vernieuwe's return to Grenoble at the end of March was a complete surprise to Berthier. Indeed, the courier's arrival created a dilemma for Berthier because he was now forced to choose between the conflicting counsel of his two top agents regarding his own escape route.[1] When Vernieuwe appeared at the apartment, nearly catatonic after three sleepless nights in transit, he discovered that concern about Berthier's exit via Mendive had propelled his comrade de Hepcée to risk similar dangers and return from what was to have been de Hepcée's final mission to Barcelona. An adrenaline-charged de Hepcée had arrived to warn the Zéro chief that the French border with the Spanish province of Navarre was about to be placed under a state of high alert. The information from British intelligence in Barcelona had led him to make all the arrangements necessary for his boss to depart the country via the eastern extension of the Pyrenees. Before he left France, regardless of which way he chose, Berthier needed to meet with Pérot in person to brief him about the plans for the relocation of Zéro headquarters as well as the succession of new personnel who would administer both the Zéro network and the Belgian underground coordinating organization.

Berthier decided to pursue the plan that Vernieuwe proposed, but first to travel to Perpignan to confer with de Hepcée's contacts and confirm the feasibility of the itinerary. Berthier sent de Hepcée ahead to allow Vernieuwe a day to recover before departing for the next expedition. The two stayed in Perpignan only a few hours once they realized their safe house was under German surveillance. It quickly became evident Berthier had no choice but to make his passage to Spain via Mendive. De Hepcée decided to continue on to Barcelona, while Vernieuwe and Berthier boarded a train for Oloron. If all went well, within a few weeks the two Zéro couriers could at last fulfill their dreams of becoming RAF pilots and Berthier would become an officer in the new Belgian secret service office in London.

Each of the Belgians had developed his own personal travel style honed by three years of traveling back and forth across the Line of Demarcation, and thus they rode in separate railroad cars. Vernieuwe preferred sitting in the crowded third-class compartments, where a boisterous atmosphere and fewer spot inspections of papers prevailed. Berthier, who naturally projected a bulldoglike aura, felt more secure traveling in first class, where a condescending attitude seemed to fend off the threat of interrogation by the German or Vichy police. The odd couple did not travel together for another reason: they were actually two "Monsieur Berthiers" on board the train with only one *ausweis*. Berthier prided himself on his counterfeiting skills and, whenever he could, enjoyed adding devious touches to official documents. Before their departure he had created two false identity cards for "Monsieur Berthier," each of which bore the authorizing signature of a certain fictitious Monsieur Cemoi (a contraction in French meaning literally "it's me.") One card had his own picture, and the other had that of Vernieuwe.

The train trip proceeded without incident, but when the two Berthiers arrived in Oloron it was Vernieuwe's chance to demonstrate his own skill at deception. Bearing the *ausweis* he passed first through the checkpoint in the train station then enlisted a station employee to approach the other Berthier, who was still standing in line, with an envelope containing the permit and to explain that it was a message from Monsieur Pérot. They used a similar ruse in the restaurant of the hotel in Oloron when the Vichy police came through the dining room to check the papers of the guests. This time Vernieuwe disappeared and reappeared with enough time to elapse for the inspector not to take note of the repetition of the use of the travel pass. To reduce any chance of the ruse failing while en route to Lecumberry, Monsieur Pérot had arranged that he would drive Vernieuwe via Hosta in the *gazogène* while Haurat, the Oloron garage owner, transported Berthier (that is, Ugeux), who held the official permit.

Immediately upon entering the Pérot household Berthier remembered being enveloped by the warm family atmosphere, admittedly a bittersweet experience for a fugitive. In fact, his three-day stay was a sort of pleasurable captivity since Pérot had instructed him not to leave the house nor go near the windows. Among the "charms" of the country farmhouse were the fish swimming in his morning wash basin. Cette recalls him, tongue-in-cheek, "thanking her for the little surprises from the river." To pass the time he wrote a detective novel, which he regretfully remembered burning in the fireplace before his departure.

While Berthier was exercising his literary talents, Pérot was still at work on an alibi for their daytime passage through the Forêt d'Iraty. On the day of Berthier's arrival Pérot had spent a sleepless night reviewing the alternatives and finally talking himself into having them pose as technical consultants brought in to evaluate the feasibility of installing a funicular to augment the operation of the existing cable system. Using this guise Berthier could be transported up to the Plateau d'Iraty via mule for an "inspection," and from there they would only have a distance of seven kilometers through the forest to reach the Casa del Rei. With the same precision that he had practiced in planning their Boy Scout expeditions to the Ardennes almost fifteen years before, Pérot spent the next two days choreographing all of the details of the hoax and the timing of their passage.

At six in the morning on the day of their escape, the rogue director of the sawmill left Lecumberry in the company of his two phony *seilbahningenieurs* (railway engineers), with Berthier aboard Pérot's bicycle and Vernieuwe on foot. Pérot stopped at his office to get a set of drawings of the cable system and outfit his "consultants" with various measuring devices. Their knapsacks, filled with currency and clothes, were loaded into one of the trunks transporting other company material via the cable to the Plateau d'Iraty. The group continued down the main road to the Irigoin farm, where Jean Sarochar was waiting with his dog. He had descended from his hut (a few hundred meters up the mountain directly above the Irigoin farm) with a mule intended as Berthier's mount for the trek up to the plateau.

Both men remember the comic drama of Berthier's attempt to ride the animal during the three-hour climb, particularly the contrast of the agile steady Sarochar chattering away as he led the tottering and speechless passenger along the dangerous, stony paths hugging the mountainside. En route the caravan encountered several groups of Grenzschutz that were returning from the frontier; Pérot cordially greeted them and identified his companions as "two eminent *seilbahningenieurs.*" The Germans saluted and continued on.

Pérot had carefully planned their lunchtime arrival at the plateau, where they were introduced to Modesta's Spanish cuisine. After a hearty lunch, including ample quantities of wine drunk from a communal gourd brought along by Pérot, the group went off to the cable station to "perform their inspection." Pérot recalls with amusement how admirably Berthier played his role as chief engineer, "studying, pointing, and shaking his head like a true professional." They then resumed their trek through the forest; several times Pérot instructed his two "consultants" to pretend to examine the rusted remains of one of the feeder lines that dated from the Pédelucq era and the relics from the failed Swiss funicular installation of an even earlier age.

When the threesome reached the Rio Iraty, Sarochar and the dog were waiting for them. While Pérot and his advisors had been acting out the masquerade of the previous few hours, Sarochar had continued on to the Casa del Rei a few kilometers further in order to verify that there were no German or Spanish guards in the vicinity. Discovering a group of Carabineros with a recently captured group of French draft dodgers in tow assured him that the Spanish patrol was preoccupied. Pérot, relieved that the hoax had ended successfully, entrusted his Belgian colleagues to the expert service of Sarochar for the final leg of the journey to the Casa del Rei through the Spanish portion of the Forêt d'Iraty.

From under a pile of leaves Sarochar produced their belongings and, armed with his walking stick, eagerly assumed the leadership of the caravan. Shortly after beginning their march Vernieuwe went back to find Pérot to get sandwiches, which Pérot had promised for their journey and forgotten to pass on. After this brief delay the threesome continued through the forest on a rambling path, which under different circumstances would have made an agreeable outing. Berthier remembered being mesmerized by the strange antics of their Basque guide as they proceeded along: how could morsels of salt sustain this man who seemed to be perpetually in forward gear and who had not eaten or drunk anything since their departure? What and why was he chanting to himself? Did he have some special form of communication with his dog? The sound reverberating through the woods of "Alemanos! Alemanos!" — the call by which the Spanish border guards alerted the German patrol of a capture in the border zone — ended Berthier's ruminations. Sarochar quickly herded the group down to a ditch below, where they lay prostrate until the patrol had passed with their prisoners.

When they arrived at the Casa del Rei late in the afternoon, Berthier and Vernieuwe waited in a dense thicket nearby while Sarochar went inside and discovered a group of Carabineros ensconced there.[2] A messenger sent from the inn later in the evening informed Sarochar that their hope of gaining entry was not possible, and they would be forced to spend the night in the woods. After an extended discussion the two Basques then led the Belgians to a site well removed from the grassy opening surrounding the stone lodge. Before retiring in their cold sylvan shelter Vernieuwe and Berthier consumed a plate of tortillas sent by the innkeeper (who demanded payment of his exorbitant bill on the spot) while Sarochar contented himself with more salt. Sometime in the night an early April snowstorm began and did not let up until after dawn. Berthier remembers that it was so cold and wet, he and Vernieuwe spent most of the night strapped by their belts against the trunk of a tree. The same alfresco catering service from the inn produced a hot breakfast the next morning, which further diminished their reserves of pesetas and only briefly staved off the chills that both men were now experiencing in their wet clothes. The news that the Carabineros would not be departing also further dampened their spirits.

After spending almost twenty-four hours in their inhospitable quarters they proposed to Sarochar to return to Mendive. He was hesitant to depart from his leader's orders, and decided to return to Monsieur Pérot by himself to obtain new instructions. While Berthier and Vernieuwe shivered through another night of chilly rain, Sarochar, imbued with the superhuman determination comparable to his ancient Basque heroes, strode back down to the valley in the pitch dark.

After an extended six-hour trip (without his dog) the Basque shepherd landed, completely drenched, on the threshold of Monsieur Pérot's house in the middle of the night. This unexpected visit made a profound and lasting impression on the Belgian. As he vividly describes the experience, "Sarochar was apologetic, and told me the story of what had happened and then relayed their message of wanting to come back to Mendive. I knew if they tried to come back down they would be arrested. And there would be no way to get them back up again by using the same ploy. They would have to wait. Sarochar dried off, and we fed him some cheese and bread. Then he insisted on going right back up to deliver the message." Not since his youthful friendship with Oleg Pomerantzeff had Pérot experienced this degree of loyalty.

Schepens's reflective commentary on the traumatic series of events is revealing: "You know, there are few people who will risk their life to do things that are dangerous and not very pleasant. Once Sarochar had confidence in you, he would risk his life!" In these words, indeed, lie the key to understanding the common psychological trait—trustworthiness—that shaped the decision of these men of such different cultures to provide active service to the resistance, and to enter into such an unusual alliance. While the Belgian does not discount the influence of the Basque heritage of resistance to occupying forces and mountain subterfuge, nor the shepherd's latent appetite for heroic combat, he attributes "his intuitive confidence in me" as the overriding motivation for engagement: "I knew he would not betray me, and he knew that I would not betray him."

Thus, later that night the intrepid shepherd, blazing his own path over the treacherous, heavily wooded terrain, re-ascended and carried the harsh message back to Berthier and Vernieuwe. Monsieur Pérot learned the resolution of their predicament from Sarochar two days later, who again appeared late at night at his home in Lecumberry to deliver the news in person. Once the disheartened fugitives accepted that they must remain in Spain, Sarochar agreed to find someone to relay a message about their situation and their need for transport out of the mountains to the Belgian consul in San Sebastian—a Spanish Basque businessman also working for the Zéro network. The messenger to San Sebastian was a relative of the innkeeper, one of the most well-known bandit-smugglers in the region. Berthier dispatched the courier with a cryptic message and one thousand Swiss francs that he wanted converted to pesetas.

After a third rain-free night in the woods the Carabineros finally departed and the fugitives were at last allowed to enter the inn. The two Belgians stripped off all of their miserable garments, thawed, and bathed by a huge open fireplace and then consumed their sixth exorbitant meal of tortillas. Meanwhile, Sarochar, a man who inhabited his clothing the way an animal wears its pelt—and with far less attention to its cleanliness—preferred to maintain a vigil with his dog in the surrounding forest. After

Berthier and Vernieuwe were restored, however, the innkeeper informed them that the threesome would have to spend the night in the barn because of the likely return of the Spanish border guards.

Finally at noon the next day the professional smuggler reappeared with the pesetas and a reply: in four days an agent would pick them up at a designated site further west in the mountains. After the bandit-smuggler was paid his fee he offered (through Sarochar) to conduct the pair via his network of guides to their rendezvous point. Sarochar negotiated a price for the Spaniard's services, half to be paid on departure and half on completion. He was not completely confident of the integrity of the smuggler's associates; Sarochar later told Monsieur Pérot that as they got ready to depart he reminded his Spanish Basque confrere that if any harm befell his convoy, a vendetta would have to be reckoned with.

Only months later did Pérot hear the full story of what had happened after the pair left the Casa del Rei, but when Sarochar told Pérot of the involvement of the consul, "I knew they would eventually make it safely either to Pamplona or Madrid. He [the consul] had access to train tickets, false passports, whatever was necessary." It had been another six days of waiting and walking until they reached San Sebastian. Not surprising, from this ordeal Berthier gained an even deeper appreciation of the value of the sawmill in Mendive, which in turn reinforced his determination to conceal its operation as long as possible.

Chapter 12

For Jacques Pérot the return of Señor Compains and his crew to begin another logging season in the Forêt d'Iraty was the true sign of the arrival of the spring of 1943. Within a year of his first visit to the Laurhibar Valley, Pérot could rightly be proud of the commercial and clandestine feats he had accomplished in the Basque borderland. The secondary feeder cables to the main line on the Plateau d'Iraty had been installed, and the second year of his tenure as director of the sawmill held out the promise of even greater productivity and the possibility of financially breaking even.

As in the Pédelucq era, the SNCF was the major customer for the lumber processed by the Compagnie d'Iraty.[1] Pérot remembers that the railroad's procurement agents regularly came on site to inspect their order and to verify its proper dimensions ("two meters, eighty centimeters"). Almost weekly Jean Bouleux drove the company tractor to haul a flatbed full of railroad ties and lumber to the train station in St.-Jean-Pied-de-Port. Every two weeks he and José Izquierdo drove to Pau in the company truck to deliver orders of furniture squares and other unfinished goods for export to other factories in eastern France; Bouleux still remembered the temperamental *gazogène* truck and how often his mechanical skills were put to use keeping it going.

A siren at seven A.M. announced the beginning of the workday for plant employees, who worked six days a week. Wages, paid in cash once a month, ranged between six hundred and one thousand French francs per week, a little more than the amount employees made under the company's previous regime but competitive with those of other industrial enterprises still in operation during the war. Though memories of both Paul Pédelucq's death and a subsequent accident in which one of the sawyers had his leg amputated by a circular saw still hung over the factory, under Pérot's direction the only injury at the mill that had required an emergency trip to the hospital in St.-Jean-Pied-de-Port was the time a wooden shoemaker chopped off several of his fingers.

Transforming a tree into a railroad tie took a minimum of four weeks. Every ten minutes workers on the plateau attached a log—from 2.5 to 3.5 meters long and .5 to 1.5 meters wide—onto a suspended steel trolley to begin the eighteen-kilometer ride along the grand cable to the valley floor. At the three relay stations along the route where the cableway changed directions, workers would oversee the transfer of the log to the connecting line. If no problems were encountered a log could make the journey in several hours.

On a daily basis the normal flow of material along the cable consisted of logs and sacks of charcoal descending from the plateau, trunks loaded with company provisions, and the Germans' gear ascending from the station in the valley. Every few weeks the special burlap bags containing the contraband materials would also be a part of the goods making their way to the plateau. The frequent breakdown of the cable, however, presented an ongoing problem for the plant's operation. Although the cable crew greased the trolleys on a systematic basis, a derailment occurred at least once every few days. When the cable stopped the wires hung a few meters above the ground in several places, and local farmers would occasionally help themselves to the contents of the trunks—a situation that Pérot knew about but chose to ignore.

In late April 1943 another type of cargo was transported from the upper station: a permanent worker on the plateau named Bengochea found the dead body of an older man in the woods, and on Pérot's instruction relayed the cadaver down to the village via the cable.[2] "He was a fugitive who probably died of a heart attack but not someone who had come through Mendive," Pérot recalls. One of the transient workers on the plateau, Elie Dyan, witnessed the grim event. Dyan's case history is both typical and unique among the revolving cast of young men who briefly worked for the Compagnie d'Iraty on their escape out of France. Like many others seeking to avoid conscription or persecution who were temporarily absorbed into the company's workforce, Dyan was not French by birth but rather a Tunisian Jew educated in France who had served in the French army during the German invasion. Until 1943 he had done clerical work in an office in Montpellier, but the Vichy government's effort to round up Jewish foreign nationals and the imposition of the Service du Travail Obligatoire had convinced him to attempt an escape via the Pyrenees. Like the other fugitives who traveled under a pseudonym and landed by chance in the Laurhibar Valley, Dyan was first interviewed by Pelfort about his occupational background and educational training, then issued a company card and sent to work and live on the Plateau d'Iraty. Because of his education at the Polytechnique Supérieure in Toulouse, Dyan was assigned the job of scaler, which entailed measuring the length of the logs prior to their transport on the cable. After studying a map to develop an itinerary for his escape he paid one of the younger Basque shepherds in residence near the Chapelle St.-Sauveur to conduct him over the border into Spain, but was arrested by the Carabineros before he got to Orbaiceta. Dyan then endured the fate similar to that of a great majority of persons in flight: several weeks of internment at the overcrowded camp in Miranda. While there he discovered an occupant of cell 14 was a Frenchman who had also worked for Monsieur Pérot.

What makes Dyan's story atypical is the fact that he was one of the few fugitives who ever came forward and identified himself to Monsieur Pérot after the war's end. In a long letter sent in the mid-1960s Dyan recalled the details of his flight, including the sobering experience of seeing the cadaver making its way down the cable.[3] His story is also exceptional because he was the only unknown refugee whom Monsieur and Madame Pérot allowed to stay overnight at their house in Lecumberry, a good deed done at the insistence of Cyrille Pomerantzeff. In his letter Dyan recounted how he arrived at the Hotel Bidegain in Mauléon only to discover it teeming with German soldiers; how Maitena and her father were expecting Monsieur Pérot and Monsieur Pomerantzeff on their return trip from Pau but had agreed to hide him temporarily; how the two men voluntarily picked him up late that night and concealed him among sacks in the rear of the *gazogène* on the drive back to Lecumberry; how Cette and Cyrille made up a bed for him; and how the next morning he awoke to his first true breakfast in three years.

Interestingly, while his hosts have little memory of the visit of this unexpected guest, the few hours spent as part of their cultured household were long cherished by Elie Dyan. Although Pérot knew the identity of all of the plant workers, he made it a firm policy to maintain as much distance as possible from his short-term employees. As he reasoned, "They might have been confronted by the Germans. Or I might be confronted by the Germans. I didn't know them. I didn't want to know them."

Dyan's overnight stay was one of several unexpected events in the spring of 1943 that collectively had an unsettling effect on Jacques Pérot. Another occurred late one night when he heard someone banging at the front door of their house, calling out in German. Pérot hesitated for a long time about whether to open the door or to escape by the rope. When he descended he discovered, thankfully, that it was only a drunken soldier who had lost his way to the chateau. A second encounter that took place during his normal inspection rounds in the mountains with a pair of German guards and their dog also gave him a brief scare: they marched towards Pérot, who was relieved to discover they were new arrivals who simply had lost their way in the forest. The sawmill director became the helpful Boy Scout and guided them part of the way to their destination.

In contrast, the arrival of a letter bearing a salutation to "Dr. Schepens" was true cause for concern, although he was careful to show no emotion. The note (in a blank envelope) was delivered to his office at the factory by an anonymous messenger. It held a request from the son of a Belgian friend of the Schepens family who was imprisoned in Puyoô eighty kilometers away, and who was seeking his assistance. Pérot took the letter home and burned it, deciding he would not risk following through on the young man's appeal.

Pérot's most serious and enduring concern, however, was the unplanned visit of Vallier, the Frenchman providing courier services to Zéro in Grenoble. During his stay at their house in April, Berthier and Pérot had reviewed the arrangements needed for continuing the Zéro network under new leadership. Berthier had indicated a hiatus in the evacuation work would likely occur, but that Pérot should anticipate the July arrival of "Antoine," the last of the original Zéro agents, on his route out of France to London. Packages would continue to be delivered to Oloron. In addition, sometime in May, Vallier would deliver there the final deposit from Berthier's reserve funds in Grenoble, and that the money should be held in the factory safe until "Antoine's" passage.

On his expedition from Grenoble the young Vallier decided to bring the money in person to Monsieur Pérot, whom he had never met, instead of leaving an envelope with the garage owner as he had been instructed. He rode a bicycle all the way from Oloron to the factory in Mendive on the main roads, passing without problems through all the German checkpoints. Pérot recalls, "I was furious. Out of curiosity, he did not follow orders. I told him he could not stay. He wanted to go back that night the same way he had come, which meant crossing the Zone Interdite twice to get out on the main road and then back into the formerly unoccupied French territory. I told him that he would never make it at night. Never. I offered to take him to Hosta to show him the way, but he was so sure since he had made it through the first time, that he could make it the second time." Pérot's misgivings were well-founded, because several weeks later he learned that the young Frenchman had been captured that night.

During the spring months Pérot also began to sense a change in the attitude of the Grenzschutz toward him. He recalls, "There was something different. There was more turnover in the patrol. They seemed a little less friendly; they asked more questions." For the first time since taking up residence in the valley he questioned his immunity from German surveillance.

Late in June 1943 Cyrille arrived for his regular monthly visit in the company of sixteen-year-old Bernadette Lafitte. As Monsieur Pérot remembers, "Life had become very difficult for Lafitte and his family in Paris, and he had contacted us through Cyrille to see if we would be willing to have Bernadette come down and stay with us for the summer.

We figured she could help Cette with the children, so we accepted." When she arrived she knew only that the Schepens family had fled the Germans in Belgium and were living in the Basque country under an assumed name. Cette remembers her fondly as a "very idealistic, very confident" young woman. It took Bernadette only a short time to adjust to her new life as a member of the Pérot household, and she especially enjoyed spending extended periods of time outdoors. After Bernadette's arrival Cette began to range a little farther from her home base as well, organizing small jaunts in the surrounding countryside. The presence of the teenaged Parisian guest also led to Cette's first contact with the Pédelucq family: Bernadette met Léon Pédelucq, also in residence for the summer in Mendive, and frequently invited him to accompany them on their outings with the children.

One Sunday in late July 1943 Monsieur Pérot organized a daylong excursion up to the Forêt d'Iraty for the entire household, including Bernadette and Beppina. He had spent the previous week marking 350 cubic meters (12,000 cubic feet) of timber with the forest rangers and knew that the woods were filled with tiny wild strawberries. Beppina remembers they picked more than four kilos of fruit over the course of several hours, an unexpected bounty that changed their plans for the return trip to Mendive. It was decided that Beppina would stay with the children at the mountain chalet for an extra day, while the others returned to the valley with the berries to make jam. Monsieur Pérot was anxious to get back to Lecumberry because he knew that Cyrille Pomerantzeff and Nicolas Rosenschild were expected to arrive at the factory the next day to review the company's bookkeeping system and the status of its finances.

Chapter 13

Jacques Pérot began the workday of 21 July 1943 with the news that the Germans were at the factory and wanted to speak to Monsieur Pérot. Nicolas Rosenschild had gone ahead to the Compagnie d'Iraty plant, while Cyrille had breakfast with Pérot and his wife at their home in Lecumberry. Soon after Rosenschild's arrival at the office early that morning a black sedan with yellow wheels pulled up in front of the building and four plainclothes Gestapo officers emerged. The officers would not state why they had come; although Rosenschild talked to them in fluent German they insisted on speaking to Pérot. Pelfort dispatched Rosenschild back to Lecumberry to alert his boss to the situation.

Pérot decided to send Cyrille instead, "because he spoke better German." However, Rosenschild returned with the message that they insisted on meeting with Monsieur Pérot. Pérot departed wearing his normal work clothes—khaki shirt, shorts, and espadrilles. He added a cache of a few large-denomination American bills to his pockets, should an immediate exit from the country be necessary. When he arrived at the factory Pérot discovered that the agents were not part of the local Gestapo but rather a group of officers from Paris. He and Cyrille ushered them into the tight quarters of the director's office, where the Germans announced that someone had been arrested near Mendive who admitted that Monsieur Pérot was passing people into Spain and that a large sum of money had been brought in by an unnamed man to be deposited in the company safe. At that moment Pérot realized that Vallier had in fact been caught. Though he could not show his anger, he realized (as he had observed in the early work of the resistance in Belgium), that betrayal by other volunteers in the amateur secret service posed as real a threat as German surveillance did. Loyalty and total discretion were cardinal virtues that he lived by and expected of his family, his friends, and his underground associates; yet even his selectivity in personnel and his efforts to be invisible could not protect him from the impulsiveness and foolish mistakes of a young fellow *résistant*.

Pérot calmly denied the accusation and attempted to use the false order for material for the Atlantic wall to show that the factory was working in cooperation with the Reich. The Gestapo officers questioned each other in German to see who was armed. From their exchange Pérot realized that none of them were carrying guns, which gave him a degree of confidence. After forty-five minutes of interrogating the factory director the Germans indicated that they believed him, but they needed to take him to Paris for questioning. He agreed to go with them, but said, "You'll have to give me a few minutes. I have over a hundred workers waiting to receive their orders. I want to make sure that production of lumber badly needed by the Wehrmacht will not be interrupted." With that statement he got up, closed the door, said a few words to the secretaries, and walked out onto the porch and down the stairs to the factory floor.[1]

In his first minutes as a fugitive Pérot headed to the cable terminus and told one of the Moretti brothers to cut the telephone lines up to the Plateau d'Iraty. He then happened to meet Nicolas Rosenschild who, almost fifty years later, could still recite Pérot's parting words: "They know who I am. I've got to escape to Spain. Tell Cette to meet me with the children at the border." Permanently etched in Rosenschild's memory was the "perfect sangfroid and tranquility" with which Pérot delivered this directive.

After his brief encounter with Rosenschild, an adrenaline-charged Pérot dashed through the obstacle course of sheds and lumber piles, much to the consternation and confusion of the factory workers. Never did he look back, but when he reached the edge of the millyard he unexpectedly came upon the local Basque named Bainam, who was in the process of surveying the operation of his dam on the Laurhibar River. For half a minute Pérot gained composure and exchanged a few words with the man. Pérot then slowly walked further along the bank, but as soon as Bainam was out of view he scrambled down into the ditch and began bounding like a deer being tailed by bloodthirsty dogs.

For the first time in his resistance career Pérot knew that physical endurance was the one thing that could save his life. He tried to maintain his accelerated pace as he continued running along the ditch a few kilometers to a spot just at the edge of the Irigoin farm, all the while desperately reminding himself that every minute lengthened the distance between him and his captors and brought him closer to the temporary safety of Sarochar's mountain hut. Relieved that neither the Grenzschutz nor the Gestapo were anywhere in sight, he sprinted across the road and headed along a hedgerow up the mountainside toward the shepherd's compound. As he made the ascent he came upon Monsieur Irigoin with his flock, who happened to be in the valley rather than the mountains because his wife was expecting their first child. Pérot asked him to go down and cut the telephone line that paralleled their house on the opposite side of the road.

By noon, after an hour and a half on the run without ever stopping for water, Pérot reached the shepherd's hut. As he caught his breath Pérot told his Basque comrade what had just transpired and stated his need for shelter in the mountains while he waited for his family. Sarochar led him to a hiding place in a rock outcropping about one hundred meters away, which was higher up the slope and on the lee side of the mountain amidst a gloomy tangle of moss-covered ledge, strewn boulders, and tentacle-like tree roots. The site easily conjured one of the hangouts of the supernatural creatures of Basque legend. Within one of the ledges was a crevice just large enough for a man to stand. There, in the shadow of the Pic de Behorleguy, Pérot would remain for the next two days while Sarochar, like a "chien fidèle" (loyal dog), maintained watch.

Pérot's flight had set in motion a number of events in the valley. After their encounter in the factory Rosenschild headed to Lecumberry to deliver a third round of bad news to the Pérot household. When he arrived Cette and Bernadette were in the kitchen making jam, and he asked to speak to Cette alone. He informed her of the situation and of her husband's message. Her resolve to follow her husband was as striking to him as Pérot's composure in the face of mortal danger, and it, too, left an indelible impression in the man's memory. Before she departed she told Bernadette that she was going back up to the mountains to the forest rangers' cabin to get the children and that Bernadette should burn certain family papers and photographs. Cette also grabbed a handful of French currency and concealed it in a scarf that she tied around her leg.

Meanwhile, after Pérot left the office ostensibly to make his morning rounds, Cyrille continued to defend the operation of his plant and to distract the Gestapo officers as long as he could. When a half hour had elapsed and the director of the sawmill had still not reappeared, the Germans realized that he had slipped away. Sensing their anger, Cyrille decided to alter his tactics and proclaim indignantly that he had been duped by his business associate and labeled him a "grosse bandiet" and a "schweinhund." In his pretend role as turncoat victim, Cyrille told them he too wanted an explanation from this scoundrel and would help them however he could. Soon after the Gestapo had arrived at the factory they had alerted the Grenzschutz — both at the chateau and in the mountains — of the purpose of their visit. The Grenzschutz were in total disbelief, especially Müller. When Pérot disappeared the Gestapo then mobilized the mountain patrol to begin a manhunt, and sent word to the equally shocked local Gestapo unit in St.-Jean-Pied-de-Port to organize an additional fifty men for the search.

Soon after Cette's departure and while Rosenschild was still at the house in Lecumberry, several officers came swooping in to search the Pérot dwelling. Rosenschild watched and inwardly trembled as they rifled through the cupboards, barking questions about their contents. He also recollected Bernadette's hysterical laughter, which only heightened the tension. When Rosenschild was questioned he replied in halting German. Still, to his amazement they did not interrogate him about his identity or connection to the family and left the house frustrated and empty-handed. Similarly, sometime later that morning a frightened Beppina confronted two Grenzschutz who appeared at the mountain chalet and in broken French announced "Pérot, grand capitaliste," making the gesture of a bankrobber. She and the children did not share the fate of their counterparts in the valley but instead became hostages at the chalet.

Cette realized that it would be too risky to make the direct ascent to the Plateau d'Iraty and that she would have to pursue a much more circuitous path. She recalled that on one of their excursions to the Chapelle St.-Sauveur, as they studied the landscape below her husband pointed out the little hamlet of Gasnateguy in the neighboring valley. Now, though she had never taken this route before, it seemed that her only option was to cross over the western wall of the Laurhibar Valley, pass through Gasnateguy, and then follow the streams up the mountain. The only people she encountered during her eight-hour walk were some Basque shepherds near the southern edge of the forest, who redirected her northward just as she neared the Spanish border.

Cette did not encounter any patrol unit until she reached the forest rangers' cabin. As she neared the chalet exhausted, drenched in sweat, and covered with scratches, she spied two Germans standing with rifles in front of the door. Of the many emotional trials she had endured since the beginning of the war, this sight posed the greatest dilemma of all: "When I knew Charles had fled my first thought was to go up to the children in the mountains. Only when I arrived at the chalet and saw the Germans guarding did I have a moment of indecision: to flee or to go to the children. I decided to go to the children."

Once reunited with her children (joining the company of hostages) she confirmed Beppina's suspicion that Luc had a fever and insisted that they remain overnight at the cabin. She also was determined not to let the Germans confiscate her cache of money and used the excuse of having to go outside to relieve herself as soon as darkness fell. She buried the money under a pile of stones and brush. She now bemusedly recollects her frustration at not being able to find the hidden treasure before dawn.

The next day the guards marched their party of hostage women and children back down to the valley by way of the Plateau d'Iraty, in full view of the company workers. As the forlorn convoy made their descent they also encountered Cyrille, dressed in full hiking gear. He had gotten permission from the Gestapo to travel up to the mountains to see if he could locate the "bandit director." Cyrille informed Cette and the others that he was "off to find Pérot." When they reached the Chapelle St.-Sauveur toward noon Cette demanded that they stop so that the children could rest and have something to eat. She now looks back on this move as a lifesaver, because by the time they got back to Lecumberry the Gestapo had gone. They were marched to the chateau by the pair of Grenzschutz soldiers, however, and placed under house arrest. Rather than send them to prison the Germans had decided that the best way to lure Monsieur Pérot back to the valley was to let his family stay at their house as bait. Cette was ordered to report to the chateau every day to sign a register. As she discovered that night, guards and a dog were posted outside to block entrance or exit of the Pérot house after dark.

Bernadette had much to report when the women and children returned to the farmhouse. She described the Germans' arrival immediately after Cette's departure, and their unsuccessful effort to retrieve any incriminating material or helpful information. She told Cette that a Basque shepherd had appeared during the night to deliver a note from Monsieur Pérot, which she still had concealed in her sandal. Unfortunately, when Cette read the note she discovered that her husband had asked her to send a set of warmer clothes and hiking shoes with Sarochar, and now it was too late to help.

What Bernadette did not know was that after Sarochar delivered the message but before heading back up to the mountains, he went next door and slept in the Argains' hayloft for a few hours just in case the Germans reappeared at the Pérot house. She also did not know that as part of his secret mission to the valley he had first gone to see Pelfort with instructions to bring up to Monsieur Pérot the one thousand dollar bill stored in the safe. When Sarochar returned to the mountains with the money but without the clothes, he also brought the bad news from Pelfort that Pérot's family had been taken prisoner.

While the former sawmill director remained immobilized in his hideout, Mendive and the surrounding mountains had become a multistage the-

ater. Despite Pérot's well-concealed position he was not completely removed from the action and a few dangerous moments ensued. Twice he
heard trucks loaded with German soldiers pass above him along the crest
of the mountainside. At another point, after a flock of sheep passed
through the area a young shepherd returned to look for an injured ewe.
Sarochar volunteered to help him, thus avoiding the possibility the young
man could catch a glimpse of the most wanted man in the valley.

Most of all Pérot remembers that the tense and agonizing hours spent in
his mountain hideaway deepened his affection for this "être primitif"
(simple soul) and increased his admiration for the Basque shepherd's innocent heroism. During Pérot's confinement Sarochar shuttled back and
forth to his hut to bring food (bread, cheese, and eggs) and a blanket,
insisting that Pérot bed down under it on the forest floor while he curled
up on an exposed rock to sleep. "Sarochar had the courage of a hero. If he
trusts you, he trusts you unto death. What intellectual would die for you
without asking any questions? It was almost like religion. I had never
witnessed that before."

On the morning of 24 June, the third day after his initial escape, Pérot
joined Jean, Jean's brother Raymond, and their brother-in-law Louis
Etchepare for a conference at their nearby family hut. Collectively the
members of the Sarochar family decided it was too hazardous for Pérot to
remain in his hiding place any longer and that he should head to the
border — by himself. Jean outlined an "easy" backcountry route through a
remote section of the mountains that he could follow to get to the Spanish
lumberjacks' camp without encountering either shepherds or Germans.
Pérot remembers Jean Sarochar's full confidence in his ability to make it
and the shepherd's belief that it was less dangerous for him to travel alone,
since a twosome might draw more attention. Pérot, however, was less
assured. Despite his extensive experience roaming the Forêt d'Iraty, until
he arrived at the Pic des Escaliers the majority of the proposed route
would take him through unfamiliar territory; he would have to use the
Chapelle St.-Sauveur, the cableway, and the course of different mountain
streams as points of orientation. His lightweight espadrilles were also less
than ideal for clambering up and down the coarse and open terrain. Indeed, the experience would be the true test of the merits of the man's
mental and physical training at Verberie.

Pérot waited until that afternoon to set out on his solo journey, once the sun had burned off the moisture from the grass. His parting with Sarochar was, in certain respects, a reprise of Oleg's leave-taking several years before. As with his Russian friend, Pérot had formed a transcendent relationship based on "total trust and total forgiveness." This time, however, he was the one setting out on a perilous journey. Pérot remembers his Basque friend giving him bread and cheese, and Pérot "thanking him and kissing him on both cheeks."

It did not bode well, however, that soon after he began his ascent he saw people emerge from a remote farmhouse far below to watch his passage. He remembers wondering whether the Germans had enlisted their help in his capture. But he continued on and maintained a steady pace until it got too dark to see. That night he bedded down on an exposed slope, straddling a thicket of bushes to prevent sliding down the steep incline.

Pérot resumed his march before dawn the next morning, reassuring himself that once he had located the Chapelle St.-Sauveur far below he would be very close to the logging camp. Sometime midmorning he arrived at the camp hungry and dehydrated and found only the camp cook in residence. For the first and only time in his life he had a lumberjack breakfast: a stew of potatoes, meat, and lentils accompanied by bread. Pérot then dispatched the cook to find Compains while he hid in the surrounding forest. Through their association over the previous year Pérot had picked up enough Spanish to carry on a conversation, and enough to understand that Compains had been a prisoner during the Spanish Civil War but had escaped and walked six hundred kilometers back to Orbaiceta. Pérot also knew that Compains was not afraid to kill. Thus when Compains returned and saw Monsieur Pérot, the *contratista* smiled broadly and told him in Spanish not only that "Señor Pomerantzeff" was up in the mountains looking for him, but that the Germans had offered a reward of one hundred thousand francs for his capture. Compains immediately volunteered to try to rescue Cette and the children in a commando operation, but Pérot dissuaded him saying that the Germans would slaughter the village in retaliation. Pérot told him that instead he wanted to hide out and wait for Pomerantzeff at the logging camp and then together the two would travel to Spain. The Spaniard agreed and maintained a vigil while his boss-turned-outlaw hid in the forest.

Around two o'clock that afternoon Pomerantzeff wandered into the camp. Compains led the Russian to his fellow fugitive, and the two embraced as if they had not seen each other in decades. Immediately Pomerantzeff recapped the events of the previous three days in greater depth than Pérot had heard from Sarochar, proudly describing the effectiveness of his improvised deception scheme as well as Pelfort's flawless performance as the innocent company engineer. Pérot also learned that one of the company truckdrivers had driven Rosenschild to the train station in Dax, and that by now Rosenschild should be back in Paris.

Pérot, Pomerantzeff, and Compains then turned to a discussion of the future. To Pérot's amazement his Russian friend "proposed the idea of transplanting the logging camp to the other side of the border, and restarting the enterprise there." Pérot laughed at the absurd and impossible idea and promptly vetoed it, as did Compains. Pérot wanted to get out of France as soon as possible, and he asked the *contratista* to take them to the Casa del Rei. Compains agreed and the three set out around four o'clock.

Yet again Pérot found himself in unfamiliar territory and grateful for Compains's guiding skills. Their route took them across the Col d'Orgambidesca and along the ridge of some of the highest peaks within the Forêt d'Iraty, areas that the Spaniard knew were far above the normal circuits of the Grenzschutz. As they approached the Casa del Rei later that evening Compains went ahead to consult with his sister, then came back with the bad news that both the Germans and the Carabineros had staked out the inn. They would have to spend the night in the woods in the rain. Before they retired someone from the inn brought them a meal. Compains told them that he would stay at the Casa del Rei and bring them food the next day. Though for several months the *contratista* had been involved in the relay of secret documents from the mill into Spain, Monsieur Pérot knew that he was motivated by money. "I wasn't completely sure whether he could be fully trusted and whether in the end he would sell us out."

That night the two fugitives bedded down in a sheltered site under a thick-canopied tree that afforded them a view of the inn below. Pérot remembers receiving a second meal the next morning and then spending the rest of the day watching the activity around the Casa del Rei, waiting for their next alfresco Spanish repast. They saw a few Germans enter the building who did not reemerge, which caused a mounting fear that they might be ambushed. The pair decided to decamp before darkness fell, without a meal or any directions to follow. The former sawmill director knew, though, that rather than proceed on a course parallel to the nearby Rio Iraty they would first have to make a big detour to the southwest.

Pérot recalls how they made their way through the Spanish side of the Forêt d'Iraty: "We traveled by night and tried to sleep during the day. Our hiding places were the woods when it wasn't raining, and vacant shepherds' huts when it was. We would listen for the sound of water; if there were no dogs barking, we would head in that direction. In the dark we would drink the water if it did not smell foul." After three nights on the move they gradually became optimistic that they had passed out of the zone where the Carabineros would turn them over to the Grenzschutz if they were captured. Having existed on some bread they were given by farmers, raw potatoes they picked from a field, and water from the streams, the two Verberie disciples decided to make a detour into one of the mountain villages to buy food and new shoes, as well as replace Pérot's shorts. From the very limited stock of a small general store they bought a five-kilogram tin of biscuits, another pair of espadrilles, and a pair of wedding pants a few sizes too small.

For the next ten days Cyrille carried the tin box strapped to his back by his belt—the cookies were the mainstay of their diet. One night the Russian lit a fire and made soup with the biscuits in a tin can they had found and added to their possessions. To his great chagrin, however, Pérot "clumsily upturned the pot before they got to taste his preparation," so once again they had to subsist on the dry sweet snacks. Since they were now walking at a lower elevation and passing upland farmsteads, at one point Pérot proposed catching a lamb and killing it. Pomerantzeff was strongly opposed to this; as Pérot remembers him saying emphatically, "No, that's stealing. If you do that, I'll go my own way."

In fact the dangerous trek brought out the differences in the personalities of the Belgian and the Russian. Soon after Pérot donned his new striped woolen trousers he ripped the center seam. As Pérot remembers it, Pomerantzeff insisted on stopping to repair it "because he did not think I was presentable, even though I was less concerned." Using hairs that he plucked from a cow's tail and a penknife he was carrying to punch holes in the fabric, the Russian restitched the garment for his companion. As it turned out this was the first of several tailoring repairs made to the ill-fitting pants, which seemed to rip every time Pérot had to dash for cover when they heard a threatening sound.

A second incident involving a difference of opinion had more substantial consequences. Pérot was constantly checking to make sure he had not lost the one thousand dollar bill. As he recalls, "That was reason for worry because I was putting it here and there, in my pocket and in my shoe. Finally Cyrille got impatient and said, 'You give it to me, and I'll put it away once and for all.' He put it in the lining of his shoe. . . . That night we were walking along railroad tracks, but his boots were making so much noise he took his shoes off, put on his espadrilles, and carried the shoes on his shoulders. Later we decided to walk on the road, and saw a large group of people walking toward us, so we tried to escape up the mountainside. We got separated and Cyrille ended up surrounded by several Spaniards. They did not try to capture him because they were afraid he might be armed. One of the Spaniards who was supposed to be guarding him fell asleep, and then Cyrille started to make his getaway. Some of the others heard him and attempted to follow him, but then a terrible thunderstorm erupted and they gave up. But while Cyrille was running farther up the mountain he lost the boots." The two men ended up in different places on the slope and regrouped the next morning back at the railroad tracks, as they had agreed to do when they started to run for cover. To his embarrassment Cyrille, however, had not been able to find the precious shoes when he made his descent, nor would he allow his friend to retrace his steps. They chalked up the loss of the small fortune to bad luck and moved on.

To accommodate their different styles and relieve the emotional pressure of their flight they decided to take turns planning their nocturnal itineraries. They continued to rely mostly on the position of the sun and moon for guidance, and occasionally stopped to ask for directions from road workers who were prisoners of the Franco regime. Elizondo was always the destination they mentioned, because Pérot was hopeful that if he could get there and contact his friend the cafe owner, they would be able to arrange passage to San Sebastian. As Pérot reflects on their escape journey, "I had bouts of anxiety and depression about the fate of my wife and children, wondering if they would be taken to a concentration camp and whether I should surrender and try to replace them. Cyrille had bouts, too, of anxiety and depression about his whole future. He was especially worried about his employees at Trait D'Union. Luckily we never had these down moments simultaneously."

Their progress was frequently retarded when clouds covered the moon. On one of these dark nights Charles remembers Cyrille losing his footing when he was looking for an easier way to proceed. As he clutched the bushes Cyrille "forbade me to come and help him because he was afraid that I would also find no footrest and we would both die falling off this cliff. A very tense moment followed, and Cyrille made an extreme effort to pull himself up with no avail. He said, 'I can't hold on, I will let go.' I was positively horrified. Then I heard nothing for a moment and Cyrille said, 'I'm okay, I fell about eight inches and my feet hit a rocky outcrop.' With my help he pulled himself back up." Throughout the rest of the journey whenever their spirits were low they reminded each other of this comic scene.

As the pair made their way westward through the foothills of the Spanish Pyrenees they once stopped at a village to buy wool overcoats that they could use as blankets and as protection from the frequent rainshowers. As Pérot remembers, "I had pants that were too short and a coat that was too long." In hope of replacing his espadrilles one day he approached a road worker and offered to pay him handsomely to go buy boots for him, but the convict was afraid to leave his job. Pérot continued on wearing his worn-out sandals.

Each night they tried to cover at least fifteen kilometers, walking eight to ten hours. The sight of the Carabineros somewhere between Burguete and Elizondo made them realize that they had gone astray and were almost back in France. Again they had to make a lengthy detour to avoid a string of villages near the border. When they finally reached the outskirts of Elizondo they sent a little boy to the village to tell the Spaniard of their arrival. The child returned later with the news that Pérot's friend was showing a film at his cinema but would come later that night. However, after waiting more than three hours past the appointed time, Pérot and Pomerantzeff grew agitated and decided to continue on their own.

Near the end of their trek from Elizondo to San Sebastian, after several hours of walking they decided to stop and sleep for a few hours. They lay down on a steep bank with their feet dangling in a ditch. "We awoke two hours later because our feet were so cold and wet. It had rained and the depression had filled with water," Pérot recalls. On what turned out to be the last day of their pilgrimage the two travelers spent a few hours in a stone shelter filled with sheep. Pérot can remember the shepherd opening the door but to his never-ending amazement the sheepdog did not detect their presence amid the sheep. Later in the day they trekked to a nearby farmstead to ask for food and directions. "An old woman apologized and said she was so poor she had nothing she could give us. She advised us to go down to the village of Yanci to the little store, where the people would help us."

When the two travelers appeared at the store the two young women there, daughters of the owner, realized immediately from their drenched overcoats and their air of exhausted desperation that these foreign vagabonds were escapees from France, and gave them food. The teenagers also asked their destination. Pérot indicated that he wanted to go to the Belgian Congo, and Pomerantzeff to South America. When the men inquired about a walking itinerary through the mountains to San Sebastian the women sought the counsel of other family members. In the end the family offered to arrange transport that would enable them to get to the coastal city in a few hours rather than six days. After more than two weeks on the move the fugitives decided to accept the offer. While they waited they bought suits in the store (which almost fit their frames), intending to change into these garments once they arrived in San Sebastian. The men also rediscovered the simple pleasure of soap and warm water. Jacques Pérot symbolically shaved off his mustache.

A car loaded with Spanish peasants on their way to a local celebration was their promised ride. After the two freshened travelers climbed into the crowded interior each was given a hat and a neckerchief, and Pomerantzeff was handed an accordion to play. In Pérot's words, "The Spaniards told us that we must not speak, and that we should act drunk and sing every time we saw the Guardia Civil." As their benefactors had predicted, when they approached the major crossroads where Franco's national police were posted, the vehicle was repeatedly stopped but then waved on. The former owner and the former director of the sawmill of Mendive ended their dangerous masquerade performing one last comical role.

When they reached San Sebastian the pair were taken to the back room of a small hotel to change into their new clothes. Pérot chuckles as he remembers "throwing our heavy, mildewing overcoats on top of the armoire in the room to ditch them." The twosome then walked to the office of Señor Lizariturri, the Spaniard who was serving as the Belgian consul as well as an operative for the Zéro network. He invited them to join him that evening for dinner at Hotel de Londres Y Ingleterra, the biggest resort hotel in San Sebastian.

Charles Schepens's resistance career as Jacques Pérot ended on a note of absurdity. After a sumptuous meal that night he and Pomerantzeff retired upstairs to a luxurious room booked for them by the consul. As Pérot recollects, "We were standing on the balcony of the hotel, having a huge, intellectual argument, probably about a theological issue, which had nothing to do with our situation. It was just like old times." Indeed, sixteen months after his arrival in Paris the Belgian ophthalmologist had fulfilled his ambition to continue his resistance work in the Pyrenees. As a result of his efforts dozens of people and countless secret documents had crossed the border. Yet even today he does not know exactly how many fugitives he helped, because he never saw most of the people being passed along through the Zéro network. "They did not come through Mendive, but were picked up by Sarochar in Hosta." He can remember that on ten or twelve occasions he was contacted for assistance by Vernieuwe, and that beginning in November 1942 the factory was losing ten workers a month. Though the tally is imprecise, it is probable that of the thirty thousand people who crossed the Pyrenees during the war, the lives of more than one hundred people were saved as a result of Charles Schepens's imagination and courage and Cyrille Pomerantzeff's generosity.[2]

At the same time a stinging irony clung to his accomplishments. Schepens and Vernieuwe had originally conceived the daring scheme with a dual purpose: to serve the underground and to provide a means to reunite the Schepens family for the duration of the war. Unfortunately, an international boundary once again separated him from Cette and the children. He was once again at large but they were hostages.

Part Four

Aftermath

(*Previous page*) Madame Pérot with
son Luc and daughter Claire, 1943.
(photo courtesy Dr. Charles Schepens)

Chapter 14

As the two fugitives trekked across the Spanish highlands a new chapter in the saga of the Mendive sawmill was already unfolding far to the north. Within a week of Nicolas Rosenschild's arrival in Paris, Oleg Pomerantzeff, his wife, Irène, and their daughter Marina were able to emerge from a train at the Gare de l'Est.

At the outbreak of the war in Yugoslavia two guerrilla groups were fighting the Germans and each other: Tito led the communist forces, Mihailovic the nationalists.[1] Oleg sided with Mihailovic's partisans because they were royalists, and assisted them by using the mining company's trucks to transport food and ammunition to their mountain camps. When he was arrested by the Germans Oleg was convinced that he was going to die because "one by one the other prisoners in the overcrowded cell were taken out and shot, until only another man and I remained." A large bribe (the equivalent of a full year's salary) offered by Nicolas Rosenschild on behalf of Cyrille to a high-ranking German general in Paris had bought Oleg's life and freedom after six months of incarceration.

Since the beginning of the war Oleg had been completely out of touch with his family in Paris. He had no idea about the existence of Trait D'Union, its purchase of the Mendive sawmill, or Charles Schepens's service as the sawmill's director. Rosenschild briefed Oleg about the unusual history of the enterprise as well as the current fiasco it faced.

At the same time that the two former sawmill directors landed in Elizondo, two members of the Gestapo burst into the Trait D'Union's company office on the rue St.-Lazare in Paris, announcing that "the 'brothers' were in Pamplona" and that they had come to interrogate the staff. Oleg did not correct their faulty identification; instead he acted as though he were a lowly employee. The Germans also did not even bother to read an incriminating letter that one of the secretaries happened to be in the process of typing. Before leaving the office one of the German officers informed them that "they knew that the Paris office had destroyed all the documentation and warned that if they were lying, they had passed the majority of their days." After the encounter Rosenschild advised Oleg to "disappear" until the situation calmed down and it was safe to make the journey to see their subsidiary operation in the Basque country. For the next several months Oleg and his family used the chateau at St.-Brice as their hideout while the Russian accountant maintained a distant relationship with key personnel at the ever-functioning mill in Mendive.

In fact, the two fugitives from France were not in Pamplona but on their way to Madrid. They spent only a few days in San Sebastian, just long enough to recover from their fourteen-day march and to acquire new false identity papers. Charles Schepens rechristened himself "Jacques Wielemans" because "Wielemans was the name of a popular Belgian beer." Señor Lizariturri issued a Belgian passport that identified Wielemans as a military officer, a document that would enable him to collect a regular salary from the Belgian consular offices during his temporary stay in Spain. Cyrille Pomerantzeff, who had been stateless since his arrival in France in the 1930s, acquired his first official passport even though it bore neither his true name nor his authentic nationality.

The two travelers arrived by train in Madrid in mid-August 1943 and took up residence in a pension across from the Ritz Hotel, which they quickly realized was full of German spies. Uppermost in Schepens's mind was sending correspondence to Cette, notifying her of his safe arrival and detailing the escape plan for her and the children that he had worked out during his long hours of waiting and walking. Charles had decided the safest strategy would be to write a letter to a trusted accomplice who could relay the news to Cette and Pelfort. He drafted a letter to Señor Murillo, who had served as a messenger for Vernieuwe several times. He sent the note to Murillo's home in Mauléon to avoid any possible suspicion that a letter postmarked "España" might arouse. Cyrille was anxious to make contact with his own family and office but held off doing so because Señor Lizariturri had adamantly stressed the importance of not sending any kind of communication to Paris.

Immediately after they arrived in the Spanish capital both men began the process of negotiating their passage to Britain. Schepens hoped that the Belgian secret service in Madrid would expedite his departure, but was disappointed to discover that "they were in no hurry to send me to England." Only later did he learn about a rift between the operatives in Spain and Ugeux, who was now directing all clandestine operations on the continent for the Belgian government in exile. Pomerantzeff decided to petition the British government for permission to immigrate as a French military officer (due to his prewar service). To his frustration the British refused his request on the basis that he had been born in Russia.

Thus the two men spent almost two months in Madrid—the first time either had been idle in several years—and experienced daily life under Franco's repressive dictatorship. Access to transportation was extremely limited which made it impossible to leave the city. For the Belgian the Spanish capital was "much like living in Brussels under the Occupation, although food was in greater supply. The biggest difference was that Spain was poorer, and you could bribe the Guardia Civil. Also there were prisoners everywhere working on the roads."

"Wielemans" and his Russian roommate quickly made friends with the chambermaids at the pension, who were all "anti-Franco and eager to help us get out of Spain." The two pensioners learned that a brother of one of the employees was plotting his own escape from the country and might be willing to include them, so Schepens met the Spaniard at a cafe. "From the start I did not trust him. Then when I paid for our drinks he was so insulted that I thought he was going to kill me. So, I insisted that we have another [round of] drink at his expense." Indeed, he remembers this encounter as one of the most disappointing moments of his months as a fugitive, and was glad to emerge unharmed from the rendezvous.

Their stay in Madrid also created a curious role reversal. From June 1942 through July 1943 Cyrille Pomerantzeff had invested at least ten million French francs into Jacques Pérot's resistance operation. Now it was Schepens's turn to be the financier, using Wielemans's modest military salary as a joint bank account for them both. Each bought new clothes and treated themselves to a daily sweet from one of the bakeries. Schepens remembers that "we both had a terrific craving for sugar. We were so ashamed that we would go separately to different pastry shops, but every evening we had to tell the other what we had eaten."

Indeed, to get food and to learn how the war was going were the two primary concerns of their life as restless transients. For the first time in several months Schepens had access and time to read a daily newspaper, albeit a pro-fascist one. As he remembers, "I found out generally what was happening in the war—the invasion in Italy, the new Russian offensive— but I could not tell who was winning." He taught himself Spanish using a book he had bought about ophthalmology. Several trips a week to the

Prado Museum were another benefit of being an uninvited guest of the Spanish government. Schepens remembers spending hours looking at the paintings by Velazquez and Brueghel. On one occasion the two friends even went to a bullfight.

When they arrived in the Spanish capital in late summer 1943 the city was awash with people like themselves who had escaped from France during the war. Unlike Schepens and Pomerantzeff, a large percentage of the other refugees — not only Europeans but Americans and Canadians as well — had spent several months in one of the Spanish prisons;[2] for these escapees time in the capital was a welcome period of recuperation before being shipped off to Africa or to England. Well aware of the polyglot character of the city, Wielemans was not tempted to fraternize with other expatriates on the loose. Fear of being exposed still haunted him.

A chance encounter in the Prado with a former sawmill employee who had recently been released from the camp at Miranda was the only occasion that Schepens let down his guard. Pleased to know that the young man, Jean Tabary — an engineering student from Paris who had worked in the company office with Pelfort and then been assigned as an "apprentice" to the mountain crew — had been successful in getting out of France, Schepens invited him to join them for dinner the following night. During the course of the evening the ever-cautious Schepens only revealed in general terms the secret mission of the Mendive sawmill and his own Belgian origins.

In early October 1943 Schepens received word through contacts in Madrid that arrangements had been made for his departure to England via Portugal at the end of the month. By then Pomerantzeff had decided to emigrate to South America and he was actively casting about for transatlantic passage. A chance encounter fulfilled his wish. According to Schepens, "One day we were walking in the center of Madrid and I overheard two men talking loudly in Russian. Cyrille approached them and struck up an immediate friendship." Subsequently, Pomerantzeff met one of the men alone on several occasions, and decided to join him in a business venture in Paraguay. The man was able to obtain a visa for Pomerantzeff, which finally allowed him to leave the continent.

In late October Schepens and Pomerantzeff were at last on their way to Lisbon. As they waited at the train station in Madrid the former sawmill director had an unexpected and quite unsettling encounter. A stranger approached him on the platform and said, "Bonjour, Monsieur Pérot." Schepens replied, with as much sangfroid as he could muster, "Je ne suis plus Monsieur Pérot" (I am no longer Monsieur Pérot) and walked away. During the train ride to Portugal he overheard conversation indicating that this young man was the son of one of the French customs officers in the Laurhibar Valley.[3] Apparently he had attempted to escape from Mendive in the spring of 1943 with a large group of local Basques seeking to avoid the STO. The group had been captured just over the Spanish border in Orbaiceta and had spent several months at the miserable internment camp in Totana, the topic of a lively conversation among many of the passengers on the train. From discreet cavesdropping the former Monsieur Pérot also learned that the Frenchman's release from the camp, like that of many others from Mendive, was a result of American humanitarian aid, since for every sack of wheat sent to Spain, Franco had agreed to free one foreign detainee.

Schepens knew that he would have to wait once he arrived in Lisbon, because the secret service determined the passenger lists for the nocturnal evacuation flights. In their ranking system Allied pilots had precedence over all others. During his weeklong sojourn in Portugal the Belgian continued to be cautious because he knew he was not yet beyond the reach of the enemy. Like Madrid, Lisbon was a center of both Allied and German espionage and counterespionage efforts. It later became clear that Pomerantzeff had already unknowingly been seduced by one of these double agents. As the Belgian learned several months afterward, Cyrille had been too easily taken in by the Russian businessman from Madrid, who was actually a German spy. After they left Lisbon the British intercepted their boat somewhere in the Atlantic and arrested both Pomerantzeff and his colleague. Fortunately, after being interrogated Pomerantzeff was let go. Schepens's Russian friend eventually arrived in South America "penniless, but as always, ready to start over."

As Schepens awaited his evacuation from Lisbon, Cette was preparing for her escape from France with the children. After Jacques Pérot's disappearance, Pelfort assumed control as director of the plant. He oversaw the continuation of both its legitimate and its clandestine activities. The ever-wily engineer, unfazed by a warning from the chief of the local Gestapo that they would be keeping a close watch on him, maintained the company's role as a way station for young people seeking to avoid the STO. About a month after Pérot fled the valley Pelfort came to the Pérot residence in Lecumberry to deliver the letter to Cette that Murillo had received and to tell her that sometime during the next several weeks he would help execute the escape plan her husband had sketched out. The scheme outlined in the letter instructed Cette and the children to go to the market in St.-Jean-Pied-de-Port with the rest of the local population. Instead of returning at the end of the day she was to proceed to the Hotel Baillea in Les Aldudes, where Madame Erreca would expedite their passage to Spain. Pelfort assured her that he would line up transportation and other necessary details for the journey.

Cette was extremely gratified by Pelfort's ongoing attentiveness and assistance because her current situation as a hostage and bait made her feel even more isolated from the rest of the community. As she recalls, "I was not surrounded by sympathy when Charles left. His escape confused and shocked people. They weren't sure why he had left. Was he dishonest in his affairs? Was there a drop in business? People were afraid of being implicated. I think the Argains must have wondered if they would get their rent, and if the children might be left behind. Not until the end of the war did the real story emerge."

Like so much of what happened during Cette's stressful, yearlong residence in Lecumberry, the weeks between her husband's flight and her own escape have remained largely a blur to her. One of her vivid memories is lying in bed at night listening for the Germans and their dogs outside. To survive the emotional anguish Cette focused on the day-to-day needs of her children during the period she was under house arrest. The protective maternal instincts she had felt during her trip from Belgium were rekindled, and the only time she left the children—either in the care of Madame Argain or with Beppina (who had remained in her employ)—was to make her obligatory appearance at the chateau. In fact, after several weeks the Germans decided to relax their regime and only required her to travel to the chateau to sign the register every other day.

As much as she liked Bernadette, Cette decided it would be best for the young woman to return to her family, so in early August Cette made arrangements for Mademoiselle Lafitte to travel by train back to Paris. In addition, since Cette knew that it was important to avoid any possible suspicion of what was afoot for herself and the children, sometime toward the middle of October she also announced to Beppina that after a certain date she would be having time off. Beppina remembered Madame Pérot informing her "that her mother was ill and that she had to go take care of her." Beppina respected her employer and accepted the news without question.

In contrast to her husband's July escape when the news of the event ricocheted rapidly throughout the valley, Cette's mysterious departure with the children was not discovered for more than a day. She does not now remember the exact date of their flight, but it was sometime near the end of October. Pelfort had arranged that they would have lunch with the family of Marie Esponda in St.-Jean-Pied-de-Port and then, in the afternoon, Jean Bouleux would pick them up in a company truck, conceal them among the goods in transit, and transport them to Les Aldudes. That day Cette went to sign the register at the chateau in the morning and in the afternoon departed with the rest of the local women and children going to the weekly market. She rode her bicycle behind a cart driven by Raymond Sarochar, with Claire and Luc sitting in the back of the cart among various sacks and baskets of produce to insure that the guards in St.-Jean-le-Vieux would let the group pass the checkpoint. Hidden in one of the baskets were the few personal possessions that Cette had brought for their trip.

Everything went according to schedule until her departure from Les Aldudes, when their secret pilgrimage took on an almost biblical character. She and the children spent the better part of two days hidden away in the far reaches of the Hotel Baillea. They left for the border the second night, guided by a young Basque. Madame Erreca had arranged for a mule to help transport the children and their modest belongings across the mountains, but unbeknownst to her Luc was terrified of the animal (the result of a fall he had experienced on one of their many trips up to the Forêt d'Iraty). The trek began with Cette and Claire walking hand in hand and the shepherd leading the mule with a very unhappy rider. The toddler was crying so violently and Cette was so afraid that they would be heard by the border patrol that she ended up carrying him on her shoulders, all the while continuing to hold Claire by the hand. As Cette recalls, "What saved us was a terrible thunderstorm. The guards had all sought cover, and we were able to pass the frontier without being stopped." After a four-hour walk through the mountains the valiant young mother and frightened, exhausted youngsters arrived safely in Elizondo.

At the hotel owned by her husband's friend Cette was not only warmly accommodated by the Spaniard but found herself in the company of a number of other Belgian and French refugees. Among the group was a waiter from the Grand Hotel in Brussels who recognized her. Today she remembers with amusement her three-day sojourn in Elizondo: the daytime hours she spent distracting the children who were hidden away in the attic of the hotel, and at night listening distractedly to the other guests exchange explicit accounts of their previous romantic involvements.

The intervention of Señor Lizariturri enabled Cette and the children to finish the last leg of the journey from Elizondo to San Sebastian by car, under the protection of diplomatic immunity. Her first hours in the coastal city gave her both a tremendous sense of relief and the feeling of an unbelievable change in fortune. She was not only lodged at the same fancy nineteenth-century hotel overlooking the ocean where her husband had stayed, but in their room a huge basket of fruit sent with the compliments of the Duchess of Alba (a local aristocrat) awaited them. Her stay in San Sebastian, however, was marred by a minor tragedy. The only item that had traveled with her all the way from Belgium to Spain was the missal filled with family memorabilia. "I can't figure out how I was able to bring it along. Then to have lost it! While I was watching the children play on the beach the waves washed it away."

Though she never saw him, Señor Lizariturri performed a variety of services on her behalf during their stopover: sending word to her husband in England of their safe arrival; advancing money for the family's expenses; purchasing train tickets for the trip to Madrid; and producing new false passports. True to form, Claire and Luc once again took on a new name in Spain and became members of the Wielemans family. The family's stay in the Spanish capital lasted almost six months because of the long waiting list of escapees wishing to immigrate to Britain. The consular office briefed Cette about her husband's situation and provided her with a living allowance due the wife of a Belgian military officer. She and the children took up residence at a pension near the Prado Museum, where the galleries became a second home for them. While most of her energy continued to be devoted to taking care of Claire and Luc during their stay, she occasionally attended evening events with other expatriate Belgians whom she encountered. She enjoyed these social gatherings, not only because they provided a touch of familiarity to an abnormal existence but also because they enabled her to catch up on news gleaned from the underground journals and gossip from other sources.

Like her husband, Cette and her children began their trip to London with a train ride to Lisbon. And, just as her husband had discovered several months earlier, gaining passage aboard the Clipper seaplanes being used by the Allied forces was a matter of timing and depended on who else was on the list of evacuees, on if the weather was suitable, and on whether the absence of German spy planes would allow takeoff.[4] In late March 1944 their travel was approved. Aboard the plane Cette remembers "an officer covered with stripes and decorations, accompanied by another officer who had fewer stripes and medals, and a third one who was probably a diplomat." She and the children were the only civilians on the flight. Their nocturnal flight to Bristol lasted more than eight hours and, fortunately, the children slept through practically all of it.

Once they landed in Bristol, however, it was a group of British military officers, not her husband, who met them. One final bureaucratic hurdle had to be overcome before they could officially gain entrance to the country and have a family reunion: like all the other Belgian *résistants* who had escaped via Mendive and had eventually been airlifted to England, Cette and the children were immediately transported to a transit center (with the curious name of "Patriotic School") that was located in Wimbledon on the outskirts of London. The transit center functioned as a screening facility operated by the British counterespionage corps to filter out Nazi spies — not only Germans but all kinds of people from all over the continent who were trying to establish residency in enemy territory. Over the course of two or three days Cette was interrogated about her family history and about her husband, and tested on her knowledge of other facts about recent political history. She attributes her short residence in Wimbledon (where the usual stay was five days) to the fact that she was carrying correspondence from the Belgian consul in Lisbon for Hubert Pierlot, the Belgian prime minister in exile.

After nine months of separation and fifteen months embroiled in an underground existence of lies and secrets, Cette and Charles Schepens had regained their former identities and could together begin the process of rebuilding normal lives, albeit in a foreign country in an active theater of war. Charles, who had summoned the courage to act and then to lead, and Cette, who had found the fortitude to endure — both were now different individuals from the young Belgian doctor and his wife living on the chaussée de Haecht or the impostors Monsieur and Madame Pérot in residence in the Basque country.

The circumstances of their initial reunion in London were only slightly less hectic and stressful than their rendezvous in the train station in Paris in 1942. Charles remembers a taxi pulling up in Sloane Square, and getting into the back seat to join Cette and the children. "Claire was overjoyed to see me, but Luc did not recognize me dressed in a military uniform and not having a mustache. He was scared and started to cry." On their trip out of London Charles explained that with the bombing raids both in the daytime and at night, they would be far safer staying in the British countryside with the Wells family, near Bedford.[5]

Cette credits the kindness of Sir Richard and Lady Wells for helping them through a period of emotional transition. Soon after Charles's arrival in England in November 1943 he reestablished contact with the displaced Belgian military command in London (who accorded him status as a reserve officer) and with Moorfields Eye Hospital (where he gained an appointment). To Charles's amazement the same doctors who had earlier given him the cold shoulder during his medical residency treated him as a long-lost associate and welcomed him into their social circle. One of these colleagues introduced him to the Wells family, and he became a regular guest at their lovely estate. When Lady Wells learned that Cette and the children were arriving in March she insisted on housing them all, knowing well the anguish of war having lost two sons of her own, and fearing the death of a third. Cette and the children were immediately absorbed into a large and congenial household of daughters-in-law and grandchildren in the Wells' estate in Felmersham.

Charles continued to maintain a small apartment near the hospital and commuted to the country on the weekends. Cette remembers traveling into London on a few occasions only. The advantages of living outside the city were confirmed when she experienced a bombing raid on one of her urban visits. Though her life continued to revolve around her children, the matriarchal atmosphere of the Wells home provided a ready source of supervision and support. In fact, during her eighteen-month stay Cette joined the in-house schooling effort that the Wells women had instituted for the youngsters in residence, taking on the role of art and French teacher. Cette resumed her own painting as well, and produced many portraits of the three generations of this spirited English family. The cheerful palette and airy brushwork of the paintings done in 1944–45, in contrast to the solemn mood of the paintings of young Jean and Charles Moretti, signal the tonic effect of the Wells' hospitality.

Moreover, although they were still living in a war zone, for the Belgian doctor and his wife the Normandy landing was a potent symbol that both the end of the conflict and an Allied victory were in sight. For the first time in several years they could begin to think about their own future. While they were in England Bernadette, their third child, was born in 1945. And once again Charles could resume his personal quest to wage war against eye disease. Since his fellowship at Moorfields entailed seeing patients only two days a week, Charles had renewed his interest in the problems of diagnosing and treating retinal injury and disease. As soon as he began his employment at the hospital (recently hit badly in a bombing raid) he initiated a project that he had envisioned for several years: development of new optical equipment enabling an ophthalmologist to study the rear wall of the eye. From glass lenses, screws, and scraps of aluminum and other available hardware salvaged from the ruins of the hospital laboratories Dr. Schepens fabricated two crude model instruments: one, an indirect binocular ophthalmoscope, would prove revolutionary in the postwar world.

Despite the end of his unexpected career as a resistance fighter and his reentry into official military service and the medical profession, Charles Schepens could not forget his months in the Basque country. Once he arrived in London he reestablished contact with Anselme Vernieuwe (who was flying for the RAF), and William Ugeux (director of the Belgian secret service). They compared notes about their experiences trekking across Spain and stopovers in San Sebastian, Madrid, and Lisbon. Charles learned that his friend Selmo had suffered from the flare-up of an old hernia problem en route to San Sebastian, and had daily drunk almost a liter of anisette to counter the pain.

Charles also learned the tragic fate of other members of the former Zéro network who had not made it to England. "Antoine" had been arrested in Grenoble before his projected trip to Mendive and then sent to a concentration camp. Ugeux had learned from intelligence sources in Spain and France that de Hepcée had been sold out by one of his *passeurs* and never made it back to Barcelona in the spring of 1943. The information included an unconfirmed story that, after he was arrested by the Gestapo in France, he was forced to dig his own grave and then shot.[6] The news of what had happened to the courier's wife and children, who were close in age to Claire and Luc Schepens, struck a particularly poignant note for the former Monsieur Pérot: "The Germans subsequently arrested his family at their apartment in Villard-de-Lans, but separated the mother from her children on the platform of the railroad station as she was boarding the train for a concentration camp. By sheer luck someone in the station happened to recognize the two abandoned youngsters and rescued them."

Charles could not stop wondering as well about the fate of the people left behind in Mendive, especially Pelfort and Sarochar and others, like Oleg, who were still in danger on the continent.

Chapter 15

When Jacques Pérot hired Marius Pelfort in August 1942 he knew of Pelfort's impressive military training and experience, but was unaware of several bold actions that Pelfort had undertaken when his unit was fleeing Normandy in 1940. To thwart the Germans during the invasion Captain Pelfort had overseen the destruction of the fuel depots and various construction documents of the aerodromes at Caen and Rouen.[1] As his regiment headed southward he learned that several fuel tanks had not been torched, so he alone went back to complete the chore. By the time he reached Evreux the Germans had already blockaded passage out of the town. Determined not to get captured, he drove his car through the barriers under machine-gun fire, then rejoined his men. Like Pérot, Pelfort possessed remarkable sangfroid in the middle of dangerous situations. Unlike his colleague, however, the Toulousain also had a dangerous confidence in his own invincibility, which proved to be his undoing.

When Pelfort assumed the position of general manager of the Compagnie d'Iraty in the summer of 1943 he worked diligently to keep the factory in full operation in order to insure the ongoing employment of the workers, as well as to continue its function as a point of passage for escaped POWs and young French draft dodgers.[2] During his tenure he made a few minor changes to operations, including the promotion of

Faubert and Bouleux to managerial positions. In addition he set up a new canteen for the plant workers behind the Pédelucq house, and hired Murillo's wife as the cook, since he was not eager to see the employees spend their wages on food, drink, and cigarettes at the overpriced Auberge Pedro. Pelfort traveled much more extensively than his predecessor had after his family's arrival in November 1942. He made frequent trips to Bayonne, Biarritz, Pau, Toulouse, and Bordeaux to negotiate contracts or to confer with Vichy government officials. On a few occasions he also went to Paris to review company affairs with Nicolas Rosenschild.

After Monsieur Pérot's departure some significant differences transpired behind the scenes at the factory. Now several employees in the company office knowingly participated in the counterfeiting of company identity cards, and the distribution system had been expanded. No longer were the special company passes only issued to people after they had been interviewed and hired at the plant office; in certain circumstances the documents were being conveyed elsewhere to draft dodgers, mostly university graduates, to facilitate their arrival in the Restricted Zone. And, in marked contrast to Pérot's strategy of independence, Pelfort and Faubert established contact with the French resistance, which included a secret visit to Mendive by Colonel Rémy (de Gaulle's chief intelligence agent working inside France) in the winter of 1943–44.

Moreover, until the summer of 1943 neither the workers nor the Germans knew of the resistance activities within the plant. The flight of both the director and the owner, compounded by the continuing disappearance of new inexperienced workers, were suspicious signals to the employees, especially to those working on the plateau, that some kind of clandestine service was occurring. As one of the former Basque workers commented about the turnover of temporary employees, "We worked side by side with these men, and watched them serve a false apprenticeship as manual laborers. I often wondered what their true identities were in real life."

Once Cette and the children had made their escape in the fall of 1943, Pelfort also decided to reveal to Madame Pédelucq the secret services of the plant, past and present. Her daughter, Cilotte, who was a teenager at the time, remembers hearing him comment with irony to her mother on the "pourcentage des bacs" (the number of baccalaureates) who were employed by the factory. Madame Pédelucq in response urged him to escape to Spain, fearing that his days were numbered because of the Germans' stepped-up surveillance. Sure that his practice of bribing Nazi officials (throughout all of France) with cigars and other coveted items made him invulnerable, Pelfort downplayed the risk of arrest. Indeed, he took great pride in the fact that he was carrying on the work of Monsieur Pérot.

Jean Sarochar, too, continued his voluntary resistance work, on call to Pelfort as a *passeur*. Once all of the members of the Pérot family were safely out of the valley, Sarochar also began to openly claim his role in the escape of the factory director and other VIPs that he had escorted for Zéro. Although his tales were regarded by the villagers as simply the latest chapter in his long collection of heroic fantasies, the Pédelucq children remember their mother fearing for his safety and admonishing the shepherd to be more discreet.

Two stories told by current residents of the valley provide insight into Sarochar's disinformation service during the latter part of the war, and why this brave but odd man — regarded as the local buffoon — had little reason to fear exposure from his storytelling. After Cette and the children left the valley, Beppina Moretti and her older sister Katrina, who had been working as a seamstress in St.-Jean-Pied-de-Port, were both facing conscription in the STO. The Irigoin family agreed to hide the girls in their farmhouse. During their yearlong stay Madame Irigoin remembers being constantly fearful that the Grenzschutz, who often stopped at their property on their way to and from Iraty, would hear Katrina working at her sewing machine on the second floor. Then one day their neighbor, who "was very friendly with the Germans," was walking on the hillside above their farmstead as Katrina was milking a cow below, and Madame Irigoin and her husband wondered if he had seen the girl and might report them. With considerable surprise and amusement Madame Irigoin thus listened as Sarochar told her in 1944 how he had recently passed Katrina and Beppina out of France, when in fact they were at that moment sitting upstairs in her own house.

One of Sarochar's favorite wartime pranks, according to Monsieur Etcharren, was to place an alarm clock underneath a pile of hay when another shepherd or visitor was staying at his mountain hut. When it went off he would go over and pretend to have a conversation, afterward announcing that he had just talked to General Charles de Gaulle. Monsieur Etcharren also remembers Jean telling him that "he had to put a device in a stream to receive and send messages to de Gaulle in London, but to send messages to him in Africa he had to go up to Iraty."

With a new logging season under way in the spring of 1944, Pelfort, Faubert, and Rosenschild were preparing final plans for Oleg Pomerantzeff's first visit to Mendive to familiarize him with the lumbering operation as well as to transport an infusion of cash needed for the upcoming purchase of new livestock. In late May Pelfort was on his way to Paris for company business, aware that the Allied invasion was imminent but unconcerned that it might disrupt travel into the Basque country.

On 30 May, soon after his arrival in the capital, Pelfort received an alarming call from Madame Pédelucq that cut short his visit: Thérèse Esponda had contacted her, and told her that the Germans were at the factory conducting an inspection of identity cards. Madame Pédelucq advised Pelfort not to return to Mendive where he was sure to be arrested, but instead to come to the family villa in Cauneille. This time he followed her counsel and made the return trip — which involved several detours due to the Allied bombing in progress — in the company of Léon and Henri Pédelucq, both of whom were then university students in the French capital.

The arrest the previous afternoon of Señor Murillo in Puyoô had precipitated the second Gestapo raid on the Mendive sawmill. Murillo had been caught in the train station passing one of the Compagnie d'Iraty's special identity cards to a young draft dodger named Géarts who was the son of an office worker at the Mendive plant. Early on the morning of 30 May members of the local Gestapo had appeared at the factory and arrested three company employees who had been implicated: Géarts, Verdier, and Denis. They also took Monsieur Werner, the bookkeeper, to headquarters in St.-Jean-Pied-de-Port for questioning. Thérèse Esponda immediately telephoned Bouleux and Faubert, both of whom were up on the Plateau d'Iraty, to alert them of the situation. Bouleux remembers the two of them being escorted by two Grenzschutz officers back to the valley, and the foursome then stopped for lunch at Auberge Pedro before continuing on to the Gestapo office at the Hotel Atherbea in St.-Jean-Pied-de-Port. There the Germans took away the prisoners' belts, shoes, and pants, and briefly placed the men in a cell. After several hours of interrogation, like Werner they were finally released.

The next day there was a wider search in the village. Jean Moretti recounts the following story he remembers from his childhood: "Once the Germans had left the company office and moved onto the factory floor to do their inspection [my] Aunt Thérèse gathered up a packet of fake cards that they had not uncovered and headed out of the building. She went to the house of the factory foreman, which bordered the sawmill property to the north, and asked his wife to temporarily hide the papers. Aunt Thérèse retrieved them later that day and brought them to our house, where she lived. I put them in a little iron box and buried it in the garden that night." The next morning a group of armed Grenzschutz officers appeared and ransacked the Moretti house. Luckily they did not go to the barn, where they would have discovered Jean and his brother under the care of Beppina Moretti, who was still trying to avoid STO conscription. "The only thing they found was a letter from Madame Pédelucq to my aunt requesting some counterfeit passes. Aunt Thérèse was saved because the Alsatian guard who found it told her to burn it. Although we never knew, we wondered if the foreman's daughters, who worked as domestics at the chateau, might have heard their parents talking and tipped off the Germans about my aunt."

Although some people in the village today still speculate about the role these two teenage girls played in the second round of arrests in 1944, Pelfort soon discovered that the apprehension of Murillo and the others was the result of a typed letter of denunciation. That information was revealed, along with cryptic notes about the ensuing series of events, in a heartbreaking personal journal written by Pelfort, the only contemporaneous wartime account about the factory that survives and provides a chronicle of the tragic conclusion of his service in the secret war.[3] On 3 June Faubert traveled to Cauneille to brief Pelfort on the crisis and to warn him that Mag, chief of the Gestapo, wanted to interrogate him. Supremely confident from all of his previous encounters with the Germans that he could outsmart them and elude capture, and also convinced that the Allied invasion would save him if harm came his way, Pelfort decided to take on the mission of liberating his subordinates from the jail in St.-Jean-Pied-de-Port. Knowing Pelfort's character, Schepens today believes that Pelfort "also felt that he was partly responsible for what happened to Murillo and the others, and being their boss and a gallant officer he could not bear the idea that he would be free when the others would probably die in a concentration camp." Against the vehement protest of Madame Pédelucq, who thought now more than ever that he must escape out of France, the factory director sent a letter to Mag telling him he would come to Gestapo headquarters on 5 June. After reflecting on Pelfort's intrepid character, Jean Bouleux commented, "He was a man of tremendous integrity, a true patriot. He realized that if he did not show up the rest of the factory workers would be deported."

As all had predicted, Pelfort was searched and interrogated, then arrested and transported immediately to a detention facility in Biarritz. On 9 June he was transferred to Maison Blanche, a property that the Germans had converted into a prison in Biarritz. There, for the first time, he was reunited with the five others from Mendive who had been previously arrested, and from them he heard about the written accusation. The group remained together for the next several weeks, at first being transferred to a large-scale prisoner-of-war camp at the Fort du Ha in Bordeaux, then being shipped off to Dachau. From there they were dispersed, each eventually to die in one of the German concentration camps before the end of the war. In September 1944 Pelfort was reassigned to the camp at Hersbruck, where he died on 11 December.[4]

In what proved to be the final and most bizarre coincidence among the many in the incredible history of the Mendive sawmill, Oleg Pomerantzeff was arrested almost as soon as he landed in the Basque country in June 1944. He remembered being lukewarm about making the journey, but Rosenschild was insistent that he must take on an active role in the administration of the plant. Leaving Paris at nearly the same time that Pelfort was reporting to the Gestapo, Oleg was met at the train by Faubert in Biarritz. The Russian had obtained an identity card, with his real name, specifying his profession as an engineer; he used it for the train trip from Paris. However, on the subsequent ride in the *gazogène* to Mendive, Faubert planned to introduce him as the Spanish consul to the German guards at the checkpoints, all of whom he knew well, and hence avoid recognition of the name "Pomerantzeff." That day the men traveled as far as St.-Jean-Pied-de-Port, where Oleg was dropped off to spend the night at the Etchendy hotel. Oleg recalled that for diversion he ventured off to the local cinema, where he saw *Anticipation*, a German propaganda film about the unsuccessful American invasion of France.

The next morning Oleg was traveling on his own when he arrived at the checkpoint in St.-Jean-le-Vieux. Unlike the German guards who had waved him through without checking any papers the previous day, the soldiers at the entrance to the Restricted Mountain Zone were more demanding. Quickly Oleg's story fell apart. When they searched him and found his identity card bearing the name Pomerantzeff they arrested him, confiscated the forty thousand francs he possessed, and put him in jail in St.-Jean-Pied-de-Port. A day or so later he was taken to the Maison Blanche in Biarritz. He recalled, "The Biarritz prison was far better than the one in Yugoslavia. I was placed in a ten-by-ten cell with twelve other men. They were all curious about the outcome of the *débarquement*. Since I had just seen the movie [*Anticipation*] I told them that it had failed, although many didn't believe me."

By 10 June both Pelfort and Pomerantzeff were in separate cells in the same prison, neither aware of the other's presence. Madame Pédelucq had learned that they both were in custody and decided to try to use her influence to lobby for their release. She went to the German authorities and demanded that the director of the Compagnie d'Iraty be let off. Her efforts had an ironic effect, however: because of the association of the name of Pomerantzeff with the Iraty operation it was Oleg, not Pelfort, who was spared deportation to the Fort du Ha on 12 June.

Oleg remained in the French prison for two months. Once again, through influence exercised by connections in Paris—this time through his aunt, who was married to a French admiral—Oleg was finally released in early August 1944. He remembered that one day "a guard came and told me I was to report the next day to the commandant's office. I thought I was going to be sent on to a concentration camp, but instead they told me I was being let go. They kept the money that I had brought, but I was so glad to get out I did not care."

It took Oleg thirteen days to get back to Paris, hitching rides and walking a good part of the journey. He arrived there on 23 August, the day before the Americans liberated the city. By then his wife and daughter, whom the Germans had evicted from the family chateau at St.-Brice, were living among a dozen Russian émigrés at an apartment on rue Murat. As vivid a memory for Oleg as the celebration taking place in the surrounding streets and on the rooftops after the Liberation was the sight of female collaborators with shaved heads being driven through the neighborhood.

He also recalls the shock and disgust he felt when he and Nicolas Rosenschild tried to get out to St.-Brice, "seeing Parisians en route kicking young, dead German soldiers."

The departure of the Grenzschutz from the Laurhibar Valley in late July 1944 made an equally strong impression on its inhabitants. Each year during the months of July and August, Angèle Moretti's family joined him at the three-room chalet that he had built with his brother Baptiste in the Forêt d'Iraty. For ten-year-old Jean Moretti the most memorable event of his 1944 summer holiday was the swift retreat of the Germans and their dogs, followed almost immediately by the arrival of the guerrilla fighters known as the *maquisards*. As he recollects, "One day we saw a German guard walking under the telephone line that went up to the plateau. He told my mother that they were waiting for some terrible news. That night we heard dogs barking all over the mountains, and the next day they were all gone from the chalet. Then the *maquis* appeared. Many of them had no shoes. They wanted to put a French flag on the cable, but the only woman who sewed was Modesta, the Spanish canteen operator. She got some colored cloth, but she reversed the blue and red on the makeshift flag!"

As Moretti and others remember, most of the *maquisards* were Spanish Civil War refugees who had been hiding out in the mountains and using the Forêt d'Iraty as a base for their guerilla operations after the Normandy landing.[5] The only skirmish that occurred in the area happened on 27 July when a group of *maquisards* ambushed the German patrol at Ahusky and one of the German officers was killed.[6] While the band of commandos did not carry out any major sabotage events in the valley or the surrounding mountains, Modesta Perez remembers an abortive plot to blow up Chalet Pedro, a place where the Grenzschutz often congregated.

People from the villages in the valley recall that the *maquis*, whose numbers were about equal to the former contingent of Grenzschutz, were far more aggressive toward the local population than their German predecessors had been, especially in their demand for provisions from the farm families. Indeed, despite the dangers involved in transporting contraband and escapees that he had incurred in his role as company truckdriver, for Jean Bouleux the most frightening errand during the war was his experience on a normal provision run in the summer of 1944: "Raymond

Sarochar and I would go all over the countryside to buy goods from local farmers. One day while we were making one of these weekly trips we were accosted by a band of twelve Spanish *maquisards* who wanted a ride and who were armed to the teeth. I was very worried about the potential of encountering the German patrol, but they just climbed into the back of the truck anyway. After I left them off, about one to two kilometers beyond, we did meet up with the Germans."

Not all the *maquis* were outsiders. In the last months of the German occupation Jean Sarochar participated in the brief guerrilla war. Outfitted with a rifle he ranged the mountain terrain as part of a partisan cell. Thus, when the valley was finally liberated, along with the rest of the Basque country in late August 1944 the veteran shepherd-warrior could proudly claim a direct role in the Allied victory.

Chapter 16

"When I arrived at Patriotic School in England I was asked about what I had been doing during the war. I told the British intelligence officer the complete story of my service in the Air Force, my life in Brussels, and my underground life in Mendive. All he could do was laugh. Then he went and got another officer, and I retold the story to both of them, and they howled in disbelief. When I returned to Mendive in May 1945 I was dressed in my Belgian military uniform. When the people discovered that I was actually an ophthalmologist, they were flabbergasted." Charles Schepens thus remembers what it was like, once the drama was over, to recount his fantastic story to strangers and Monsieur Pérot's former acquaintances.

In the early spring of 1945 Schepens pulled off one final surreptitious act — this time subverting the British authorities. Several months after Belgium was liberated in September 1944, Schepens decided to cross the Channel from England to reestablish personal contact with both his and Cette's families. Nicolas Rosenschild had relayed to their relatives the news of the Schepenses' successive escapes from France, but the family had been completely out of communication during their stay in England. In early March 1945 Lieutenant Schepens fabricated a false permit that gave passage aboard an LST, a British military cargo boat, and spent ten days visiting their families in Ghent and Mouscron. He remembers the reunions with his sister and mother-in-law most of all, each gasping in disbelief and relief when they first saw him. He recalls as well that his homecoming was more a reunion than a celebration, with the still-lingering fear that the war might not yet be over. Reassured that all of his relatives had successfully survived the fifty-two months of occupation, Charles returned to England aboard one of the Allied boats, and remained in the country another two months.

Just days before V-E day was declared on 8 May 1945, Charles Schepens made his final journey of the war. As he crossed the Channel aboard another military transport vessel he remembers thinking that this time he was "back for good." Before returning to Brussels, however, he spent several weeks with Cette's parents at the Chateau de Gavergracht, which during the later years of the war had been requisitioned by the Germans for a temporary training facility for truck mechanics and was still under reclamation. He discovered Brussels had not suffered the damage inflicted on Antwerp and Tournai, and to his relief found their house on the chaussée de Haecht still intact. He was surprised to find still in residence both the Dieu family and his journalist friend Zeegers (who had been in hiding in France for four years), and described to his "tenants" the succession of places he and Cette and the children had lived since leaving Belgium three years before. Monsieur Dieu in turn told him of their experiences with the Gestapo in April 1942. Schepens recalls, "My medical office was only in slight disorder. The only thing I discovered that was missing after the second German raid was another one thousand dollar bill that I had placed behind one of the paintings in the salon before my departure."

When Charles traveled across the Channel he realized that it would be several months before Cette and the children could negotiate their passage back to Belgium as civilians. In fact, not until September did they arrive in Ostend where they, like hundreds of other women and children, were greeted on the quay by anxious relatives. After an extended reunion at the Vander Eeckens' country estate, he and his wife and three children eventually returned to their townhouse in Brussels. By then Charles had reclaimed and reorganized their former residence as a single family dwelling. Not long after their arrival a friend asked Charles and Cette to take in—for six weeks—a hungry fourteen-year-old orphan. Jeanne Postal took up residence as the family's nanny-housekeeper. Almost sixty years later Jeanne continues to be a vital member of the household.

After Charles returned to Brussels in May 1945 one of his first telephone calls was to the office of Trait D'Union in Paris to learn what had happened to the plant and the fate of both Cyrille and Oleg Pomerantzeff. From Rosenschild he heard for the first time a condensed account of the second arrest and deportation to concentration camps of Pelfort and the others. To his relief Charles learned that Cyrille had made it to South America but that no one knew of his whereabouts. (Indeed, it was not until early 1946, when Cyrille made a trip to France and Belgium, that Charles learned the full story of Cyrille's perilous voyage and eventual resettlement in Argentina.) To Charles's great amazement Oleg and his family were now living in Mendive. As Charles recalls, "When I found out that Oleg was serving as the director of the sawmill, I decided to travel down to Mendive to see him and see how I could be of help to him."

Seven years had elapsed since the last time the two had seen each other. Only a crop of premature gray hair gave evidence of Oleg's ordeals during the war, and he projected the same indomitable personality that Charles so admired. In fact, hardly had Charles landed in Mendive when the Russian insisted on showing his old classmate his plans to expand the logging operation by adding a secondary cable from Astaquieta up to the Chapelle St.-Sauveur station, so the two went off hiking in the mountains. Their time ranging the somber recesses of the forest gave Charles a chance to give his long-lost friend a detailed account of his own experiences in reviving and operating the mill. Oleg revealed that one of his unexpected legacies as Monsieur Pérot was his reputation for making the ascent to the Plateau d'Iraty in less than an hour, a record that the company employees were constantly holding up to him as the new plant director and one, to his shame, he could not equal. Charles assured Oleg, who had always been a superior athlete, that he himself had never been that swift of a hiker and that "two and a half hours was my average."

Charles also remembers that though the two swapped tales from the war, it was not long before they launched into a series of hypothetical discussions about future engineering improvements to the operation and expansion of the enterprise. Moreover, his evenings spent in the company of Oleg, Irène, and their three children in their house across from the factory proved to be an odd flashback to the lively Russian-style hospitality he had known at the Chateau St.-Brice. Yet, at the end of his stay and despite Oleg and his family's apparent adaptation to living in rural France, he could not help but think that their identity as Russian expatriates created an unavoidable social barrier in this Basque village. Indeed, he sensed that theirs was a temporary situation because it offered such limited opportunities for his expansive scientific genius.

Schepens's visit to Mendive that spring also afforded him the chance to fully unmask the character of Monsieur Pérot to the residents of the valley. When he arrived at Jean Sarochar's hut unannounced, Sarochar, spotting him in his military uniform, greeted him like a returning conqueror. They ate bread and cheese and for the first time shared a gourd of wine. The former sawmill director outlined the full story of his escape to Spain and England, and the shepherd proudly narrated his continued service as a *passeur* and his brief stint in the *maquis*. When Charles revealed his true nationality and professional identity, Sarochar laughed with gusto. Though the two did not spend an extended time together, the Belgian ophthalmologist left confident that the end of the war would not be the end of their association. He realized, as well, that the unique circumstances of his resistance work had drawn them together and that Oleg Pomerantzeff and Jean Sarochar, his two most trusted friends, would never have a similar relationship.

In contrast to Sarochar's spontaneous expressions of admiration and affection, his encounters with the villagers who had not been a part of the deception scheme or who had been only peripherally involved were full of bewilderment. To be sure, Monsieur Pérot's frenzied dash through the factory had become a legendary moment in their collective memory much like the accidental death of Paul Pédelucq. And, not surprising, Sarochar's stories had done little to bring closure to the Pérot affair. The Belgian's former employees and neighbors were still unsure whether he was an embezzler, a collaborationist, a patriot, or a mix of them all. To clear the air Charles charted his entire story, beginning with his resistance work in Brussels in the first months of the occupation all the way through the recent resumption of his medical career. To those who had known Cette, especially the Argains, he described the true tale of her disappearance with the children.

Henri Pédelucq's apprehension of the full story of Schepens's deeds as
Monsieur Pérot imprinted a lifelong impression: "He was only fifteen
years older than me but he seemed like a much older man. For me Charles
Schepens had the extraordinary bravery of General LeClerc, a man who
was made a general at age twenty-nine." Indeed, at the end of three days
and after many repetitions of the account of his career in the underground
the former sawmill director, who remained Monsieur Pérot to almost all
he knew in the valley, had earned status comparable to Roland, the superhuman hero of ancient Basque mythology who continually outsmarted
the giants of the forest.

Schepens left the village also having satisfied his own curiosity about
the sequel to his escape and the remaining months of the occupation.
Thérèse Esponda gave a detailed account of the second German raid in
1944 and the sad end that Pelfort and the others had endured, a tale he
heard retold by several others during the course of his sojourn. Moreover,
he heard the amusing account of Monsieur Haurat's discovery that he had
been duped by Monsieur Pérot's professed Vichy loyalty; Murillo had
reported to Pelfort and the other conspiratorial company workers that the
Oloron garage owner had declared, "I will kill him if I ever see him again."
From Monsieur Werner, the interim director of the plant after Pelfort's
arrest and before Oleg's arrival, "I learned that the Gestapo had raided the
company's safe before they left the village in July 1943, and had taken
about one and a half million French francs," an amount far bigger than the
sum that Vallier had brought. As for the furnishings from their farmhouse
in Lecumberry, a company employee had "inherited" them. His one regret
was that Cette's paintings had somehow disappeared.

The only disagreeable experience during his visit — and one that still
galls Charles Schepens today — was an interaction with the chief of the
local gendarmerie, the officer who had interrogated Jacques Pérot a few
months after his arrival (about his knowledge of a rumored abortion) and
someone whom he knew had been all too eager to spy for the regional
authorities of the Vichy police: "Uppermost in this guy's mind was being
decorated for patriotic service during the war. He asked me if I would help
get him recognized and I told him, 'Absolutely not.' " The Belgian knew all
too well the curious denials and delusions that the end of war can cause,
remembering the two young men his parents had harbored during the

First World War. Instead of expressing gratitude they had dismissed the Schepenses' kindness and told the family "they were lucky because they had not denounced them."

For Charles Schepens the end of the war meant, most especially, the opportunity to fully resume his medical work as a clinician, surgeon, and researcher. His recent stint at Moorfields Hospital in England had focused his interest on the severe limitations of available diagnostic equipment, the need for improved instruments for treatment, and the need for further clinical research on the causes of retinal disease: "When I looked inside the patients' eyes at Moorfields I was very frustrated when I thought I detected a detached retina, but I couldn't really see it in three-dimensional relief with the monoscope. The idea of an ophthalmoscope that would enable doctors to look with both eyes at the retina possessed me, although none of my superiors at Moorfields believed it was possible to construct such a device." Once back in Belgium he continued his experimentation on the prototype that he had built in England, and used it to examine patients in his private office.

Charles Schepens's experiences in England, in fact, had heightened both his scientific and his medical ambitions. Toward the end of his stay there Charles had written to his former boss to indicate his interest in rejoining the ophthalmology service, and to ask Dr. Hambresin to help him buy the building next to the Clinique St.-Jean and Elizabeth in the hope of creating a small research department. Though he was rehired he quickly discovered the conservatism existing in the postwar medical establishment in Brussels. Dr. Hambresin turned down his proposal for the research facility, saying, "When I was twenty years old I also was a revolutionary." Thus only a few months after resettling in the Belgian capital Charles could see that in the long run working there would be a career dead end, and that to realize his large vision he would have to leave his country once again. Much of the talk among his medical colleagues in England had been of America as the land of medical opportunity after the war, so he began to consider relocating there.

Within a year of his return Charles Schepens had already gained international renown as an innovator in the field of ophthalmology. In October 1946 he was invited to read a paper he had written at the annual meeting of the American Academy of Ophthalmology in Chicago on the development of his indirect binocular ophthalmoscope. He subsequently spent six weeks as a visiting eye surgeon at a hospital in Chicago, and then went on a six-month job prospecting tour of major medical centers throughout the eastern United States.

Both Charles and Cette Schepens remember the confusion, if down-right disapproval, voiced by their families and friends about their possible emigration to America. Coming so soon after the end of the war many thought they were going to the United States to avoid another potential conflict in Europe. As Cette reflects, "People didn't understand the need for Charles's intellectual and career advancement. I even remember some-one telling me in confidence that if we were leaving to avoid some kind of problem, he would help us take care of it."

Like Charles Schepens's fortuitous fellowship at Moorfields, the events at the end of the war enabled William Ugeux to resume his true profession as a journalist. In the months following the Liberation in Belgium, Ugeux's role as head of the Belgian secret service in London shifted to chief of information for the Belgian army in Brussels, where he was in charge of all communication media. Moreover, once the hostilities concluded in 1945 Ugeux was appointed head of a Belgian commission to confer medals on citizens who had contributed to the Resistance.

In the summer of 1946 Major Ugeux traveled to Pau to participate in a ceremony to recognize individuals in the Département des Basses-Pyrénées who had aided in the escape of political refugees during the war. He had come to award the Médaille des Evadés de Belgique to Jean Sarochar, who was simultaneously receiving a similar medal from the French government. It was a moment of supreme glory for the shepherd-patriot, whose clean but musty wool suit already displayed five medals from his World War I career. After the ceremony the prefect of Pau invited Ugeux to lunch and informed him that there was a lawsuit pending against the Compagnie d'Iraty, as a subsidiary of Trait D'Union, for economic collaboration, war profiteering, and black market trafficking. The prefect showed him the dossier and Ugeux denied any knowledge of the operation or familiarity with the list of defendants (mostly names and noms de guerre of men who were now dead or far away).

While it is still unclear who initiated the suit against the factory and the brokerage firm, the action in the wake of the war was part of an extensive and coordinated effort by the Comité Départemental de Libération (CDL) to extract retribution from individuals and businesses who, rightfully or wrongfully, were regarded as abetting or profiting from the German occupation. Three separate tribunals were established to hear cases — La Cour de Justice Militaire, La Cour de Justice Civile, and La Chambre Civique. Several nonjudicial commissions also were created, including one called to identify businesses that had made illicit profits and to recommend sanctions. Of the many postwar retaliation initiatives carried out in the region — all of them paralleled throughout France — *épuration économique* (economic cleansing) produced the least concrete results and realized only the modest gain of four million francs from the fines.[1] One of the businessmen successfully prosecuted for his wartime activities was Pedro Hernandez — as owner of Auberge Pedro and Chalet Pedro and as *passeur* of questionable integrity — who served five months in jail in Bordeaux.

Nicolas Rosenschild remembered that the CDL lawsuit against the Compagnie d'Iraty contributed to delaying the eventual sale of the lumbermill. In the year after the war ended Cyrille Pomerantzeff returned to Europe both to visit his family and friends and to discuss plans for Trait D'Union and its subsidiary. Oleg had already initiated plans to establish a factory in Biarritz to fabricate finished products from the mill's scrap wood — toys, brushes, brooms, and chairs. For the new enterprise he had designed and built a number of modern automatic woodworking machines. As Charles had foreseen, after spending a year in the Laurhibar Valley, Oleg was eager to relocate his family to Biarritz where a small expatriate community of Russian émigrés lived. The two brothers began looking for a buyer for the plant, but realized they needed to first resolve their postwar legal problems in Paris and Pau. Oleg and Nicolas Rosenschild appealed to Charles Schepens for assistance. He in turn enlisted the help of Monsieur Ugeux who, by the time he was contacted, had already discovered their situation on his own. Rosenschild credited the intervention of Monsieur Ugeux, who had practiced law briefly before switching to journalism, for finally getting the charges dismissed.

Monsieur François Apistroff, a Russian from Paris, bought the Compagnie d'Iraty in 1947 when Oleg's new enterprise, "Euskualduna," opened in a building across from the railroad station in Biarritz. Charles Schepens learned the news of the sale at a family wedding at the Vander

Eeckens Chateau de Gavergracht in the winter of 1947 — Cyrille's marriage to Cette's younger sister Jo, a postwar romance kindled during his trip to Europe the previous year. During the weekend Charles learned of Oleg's new enterprise and the state-of-the-art machines and equipment he planned for the new factory. Charles, for his part, reported on his new diagnostic invention, his recent trip to America, and his current search for a medical appointment. Though the two friends seemed once again on separate courses, Charles nevertheless harbored the dream that someday they would work together.

Part Five

Heroes' Legacy

(*Previous page*) Jean Sarochar and Charles
Schepens at the Chapelle St.-Sauveur, 1970.
(photo courtesy Dr. Charles Schepens)

Chapter 17

In 1953 Charles Schepens made his first return visit to Mendive following his immigration to the United States. In 1947 he and his family had moved to Boston, where he had accepted an appointment as a research fellow at the Howe Laboratory of Ophthalmology, an affiliate of Harvard Medical School. Within six years of his arrival in America, in addition to pioneering new surgical techniques for retinal reattachment Dr. Schepens had created the Retina Foundation — the research facility he had originally envisioned for the Brussels medical clinic. The demanding project required as much daring and imagination as the 1942 renovation of the Mendive sawmill had encompassed: not only did he establish it as a private center independent of the surrounding medical schools and hospitals, but he faced the daunting task of converting a rat-infested tenement building into a facility of modern laboratories — all on a shoestring budget. When the American Optical Company took over the manufacture and commercial distribution of the indirect binocular ophthalmoscope in 1953, Dr. Schepens felt confident that his dream to create a new center for the study and treatment of retinal disease had at last taken root.[1]

Every summer after their move to America, Schepens and his family had returned to Belgium for visits with their relatives, but the pressures of launching his maverick research center had made him reluctant to undertake an extended pilgrimage south to the Basque country. When he heard that Sarochar had died, however, he resolved to travel to Mendive to confirm the sad rumor.

On his way to the village Charles stopped off in St.-Jean-Pied-de-Port to pay a call on Madame Etchendy the innkeeper. He had seen her during his trip in 1945, but learned that soon after the war she died of cancer. Surveying the landscape as he traveled southeastward through the Laurhibar Valley, Schepens realized that though many of his contacts in the region were now dead or had moved on, the countryside had changed very little during the ensuing years of his absence. A few American jeeps were visible on the roads, as well as a small contingent of French trucks and cars and the traditional farm wagons pulled by oxen or mules. The most striking element to catch Schepens's eye was the sight of a tractor in use.

When the former Monsieur Pérot reached Officialdegia he spotted the unmistakable silhouette of Jean Sarochar's lean frame and hunched, crow-like shoulders in the garden of the farmstead. "I thought you were dead," he remembers blurting out to his Basque friend. Jean, who was just as thrilled to see his revered former comrade-in-arms, told him that it was his brother Raymond who had died the previous year. Schepens learned that Sarochar's brother-in-law had died in the late 1940s, and his older sister had recently gone blind. By default Jean Sarochar had become the designated but impoverished *jaun* of the family property.

Habit had conditioned the bachelor-shepherd to live in modest comfort. When he returned to the valley from his mountain hut (where he still spent the majority of his time), Jean occupied only two rooms in the farmhouse: the ancient kitchen and his upstairs bedroom, a virtual military shrine displaying his World War I uniform, his high leather boots, and a wooden box of medals. When Monsieur Pérot arrived Sarochar proudly offered him a new level of hospitality: not only did the shepherd prepare *taloa* for his esteemed guest, but also insisted that Pérot spend the night at Officialdegia. As Dr. Schepens remembers with amusement, "He took me upstairs, where there was a thick layer of dust on the wooden floor boards and broken glass in the windows. He cleared the cobwebs and dirt from a moldy mattress stuffed with sheep fleece, and then gave me a filthy towel." The importance of renewing his spiritual bond with this "homme éternel" (immortal man) by sharing his primitive lifestyle seemed to the surgeon conditioned to sterile surroundings a small price to pay.

As part of his visit Schepens, led by Sarochar and his new sheepdog, went for an extended hike in the mountains. As they walked the Belgian once again heard the shepherd jabber away, reciting over and over his litany of tales in Basque and French. Interestingly, though he embellished stories from the war (which the Belgian knew were exaggerations), Sarochar did not stop off to demonstrate his special system of communication with de Gaulle, a common prank that the people in the valley remember him continuing for years. As the former Pérot comments, "He was very perceptive, and knew how far he could go with a listener with his tall tales. He had remarkable intuitive intelligence about both humans and animals."

During his brief sojourn Charles also was curious to survey changes to the Mendive sawmill that he heard about over the previous two years through communication with Oleg Pomerantzeff. Facing the bankruptcy of his wood products factory in Biarritz in 1951, Oleg had decided to liquidate the company and emigrate either to North or South America. When Charles learned of his friend's serious financial straits he mounted an effort to help Oleg get a visa to come to the United States, envisioning a major role for him at the Retina Foundation. After a frustrating year dealing with the American consulate, however, the Russian decided to emigrate to Brazil where Cyrille had taken up residence.

Monsieur Barmat, the new owner of the Compagnie d'Iraty, had purchased Oleg's floundering factory for debts in 1952. Three years earlier Barmat, a Parisian financier and timber broker who was developing a forest products empire in the Pyrenees, bought the Mendive plant when it went bankrupt after the brief and financially disastrous tenure of Apistroff. The postwar market for beechwood in Britain (for railroad ties and furniture) had convinced the Parisian to acquire the lumbering operation, which in 1949 was thirty-seven million francs in debt.

Looking down across the plant yard from Officialdegia, Schepens saw a scene that at first glance seemed to have changed little from his time there ten years earlier. The only major physical improvement were large concrete kilns (used to darken the beechwood to the reddish tones preferred by the company's new British customers). One significant difference was the diminished number of workers. As he learned from conversations with some of his former employees, the new plant manager, Monsieur Ernest Martin, had streamlined operations and reduced by almost half the number of workers in the factory and on the plateau, and cut back the office staff to include just Thérèse Esponda and Monsieur Werner. At the same time a factory foreman more experienced in the processing of beechwood logs and sawyers more specialized in cutting hardwood were now on the scene. Martin's efforts impressed Schepens, who departed optimistic that the plant finally had the right leadership and the proper manpower to shed its bedeviled reputation.

Jean Sarochar's status in Mendive as *le grand menteur* changed little through the 1950s, even as his fame spread beyond the valley. Although local residents accorded him greater respect for having served in the resistance simply for the honor of it and not for money — in contrast to other *passeurs*, especially Pedro Hernandez — they still questioned the validity of his wartime accounts of heroism. Many doubted the truth of his service to Monsieur Pérot.

Of interest is the fact that his first bit of outside recognition was due to his long-established reputation as a raconteur. In 1952 Abbé J. M. de Barandiaran, a highly respected Spanish Basque priest, archaeologist, and ethnographer who was living as a political refugee in France, visited Mendive as part of a systematic effort to record Basque oral tradition.[2] After the war there was growing recognition among Basque scholars like Barandiaran of the fading and dilution of the ancient Basque culture, and the necessity of identifying the surviving tradition-bearers. Likely from Monsieur Goyenetche, the long-time priest in Mendive, Barandiaran learned of Sarochar's prodigious storytelling abilities and his encyclopedic repertoire of Basque legends and myths. The shepherd's renditions of these tales, particularly the stories relating to the dolmens, to the Chapelle St.-Sauveur, and to other sites surrounding Mendive, were transcribed and published as part of Barandiaran's comprehensive collection of Basque folklore, which today is still considered a classic.[3]

More important, in 1955 the shepherd-patriot received another prestigious medal to add to his prized collection of war badges. Ten years after the war ended William Ugeux had been successful in his nomination of the Basque shepherd for receipt of a croix de guerre from the Belgian government. (Ironically, Ugeux early on had proposed a similar decoration for Charles Schepens, but the award was still pending because of the designation "deserter" on his military record.) Ugeux suggested to Charles that they make a joint trip to Mendive to present the medal to Jean Sarochar, and the two men arranged a small celebration at Auberge Pedro for the summer. In attendance were members of the Pédelucq family, Monsieur Goyenetche, Monsieur and Madame Irigoin, and a few others. Charles remembers that the guest of honor, who did not know the real purpose of the gathering, was late to the event. "When he arrived there was an empty seat left between two of the guests, and he simply crawled under the table and popped up between them." This was a momentous occasion for Sarochar, sitting in the company of two renowned resistance heroes and hearing them praise his courage, loyalty, and selflessness. Accordingly, the shepherd adopted a noble silence.

By the time the new priest, Bernard Erdozaincy, arrived in the village a few years later, almost all evidence of the former lumbermill and cableway had vanished from the landscape and most of the company's outside employees had moved away. Indeed, Schepens's optimism about the mill's future was quickly proved wrong. The operation that originally had been hailed as an engineering wonder in the 1950s came to be considered an environmental disaster: a Breton engineer for the French forest service decided that after thirty years of intensive logging, the scope of the operation was endangering the stability of the mountain terrain and declared the woodland off-limits for timber harvest.

When the operation shut down Martin salvaged the iron structures, the poles, and some of the machines and cable lines for reinstallation at a new sawmill that the Barmat firm was building in the central Pyrenees. Through a local auction Martin sold the remaining equipment, cable, sheds, and lumber to farmers or artisans in the region. Monsieur Bernard Ardohain, the current mayor of the village, purchased the majority of the former mill site and converted it to pasture for his family's farm. Under Ardohain's guidance the commune bought the remaining section of the property to erect a new *fronton* court. Thus, by the end of the 1950s only the new kilns erected by Martin and the worn metal from the giant bandsaw (now serving as the top strand of pasture fencing on the property) provided any physical clues to the previous industrial activity on the site. High in the mountains the rusting metal and rotting chunks of logs left behind were beginning their extended afterlife as forest floor sediment. The most visible remnant of the cable was near the Chapelle St.-Sauveur, where a section of the steel wire was anchored in the ground like a mysterious giant croquet wicket.

Though the cableway no longer rivaled the Pic de Behorleguy as a dramatic fixture of this remote mountain valley in the Basses-Pyrénées, its fabled history was deeply imprinted in the memories of the valley's residents, particularly one Jean Sarochar. Indeed, Abbé Erdozaincy recalls on his first visit to Officialdegia that he spent an entire afternoon with the bachelor-shepherd, where he was shown the shepherd's precious collection of war medals and heard stories about Monsieur Pérot and the now-ghostly sawmill.

Similarly, a favorite and enduring image that Cilotte Pegorié (née Pédelucq) retains of Jean Sarochar as an older man is a scene that she witnessed during one of her visits to Mendive in the 1960s: the shepherd sitting on a bench in the yard of Officialdegia, pretending to read a small paperback book entitled *Le Passage de l'Iraty* to a group of attentive young children.

His mimicry and facial expressions reminded her of her own childhood experiences listening to Manech perform his repertoire of folk tales. However, what made this scene all the more poignant was that she knew that he was paraphrasing the quasi-fictional memoir recently written by William Ugeux about the secret work of the Mendive sawmill during World War II, a narrative that portrayed the Basque shepherd as a mysterious figure of almost superhuman powers. She realized that Manech, like a child who knows the text of a book but cannot read it, was enjoying his role as impostor village historian.

Chapter 18

Jean Sarochar's eccentricities became more pronounced during his later years and he lived an even more isolated existence. Nonetheless, Madame Pédelucq and her three children maintained their lifelong bond with the Basque shepherd and continued to make frequent visits to Mendive to spend time in the mountains, as well as to accompany Manech on foraging or fishing missions. As Henri Pédelucq summarized their affection for him, "Once he had been our guardian, and now we wanted to be there to watch over him."

People in the Laurhibar Valley remember Sarochar's pride in being both a good hunter-trapper and an occasional poacher. According to several longtime residents, one of Sarochar's favorite spoofs was walking around Mendive with a sack with a squirrel's tail hanging out the bottom and telling people that he had just caught a rabbit. Frequently he would carry around the same dead animal for days on end, often repeating his tale several times to the same listener. He knew that children were his best audience and he regularly waited at the school bus stop, hoping to entertain them with stories and pranks. Yet as he aged he also developed a reputation for being feisty, especially if he felt threatened. At one point he had a run-in with the chief of the local gendarmerie and decided to hide out in his bedroom at Officialdegia. Three days later the official broke into the house and found Manech sitting upright in bed, waiting, rifle in hand. The son of the police chief also remembers him standing in front of his farmstead with that same rifle during the student riots in Paris in 1968, promising he would defend *la France*.

Sarochar's handcarved firearm had particular value to the Basque shepherd because Monsieur Pérot had given it to him. Between visits to Mendive the Belgian eye surgeon did not keep in contact with him, and so each time he returned to Mendive like a grateful student, coming periodically to surprise and pay homage to an aging mentor. For a trip in 1964 Dr. Schepens brought along this special rifle that he had commissioned from a company in Herstal, Belgium. At the end of his brief stay in the village Schepens invited Manech to join him on his taxi ride to the airport in Pau, and was particularly delighted when the shepherd proudly brought along the rifle. As the former Pérot flew off toward Paris he further reveled in the thought that his shepherd friend was riding back to Mendive as the sole proud passenger in the backseat of the taxi.

That trip was also the first time Dr. Schepens visited Mendive with Bernadette and Catherine, his two younger (by now teenaged) daughters, whom he was eager to introduce to the Basque shepherd they had heard so much about and the remote border country that had been the site of his most important resistance work during the war. As promised, the threesome went on two extended hiking expeditions in the mountains with Manech. For the first time since Schepens had known him the shepherd got lost. True to form, Jean rambled through his stock of adventures from the two world wars as they wandered the ever-darkening forest. When one of his daughters complained about his incessant talking, Jean replied, "I have to keep talking to prevent you from going to sleep."

Ironically it was the hidden relics of the thirty-year lumbering operation that enabled them to reestablish their bearings on their two hikes in the forest. The first instance was on a return trip from Spain to visit Señor Compains, whom the former Pérot had not seen since his escape more than twenty years before. With Sarochar acting as interpreter they reminisced about the events of the escape, and Schepens learned then that "an hour after Cyrille and I left our hiding place near the Casa del Rei, he had come with a meal as promised and was shocked to find us gone." As the hiking party made their way back from Orbaiceta through the Forêt d'Iraty, Jean became confused, until by chance they landed at Errequidor and found vestiges of Paul Pédelucq's electric generating station in the spot once called "little Paris."

Another day they took a walk through Gasnateguy, intending to visit that part of the Forêt d'Iraty. On the way back they became disoriented until they came upon remnants of the cable installation that Oleg had constructed in Astaquieta. As the former Monsieur Pérot remembers, "When we discovered the old platform, then I knew where we were lost. We kept walking toward St.-Sauveur but it became very, very steep. Night was coming and it was raining. I said, 'We're going to kill ourselves.' So we had to spend the night in the forest." The former Verberie graduate found a rock formation with a generous overhang, and the foursome bedded down sardine-style after drinking a bottle of anisette that they had brought along. However, as Dr. Schepens admits good-naturedly, "I was on the outside, and not protected. I was wearing shorts and shivered awake all night while waiting for daybreak. In the early morning I was hoping to go on with our trip, but the three others were fast asleep and I had to wait two hours before they woke up."

Sunday, 23 August 1970 must have been one of the most anticipated days of Jean Sarochar's life. For the first time he was going to be a dignitary in a major public ceremony in Mendive—an event, no less, that was being organized by the former Messieurs Pérot and Berthier. When Schepens and Ugeux made their first joint pilgrimage back to the Basque country in 1955 they began to discuss the idea of creating a memorial plaque to honor the efforts of those who had attempted to escape from occupied France via the Forêt d'Iraty and those who had aided in their flight. The final demise of the sawmill in 1956 and the subsequent dismantling of the cable and plant structures underscored the importance of establishing a permanent testimonial to the significant role that Mendive and the valley had played in the underground war. In the late 1950s Charles Schepens had paid a brief visit to Mendive, both to see Sarochar and to commission an artisan-engraver in St.-Jean-Pied-de-Port to design a plaque.

However, as Charles remembers, "I was immersed in my work at the Retina Foundation and traveling a great deal to medical conferences all over the world, so I had very little time to devote to this project." The decade of the sixties, indeed, proved to be a period of accelerated growth for his research institute, an achievement that he credits in large part to the long-awaited addition of Oleg Pomerantzeff to his staff of scientists in 1960.[1] (After Oleg's daughter Marina moved to Chicago in 1959, Schepens was able to lure his friend, who had also recently become a widower, to join his expanding operation.)

As a result of the all-consuming demands of his ever-widening medical career and scientific enterprise, almost a decade elapsed before Schepens could again turn his attention to Monsieur Pérot's unfinished business. When he discovered that the engraver had not proceeded with the commission he decided to make a trip to the French Basque country as part of a visit to Europe, in order to pay a deposit to assure the plaque's completion. While there he also visited Abbé Bernard Erdozaincy (whom he had met briefly on a previous trip) to enlist his assistance. The priest, who had heard accounts about the secret work of the Mendive sawmill from both Sarochar and his own predecessor, Monsieur Goyenetche, was eager and honored to be of service to the famed Monsieur Pérot.

Abbé Erdozaincy proposed placing the plaque on the Chapelle St.-Sauveur. The priest knew that the landmark had not only played a role during the recent war, but also held profound sacred significance as the scene of the annual shepherd's pilgrimage on Fête-Dieu, a major ritual that attracted people from the two adjoining provinces. Not coincidentally, the mountain sanctuary was the setting, as well, for two classic Basque myths involving religious miracles (tales that Schepens had heard Sarochar repeat many times), each of which was represented by a sacred object there.[2]

The western entry portal thus became the designated location for the latest addition to the collection of symbolic objects at St.-Sauveur. Charles Schepens drafted the original version of the text for the plaque, which evidenced his undiminished resentment of the Germans; at the priest's urging the language was softened to eliminate specific mention of the Nazis. In the final version, which bears both a French and a Basque inscription (the latter written by the priest), the memorial identifies the chapel as a stopping place for numerous Belgian patriots "on the long road to liberty" and as a fitting "sanctuary of peace to express again their gratitude to God who protected them, and to those in the Pays Basque who acted as their brothers."[3]

Ugeux and Schepens planned the August 1970 dedication ceremony as a major event reuniting and honoring those who had played a role, large or small, in the secret work of the Mendive sawmill. The priest coordinated the festivities, which attracted as notable and international an audience as the inaugural ceremony had drawn more than forty years before. Indeed, for the Pédelucq family, all of whom were present, this commemoration was in many ways a bittersweet requiem for the legendary industrial enterprise. Among the score of people who had traveled long distances, in addition to Schepens and Ugeux, was Anselme Vernieuwe, who was now an executive of Sabena Airlines and returning for his first postwar visit to Mendive. Several people remember witnessing the emotional scene of the towering Belgian embracing the slight figure of Jean Sarochar, exclaiming "you saved my life!" Also in attendance was Oleg Pomerantzeff, on holiday in France. Conspicuously absent from this gathering, though, was Cette Schepens, who did not feel ready to return to the place that had been a source of such anguish for her. As she explains, "I could not get over the feeling that I had deceived these people."

The day began with a high Mass at the church in Mendive, including performances by a chorus of young people from the village whom the priest had specially trained for the event. After the service, on behalf of the visiting delegation of Belgians, Ugeux and Schepens placed a wreath on the Monument aux Morts, which now bore the names of the two men from Mendive who had been killed in action in World War II along with the twenty from the previous war. A pilgrimage up to the Chapelle St.-Sauveur for the dedication ceremony was the most dramatic element of the event. Most of the one hundred participants walked up the mountain along the new one-lane dirt road that ran from the Irigoin farm all the way up to the Plateau d'Iraty, while others, like Monsieur Ugeux, availed themselves of a jeep provided by Pedro Hernandez for the occasion. A feast, complete with singing and dancing at the new Hotel Ardohain (fittingly located directly across from the old factory site) was the finale to the day. As an unplanned addition to the formal schedule of activities, a few of the out-of-town guests remember also being invited to Officialdegia to tour Jean Sarochar's miniature military shrine.

Several photos taken of the chapel ceremony show the aging shepherd-patriot posing with Ugeux, Schepens, Mayor Ardohain, and Abbé Erdozaincy, all of whom were the official speakers of the event. Although the former Monsieur Pérot had recently received his war medal (sent in the mail by the Belgian consul in Washington DC), tellingly he did not wear it for the ceremony.[4] For the previous twenty-five years Charles Schepens had deliberately downplayed his resistance activities for fear that public recognition of his wartime feats would overshadow the medical achievements that he considered his true humanitarian contribution. As he now candidly admits, "I did not want to be considered a military hero."

In contrast, adorning Sarochar's ill-fitting dark suit coat were his eight medals (five from his official service in World War I and three for his resistance work in World War II), which, with the help of Léon Pédelucq, he had ritually extracted from his special wooden box for the occasion. The dedication ceremony was the first time that people from all over the region heard the revered Monsieur Pérot sing the praises of Jean Sarochar. Though diffident about his own accomplishments, Schepens was only too glad to lionize his Basque friend to the audience. In his speech Schepens highlighted the Basque's exemplary courage and patriotic service in the underground war and how it had made such an enduring impression on those whom he had so selflessly aided.

At the end of the day Sarochar poignantly confided to a member of the Pédelucq family that "ils vont peut-être se ficher un peu moins de moi maintenant" (maybe now they won't make fun of me as much). In fact, the August event was not without some letdown for Manech. Since the beginning of the year Sarochar had dictated and sent off several letters to petition his "all-powerful" friend in America for help in locating his "lost" nephew, Jean Etchepare, whom he believed was living somewhere in the West. Failing health and the news in early January that his older nephew had been killed in Paris had precipitated the shepherd's letter-writing campaign. Knowing full well the difficulty of the assignment, Schepens nevertheless agreed to help find Manech's only remaining close relative. However, even with the assistance of the consul in California, Schepens's efforts proved futile and the disappointing news was delivered to his Basque friend during their reunion.

Certain that Jean's days were numbered, Charles decided to add a trip to Mendive as part of the family's annual summer visit to Belgium in 1974. With the help of his children he was at last able to persuade Cette to accompany him on the visit, although even a warm reception in the village, especially by the Argains, did not change her enduring notion of the Basque backcountry as "tragique et triste" (tragic and sorrowful). William Ugeux joined Charles and Cette on the expedition.

When the threesome arrived in Mendive they discovered that the shepherd had recently suffered a heart attack. Though clearly weakened, he still was dividing his time between Officialdegia and his mountain hut which, as Dr. Schepens remembers, was far cleaner than the family dwelling. Manech was eager to join them on a trek in the mountains, and they walked up to St.-Sauveur along the dusty hairpin road. During the course of his short visit Schepens remembers Manech showing him the mattress where he had squirreled away his life savings of sixteen thousand French francs, money that he intended to use to pay for his medical care in his last years. The shepherd made it clear to his physician-friend that "he would not stay in a hospital or go live in the retirement home that had been established in St.-Jean-Pied-de-Port."

Jean's health continued to deteriorate, and after suffering a second heart attack the bachelor-shepherd moved in with the Bidegain family, his distant relatives living in Lecumberry. Madame Bidegain remembers that though the elderly Sarochar was far from the sprightly figure he had once been, he continued to be spirited, garrulous, and curious — and quite eager to watch news broadcasts on television. Several days before his death he even went mushroom hunting with Henri Pédelucq near Behorleguy. True to his word, when he came down with pneumonia in early October 1975 (at age eighty-three), he refused to be hospitalized and died without treatment.

Over the course of the twentieth century many ancient Basque customs relating to the *rites de passage* have become abbreviated or simply eliminated. Not so, funeral practices, and the death of a villager continues to set in motion a series of prescribed rituals — involving the family, the priest, the sexton, and "the first neighbor," who orchestrates these elaborate mourning and burial rites — that take place over a period of two or three days.[5] As Abbé Erdozaincy remembers, Jean Sarochar's funeral was no different than all of the others that he has performed in Mendive, although certainly the absence of immediate family members made it somewhat unusual. What did make a strong impression on the modest assembly of valley residents who attended the Mass was the giant bouquet of flowers on the casket, ostensibly sent by Manech's resistance colleagues, Monsieur Pérot and Monsieur Berthier. However, the gathered mourners did not know (nor did the two "donors" know until well after the event had happened), that the Pédelucq family had ordered the arrangement on the men's behalf — a sleight-of-hand gesture of homage that they knew the Belgians would have approved and that the shepherd-soldier surely would have appreciated.

Jean's funeral was not the last time his patriotic service was celebrated. A tragicomic epilogue to his death occurred at a ceremony in late December 1975 when he was inducted as a chevalier of the Légion d'Honneur, the French hall of fame traditionally reserved for presidents, ministers, generals, and important citizens.[6] After the rules for nomination were relaxed in the 1970s to include ordinary citizens, a deputy to the Assemblée Nationale from the Basses-Pyrénées had proposed Jean's candidacy to honor his exceptional service as soldier and *résistant*. Before his death Jean knew that he might soon be adding the most prestigious badge of all to his collection. Unfortunately, when the bureaucrats in the Ministry of Agriculture finally scheduled the award ceremony they failed to confirm his participation, and the honoree—already dead for six weeks—did not show up. The presiding government official, Monsieur Christian Bonnet, in a face-saving statement to the press posthumously praised the phantom Basque shepherd for his "qualités de courage, de développement, et de modestie" (qualities of courage, character, and modesty).[7]

In the last quarter of the twentieth century Mendive reverted to the identity it had possessed in the decades before the arrival of the Pédelucq enterprise: a backcountry, traditional Basque village and gateway to the fabled Forêt d'Iraty. Arguably the most observable change in the pastoral landscape is the extension of the paved valley road up to the plateau and a new network of dirt roads lacing the mountain terrain. The construction of these roads, in fact, also transformed the valley's most ancient rite: the shepherds from Mendive and Lecumberry, rather than undertaking the prolonged pilgrimage for the annual *transhumance* on foot, now herd their flocks up to the summer pastures in the spring and back down to the valley farms in the fall behind the wheel of an outdated car. It could be argued, furthermore, that on the mountain slopes, far more than in the valley, the imprint of progress can be seen, evident especially in the appearance of modern cement block huts (complete with television antennas and solar-powered electricity) to replace the older and more primitive shepherds' dwellings.

Beginning in the late 1970s the access road to the forest zone and a variety of promotional efforts have brought yet another wave of pilgrims to the Laurhibar Valley—urban sportsmen and youthful adventurers—to retrace the footsteps of previous wayfarers. The current tourist literature details a variety of self-guided recreational itineraries that explore the natural world, and, as in the earlier guides, the rich conglomeration of mystical sites and historic monuments en route to Iraty continue to be prominently mentioned as places not to be missed. Most commonly highlighted are the dolmens, the Chapel of St.-Sauveur, and the Mendive church and its surrounding cemetery, touted as a veritable sculpture garden of traditional Basque funerary stone carving.

Yet for almost two decades after Jean Sarochar's death any curious *maketo* wandering among the striking assortment of shaped crosses, discoidal stelae, and raised slab tombstones in the cemetery would not have registered his eighty-three-year presence in the village. Then, much like the mysterious overnight artistry of the *Laminak*, a crisp inscription proclaiming "Jean Sarochar, 1892–1975, Héros des Deux Grandes Guerres" belatedly appeared on the ordinary gravemarker. Indeed, had it not been for the secret benevolence of a faraway Belgian surgeon-scientist, Manech — shepherd, soldier, liar, legend-keeper — might have been an invisible anonymous figure in the community of ancestors, just as invisible as he had been in the land of the living.

Appendix A

Guide to Names and Affiliations
(in order of appearance)

RESIDENTS OF LECUMBERRY AND MENDIVE (various nationalities)

Abbé Bernard Erdozaincy, Basque priest (since 1958) of Lecumberry, Mendive, and Behorleguy

Bernard Ardohain, Basque owner of Hotel-Restaurant Ardohain and mayor of Mendive

Marie Alchouroun (née Argain), neighbor of the Schepens family in Lecumberry

Arnaud Harguindeguy, French Basque factory worker

Jean Sarochar (pronounced Sare-o-shaar), Basque shepherd and *passeur*, known locally by the name "Manech"

Raymond Sarochar, younger brother of Jean and herdsman for the Compagnie d'Iraty

Marie and Louis Etchepare, sister and brother-in-law of Jean Sarochar

Dominique Esponda, Basque innkeeper and operator of mountain guiding service

"Bainam" Ardohain, Basque owner-operator of a local electric plant and village butcher

Paul Pédelucq, French businessman from the Landes who founded the Compagnie d'Iraty in the 1920s with his brother Alexis

Maître Jean, Swiss engineer who worked for the Compagnie d'Iraty in the 1920s

François Moretti, chief Italian cable technician for the Compagnie d'Iraty during the Pédelucq period of ownership

Angèle and Baptiste Moretti, sons of François, who worked as cable operators under both Paul Pédelucq and Jacques Pérot

Henriette Moretti, daughter of Dominique Esponda and wife of Angèle Moretti

Madame Pédelucq, widow of Paul Pédelucq

Léon, Henri, and Cilotte Pédelucq, children of Paul Pédelucq

Pedro Hernandez, Spanish innkeeper of Auberge Pedro and Chalet Pedro

Monsieur and Madame Irigoin, Basque proprietors of the farm in Mendive that was the last property on the valley road

Monsieur Goyenetche, priest of Mendive until the late 1950s

Thérèse Esponda, daughter of Dominique Esponda and office secretary for the Compagnie d'Iraty from 1942 until its close

Marius Pelfort, French engineer and director of operations for the Compagnie d'Iraty hired by Jacques Pérot

Jean Bouleux, French mechanic and factory foreman for the Compagnie d'Iraty

Pierre Faubert, French marketing director for the Compagnie d'Iraty

Modesta Perez, Spanish canteen operator on the Plateau d'Iraty

Monsieur Werner, French bookkeeper for the Compagnie d'Iraty from 1942 until its close

Monsieur Italo, chief Italian cable technician during the Pérot regime at the Compagnie d'Iraty

Monsieur and Madame Argain, the Schepenses' Basque landlords (and neighbors) in Lecumberry

Beppina Moretti, youngest daughter of François Moretti, nanny-housekeeper for the Pérot family

Jean and Charles Moretti, sons of Angèle and Henriette Moretti, nephews of Beppina Moretti

Monsieur Mendury, Basque priest of Lecumberry (through mid-1950s)

Pierre Harguindeguy, younger brother of Arnaud and STO draft dodger

Etienne Murillo, Spanish Basque employee of the Compagnie d'Iraty

François Apistroff, plant manager of the Compagnie d'Iraty, 1947–49

Ernest Martin, plant manager of the Compagnie d'Iraty, 1949–56

RESIDENTS OF THE PAYS BASQUE AND SOUTHWEST FRANCE

Madame Etchendy, Basque innkeeper in St.-Jean-Pied-de-Port

Marie Esponda, Basque secretary for Jacques Pérot in St.-Jean-Pied-de-Port

Bidegain family, Basque innkeepers in Mauléon

Madame Erreca, Basque innkeeper in Les Aldudes

Monsieur Haurat, pro-Vichy garage owner in Oloron-St.-Marie

BELGIANS

Charles Schepens (pronounced Skay-pens), ophthalmologist and resistance leader operating under the names Jacques Pérot and Jacques Wielemans

Cette Schepens (née Vander Eecken), Charles's wife

William Ugeux (pronounced Oo-jeu), Belgian resistance leader operating under the name "Berthier," lawyer turned journalist, head of the Zéro network 1941-43, and later the coordinator of Belgian underground groups on the Continent

Dr. Auguste Schepens, Charles's father

Madame Henriette Schepens, Charles's mother

Drs. Gustave, Yves, and Edouard Schepens, Charles's older brothers

Monsieur and Madame Vander Eecken, Cette's parents and owners of the Chateau de Gavergracht (near Ghent)

Dr. Léon Hambresin, chief of ophthalmology at the Clinique St.-Jean and Elizabeth in Brussels

Anselme Vernieuwe (pronounced Ver-nee), air force colleague of Charles Schepens and courier for Zéro resistance network (operating under aliases Jean Vernon or Jean Villeneuve)

Claire Schepens, oldest daughter of Charles and Cette Schepens

Luc Schepens, son of Charles and Cette Schepens

Monsieur and Madame Dieu, the Schepenses' tenants in Brussels

Colonel de Saule, Belgian officer living in Poligny in eastern France, working for both the Vichy government and the Belgian resistance

Captain de Hepcéc, Belgian courier-escort for Zéro (alias Halloy)

Loulou Vernieuwe, wife of Anselme Vernieuwe

Bernadette and Catherine Schepens, younger daughters of Charles and Cette Schepens

RUSSIANS

Oleg Pomerantzeff, White Russian student on scholarship at the Jesuit high school in Namur and close friend of Charles Schepens

Cyrille Pomerantzeff, brother of Oleg and founder and director of Trait D'Union, Paris

Madame Pomerantzeff, White Russian living in Paris and mother of Oleg and Cyrille

Irène Pomerantzeff, first wife of Oleg Pomerantzeff

Marina Pomerantzeff, oldest daughter of Oleg Pomerantzeff

Nicolas Rosenschild, Russian emigre and accountant for Trait D'Union

FRENCH CITIZENS (various locations)

Robert Lafitte, director of an Hébert training center and school at Verberie

Bernadette Lafitte, daughter of Robert Lafitte

"Vallier," French courier for the Zéro network, based in Grenoble

SPANIARDS

Señor Zabaleta, Spanish Basque foreman of the logging crew during the Pédelucq regime

Señor Compains, Spanish Basque farmer from Orbaiceta, foreman of the seasonal logging crew hired by Jacques Pérot, and brother-in-law of the owner of the Casa del Rei

Señor Lizariturri, Basque businessman in San Sebastian, Belgian consul, and resistance operative during World War II

BRITISH

Sir Richard and Lady Wells, hosts to the Schepens family during their stay in England at the end of World War II

Appendix B

List of Informants

Mme Marie Alchouroun
M. Bernard Ardohain
Mlle Christiane Ardohain
M. Louis Barriety
Mme Marie Bidegain
M. et Mme Jean Bouleux
M. Serge Coudineau
Mme Maitena Dabbadie
M. Elie Dyan
Abbé Bernard Erdozaincy
Mme Aurélie Erraçerret
Mlle Marie Esponda
M. Jean Etcharren
Mme Madeleine Faubert
M. Arnaud Harguindeguy
M. Pierre Harguindeguy
Mme Jeanne Irigoin
Mme Beppina Izquierdo
Mrs. Marina Krivcov
M. Kayette Lacau
M. Antoine Lerissa
M. Nicolas Lerissa
Mme Gracianne Lissarrague
M. Ernest Martin
M. et Mme Angèle Moretti
M. Jean Moretti

M. Henri Pédelucq
M. Léon Pédelucq
Mme Cilotte (Pédelucq) Pegorié
Señora Modesta Perez
M. Edmond Pessenti
Mr. and Mrs. Oleg Pomerantzeff
M. Nicolas Rosenschild
Dr. and Mrs. Charles Schepens
M. William Ugeux
M. Bernard Urruty
Mme Loulou Vernieuwe

Notes

Introduction

1. The term "life review" was originally coined by gerontologist Robert Butler. For a discussion of aging and the reliability of memory in oral history interviewing see Paul Thompson, *The Voice of the Past*, 3d ed. (Oxford: Oxford University Press, 2000), 136–37.

2. See Thompson, *Voice of the Past*, 272–73, for a discussion of criteria for analyzing the validity of informants' oral recollections.

3. Alessandro Portelli, *The Death of Luigi Trastulli and Other Stories* (Albany: State University of New York Press, 1991), 53, identifies the tendency for informants who participated in a major historical event to narrate their experiences in the language of a literary epic. Interestingly, Portelli cites resistance fighters as a prime example of this phenomenon.

4. Thompson, *Voice of the Past*, 172.

5. Theodore Rosengarten, "Stepping over Cockleburs: Conversations with Ned Cobb," *Telling Lives: The Biographer's Art*, ed. Marc Pachter (Washington DC: New Republic Books, 1979), 124, eloquently characterizes this process as "pure listening and deliberate listening."

6. In addition to Ugeux's written works, in 1993 the Belgian French-language TV channel broadcast a docudrama entitled, "La double vie du Docteur Pérot," based on Ugeux's account of the story of Pérot and the Mendive sawmill.

Chapter 1

1. According to James E. Jacob, *Hills of Conflict: Basque Nationalism in France* (Reno: University of Nevada Press, 1994), 43, the Basques maintained the custom of undivided inheritance despite new laws enacted after the French Revolution for parceling out property among heirs.

2. Ted Morgan, *An Uncertain Hour: The French, the Germans, the Jews, the Klaus Barbie Trial, and the City of Lyon, 1940–45* (New York: William Morrow 1990), 31–33, substantiates the special treatment accorded to wounded World War I patriots. Morgan offers a vivid reminiscence of the proud participation of the *gueules cassées* (broken faces) among those in a military parade that he witnessed as a child in Paris in the 1930s.

3. The property's designation was usually a geographic name given by a dwelling's original builders.

CHAPTER 2

1. Jacques Blot, "Dolmens, Cromlechs, Tumuli: Naissance du Pastoralisme," *Le Pays de Cize* (St.-Etienne-de-Baigorry: Editions IZPEGI, 1991), 45–48, describes the arrival of Indo-European peoples in the region and the birth of a pastoral civilization in the Pays de Cize, c. 2000 B.C.; the protohistoric megaliths and necropoli near strategic points of passage on the way to the Forêt d'Iraty in both the foothills and upper elevations give evidence of this anthropological transition. However, the Basque tongue is not an Indo-European language and the ethnic origin of the Basque people remains a mystery. One of the theories still unproved postulates that the Basques are the modern-day descendants of Cro-Magnon man.

2. Jean-Baptiste Orpustan, "Du Moyen Age aux Temps Moderne: Société et Culture," *Le Pays de Cize* (St.-Etienne-de-Baigorry: Editions IZPEGI, 1991), 119–20. A French priest named Aimeri Picaud created *The Codex de Compostelle*, a twelfth-century guide in which he warns religious travelers about the rude reception they should expect to receive from the local population, and offers several Basque words to help such travelers negotiate their way through the region. Picaud's medieval publication is considered the earliest dictionary of the Basque language, as it contains the definitions (in Latin) of a few dozen words.

3. Georges Viers, "Montagnes et Terroirs," *Le Pays de Cize* (St.-Etienne-de-Baigorry: Editions IZPEGI, 1991), 24.

4. Philippe Veyrin, *Les Basques de Labourd, de Soule, et de Basse-Navarre: Leur histoire et leurs traditions* (Bayonne: Arthaud, 1975), 34. Beechwood was used for oars and keels.

5. Miguel Angulo, *Randonnées en Pays Basque* (Biarritz: Editions Lavielle, 1986), 38–39.

6. André Pées, "La Forêt d'Iraty," Map Forêt d'Iraty. Pic D'Orhy (Paris: IGN, 1995).

7. Pierre Bidart, "La Scène du XXe Siècle," *Le Pays de Cize* (St.-Etienne-de-Baigorry: Editions IZPEGI, 1991), 204.

8. Pierre Laborde, *Pays Basque Economie et Société en Mutation* (Bayonne, France: Elkar, 1994), 181–83.

9. The Pédelucq brothers operated in the Chalosse region, which has soil and a climate similar to that of California.

10. See André Valéry, *Des Hommes dans la Forêt* (Portet-sur-Garonne: Editions Loubatières, 1996), 88–94.

11. To get to the French portion of the Forêt d'Iraty, which was located approximately fifteen kilometers (nine miles) south of Mendive, required a nine-hundred-meter (three-thousand-foot) ascent to the Col de Burdincurutcheta and then a two-hundred-meter descent to the Plateau d'Iraty. Unlike the Spaniards, who for

centuries had been using spring log drives to bring down both lumber and firewood via the Rio Iraty, companies on the French side could not follow the precipitous course of the streams that veined the mountains there.

12. Valéry, *Des Hommes*, 121–24.

13. Señor Zabaleta, the *contratista* (boss), oversaw a hierarchy of workers in the logging camp: master axemen (*aizkularis* in Basque); apprentice lumberjacks gaining mastery of the axe and crosscut saw; specialized workers such as muledrivers and charcoalworkers; the camp cook; and grunt laborers.

14. See Valéry, *Des Hommes*, 158–67, for a description of the construction of a similar (but much smaller) sawmill. Valéry's novel is set in the 1950s but the work practices the characters follow were decades old.

15. See Jacob, *Hills of Conflict*, 48, for a discussion of the clergy's powerful influence on the political and social life within a French Basque village. Jacob points out that the Basque word for mayor, *hauzaphez*, literally means "priest of the district." Indeed, within rural French Basque villages the priest played a role that went far beyond the official position as the community's religious leader. Just as the system of inheritance was a means of insuring the continuity of family property, the priests used their powers to preserve the sanctity of Basque cultural life within the parish. Having repelled or endured the influence of imperial tribes and nations throughout the Middle Ages (Visigoths, Moors, Franks, Anglo-Saxons, and Castillians), and then having maintained a certain level of autonomy under the French monarchy and other centralized governments, the Basque people had successfully resisted assimilation for over a thousand years. Maintaining their distinctive way of life through the conservation of language, customs, and community structure was thus part of the pastoral mandate of the "shepherd of the shepherds."

CHAPTER 3

1. The charters were called *faceries*. See Veyrin, *Les Basques de Labourd*, 38–39.

2. See Valéry, *Des Hommes*, 180–87, for a detailed account of this hospitality ritual.

3. Robert P. Clark, *The Basques: The Franco Years and Beyond* (Reno: University of Nevada Press, 1980), 84.

4. Jacob, *Hills of Conflict*, 95–96, contends that for the French Basques the affiliation between the Spanish Basques and the Communists during the Spanish Civil War served to "contaminate the very idea of Basque nationalism." According to Jacob the Spanish Civil War and its aftermath caused a further setback to the development of a nationalist movement (begun in Spain in the 1870s) within the three French Basque provinces; in the first decades of the twentieth century the

French government had effectively curtailed the rising politico-cultural activism of the French Basque clergy, "the protonationalist ethnic elite" (61). For a full discussion of the political differences between the Basque nationalist movements in France and in Spain from 1920 to 1950 see chap. 3, "The 'Red Fish' in the Baptismal Font."

5. Nancy MacDonald, *Homage to the Spanish Exiles* (New York: Insight Books, 1987), 100.

CHAPTER 4

1. Frans van Cauwelaert, "Foreign Policy, 1918–1940," *Belgium*, ed. Jan-Albert Goris (Berkeley: University of California Press, 1945), 139–40.

2. Roger Motz, *Belgium Unvanquished* (London: Lindsay Drummond, 1942), 12–15.

3. Monsieur Vander Eecken, Cette Schepens's father, was a *notaire* (solicitor) in Ghent. In France and in Belgium a *notaire* is a prestigious office empowered with greater legal authority than that accorded to an American notary public.

4. Emilienne Eychenne, *Les Pyrénées de la Liberté 1939–1945* (Paris: Editions France-Empire, 1983), 82–83.

5. Motz, *Belgium Unvanquished*, 17–22, 32–33.

6. Motz, *Belgium Unvanquished*, 57.

7. See J. Gérard-Libois and José Gotovitch, "La Faim," *L'An 40*, chap. 8 (Brussels: CRISP, 1971), 329–41. See also Raoul Miry, "The Black Market," in *Belgium under Occupation*, trans. and ed. Jan-Albert Goris (New York: Moretus Press, 1947), 68–70.

8. For more on the impact of the less visible but equally destructive war tax that was secretly imposed on Belgians as part of the Occupation, see Paul Struye, "The Policy of Occupation," in *Belgium under Occupation*, trans. and ed. Jan-Albert Goris (New York: Moretus Press, 1947), 17–18.

9. Struye, "Policy of Occupation," 18.

10. See Richard Cobb, *French and Germans, Germans and French* (Hanover NH: University Press of New England, 1983), 4–8, for a description of citizens' daily life along the French-Belgian border during the last year of the First World War, and the constant harassment of the Feldgendarmerie.

11. Comparative studies of resistance movements in Europe identify Belgium as one of the countries in which the sense of collective threat and Belgian patriotism, rather than the persecution of the Jews and other minorities, was the reason for early engagement. When the war broke out more than 90 percent of the sixty-six thousand Jews living in Belgium were recently arrived refugees from Eastern and Central Europe living in Brussels or Antwerp. See Pierre Lagrou, "Belgium," *Resistance in Western Europe*, ed. Bob Moore (Oxford: Berg, 2000), 34, 47; and

Gay Block and Malka Drucker, *Rescuers: Portraits of Moral Courage in the Holocaust* (New York: TV Books, 1997), 117. Indicative of the isolation of the Jewish community within Belgium in the 1920s and 1930s is the fact that Charles Schepens does not remember meeting anyone Jewish before the war, although he believes that foreigners could have been among his medical school classmates or medical colleagues who had changed their names. He did buy an engagement ring for his wife — through the mail — from a Jewish diamond merchant in Antwerp (where a large portion of the Jewish population lived).

12. Jo Gérard, *Les Grandes Heures de la Belgique* (Paris: Perrin, 1990), 399–400.

13. Albert Guislain, *Bruxelles Atmosphère 10–32* (Paris: L'Eglantine, 1932), 141–43.

14. Shepherd B. Clough, "The Flemish Movement," *Belgium*, ed. Jan-Albert Goris (Berkeley: University of California Press, 1945), 119–21.

15. Clough, "Flemish Movement," 122.

16. Charles Schepens does not recall ever being approached to join "the Resistance." He points out that the term came into usage only much later.

17. Daniel Ryelandt, "The Resistance Movement," *Belgium under Occupation*, trans. and ed. Jan-Albert Goris (New York: Moretus Press, 1947), 192–94.

18. Colonel de Saule provides an example of an early resister who worked in an official capacity for the Vichy regime while also clandestinely aiding the effort to undermine the German occupation. Charles Schepens believes, moreover, that de Saule was not his true name. For a discussion of the dual service army officers gave to Vichy and to the emerging French resistance see Julian Jackson, *France: The Dark Years 1940–44* (Oxford: Oxford University Press, 2001), 402–3.

19. Lagrou, "Belgium," 35–36, highlights the important role the parcel relay system played in transmitting military intelligence to the British (since there was no radio contact with London until late 1941).

CHAPTER 5

1. See Gérard-Libois and Gotovitch, "La Faim," 333–38, for a discussion of the potato's symbolic importance for the Belgians. The two authors maintain that its scarcity in the first year of the war was a prime factor in turning public opinion against the German occupiers.

2. Through conversations with a local priest at the end of the First World War, Charles's mother became interested in the new scouting movement. According to Charles Schepens the troops were affiliated with religious institutions and tended to be segregated by social class.

3. Motz, *Belgium Unvanquished*, 53.

4. See Miry, "The Black Market," 68; and Gérard-Libois and Gotovitch, "La

Faim," 336, who point out that an unsuccessful appeal for American aid was made in January 1941.

5. Cobb, *French and Germans*, 76.

6. Jan-Albert Goris, *Belgium in Bondage* (New York: L. B. Fischer, 1943), 109–10.

7. Lagrou, "Belgium," 47, indicates that Jews were required to register at their local town hall and were under the official jurisdiction of the Association des Juifs de Belgique. They were not forced to wear the yellow star until May 1942.

8. Motz, *Belgium Unvanquished*, 74–77.

9. Motz, *Belgium Unvanquished*, 84.

10. Motz, *Belgium Unvanquished*, 66.

11. William Ugeux had trained as a lawyer at the University of Louvain, where Charles first met him in the early 1930s. When Ugeux was only twenty-four years old he switched careers and became editor of *Le Vingtième Siècle*, a Brussels daily newspaper. Immediately after the German invasion in 1940 Ugeux began his service to the Belgian opposition movement as editor of the underground paper *La Libre Belgique* and as a counterfeiter of identity cards. Ugeux continued editing the newspaper even after he assumed the leadership of the Brussels-led *Service Zéro* in October 1941.

CHAPTER 6

1. After France capitulated in 1940 the Germans divided the country into two zones: the Occupied Zone in the north under German military rule (covering three-fifths of the country's land mass) and the Free Zone in the south under the puppet government of Maréchal Philippe Pétain.

2. See H. R. Kedward, *Resistance in Vichy France: A Study of Ideas and Motivation in the Southern Zone 1940–42* (Oxford: Oxford University Press, 1978), 65–81, for personality profiles of French *résistants de la première heure*.

3. Lagrou, "Belgium," 41, identifies "career officers, war veterans, anglophile aristocracy, [and] urban patriots" as the first professional and social groups of resisters in Belgium.

4. Charles Schepens's interest in heightened participation in the resistance (and his relocation to southwest France) parallels the more well-known career of another Belgian resistance leader, Andrée de Jongh. At the beginning of the Occupation, de Jongh, a Flemish Red Cross volunteer, was part of a small resistance cell in Brussels that was providing aid (food) to British soldiers stranded there; when the Germans decimated the group she and a colleague initiated the Comet evacuation line in May 1941 to relay Allied servicemen from Belgium and France into Spain (primarily via the Basque coastal town of St.-Jean-de-Luz and its environs). For further reading on the subject see Rémy, *Réseau Comète*, vol. 1–2: *La Ligne de Démarcation* (Paris: Librairie Académique Perrin, 1966–67).

5. As Julian Jackson points out in *France: Dark Years*, 385, when Jean Moulin, de Gaulle's chief aide, returned to London from a reconnaissance mission to France in October 1941, he characterized the existing indigenous opposition as "French patriots" or "Anglophile movements" — i.e., not yet meriting the designation of an organized resistance effort.

6. In *Occupation: The Ordeal of France 1940–1944* (New York: St. Martin's, 1997), 254–55, Ian Ousby contends that until 1943 resistance activity was the strongest in the urban industrial centers of the Occupied Zone. Robert Paxton, in *Vichy France: Old Guard and New Order, 1940–1944* (New York: Alfred A. Knopf, 1972), 285, estimates that in 1942 only 2 or 3 percent of the French population was involved in active opposition. Moreover, H. R. Kedward, in *Resistance in Vichy France*, 247, emphasizes the pluralistic backgrounds of these activists.

7. Ousby, *Occupation*, 212–13, discusses the wide spectrum of political beliefs and socioeconomic backgrounds of the pioneer resisters in France, and maintains that this diversity was both an advantage and a disadvantage to their effectiveness.

8. Jackson, *France: Dark Years*, 407–9, distinguishes between the propaganda-oriented civilian work of the resistance movements and the military, mission-oriented activities of the resistance networks. Ousby, *Occupation*, 241, contends that because of the lack of funds and access to equipment from either the Allies or from de Gaulle, early resisters had to focus their efforts on newspaper publishing. Belgian William Ugeux is a good example of a first resister whose initial work was the publishing of an underground journal, a role that eventually evolved into the leadership of the intelligence and escape line Zéro.

9. Lagrou, "Belgium," 38.

10. Ousby, *Occupation*, 223–25.

11. Ousby, *Occupation*, 237. By 1942 de Gaulle had an estimated listening audience of three million. In *France: Dark Years*, 278, 282, and 402, Julian Jackson emphasizes that resistance in France began as opposition to the occupying force, but as the war progressed it grew and became anti-Vichy as well.

12. Long-standing anglophilia, compounded by the fact that Belgium was completely occupied, meant that the Belgians did not face the same battle for political leadership as the French faced. According to Charles Schepens the majority of Belgian citizens in 1942 regarded the ministers in exile as their legitimate government but considered the British as their commanders of liberation.

13. Lagrou, "Belgium," 35, points out that among the organizers of the intelligence networks in Belgium, several veterans of World War I resistance already had strong links to the British (notably Waltere Dewe and Anatole Gobeaux).

14. See Emilienne Eychenne, *Les Fougères de la Liberté 1939–1945* (Toulouse: Editions Milan), 112–20. Many of the people involved in the organization of the

first escape and intelligence lines in France had been stranded there because of the events of May–June 1940.

15. According to Jorgen Haestrup, *European Resistance Movements 1939–1945: A Complete History* (Odense: Odense University Press, 1981), 298, the sustained efforts by the Belgian government-in-exile and the British Special Operations Executive (SOE) to amalgamate the diverse resistance groups operating in Belgium were never more than partially successful.

16. In the early years of the war the external opposition movement was known by the name of its then little-known leader, Col. Charles de Gaulle.

17. Ousby, *Occupation*, 217, describes a similar assessment by the British SOE agents, who were appalled by the amateurishness of the French resisters.

18. To avoid confusion I have used Vernieuwe's real name rather than his multiple aliases in this redaction of the story.

CHAPTER 7

1. See Paxton, *Vichy France*, 164, for a discussion of the role of the Chantier de Jeunesse, a wartime national service program instituted by the Vichy government.

2. See Paxton, *Vichy France*, 365–69, for a summary of the politics surrounding the issue of forced labor in World War II France.

3. See Jacob, *Hills of Conflict*, 106–7; and Bob Moore, "Comparing Resistance and Resistance Movements," *Resistance in Western Europe* (Oxford, England: Berg, 2000), 250. Pétain's professed support of the Catholic Church, his advocacy of the virtues of an agrarian society, and his interest in a return to the country's historic regional divisions initially made him a sympathetic figure among the local Basque population (an attitude commonly held until 1942 by the rural communities of the Southern Zone).

4. Jacob, *Hills of Conflict*, 89, characterizes French Basque nationalism as "moderate regionalism," that is, advocacy for increased autonomy but not separatism. However, Jacob also points out that because of the exigencies of survival during the war, "the question of ethnic self-interest and Basque mobilization was lost on most individuals" (127).

CHAPTER 9

1. Louis Poullenot, *Basses Pyrénées Occupation Libération 1940–1945* (Biarritz: J & D Editions, 1995), 122.

2. Poullenot, *Basses Pyrénées*, 138.

3. Poullenot, *Basses Pyrénées*, 139.

4. See Eychenne, *Les Fougères*, 238. For several firsthand accounts of daily life at Miranda see 234–38.

5. Eychenne, *Les Pyrénées*, 91–92.

6. Eychenne, *Les Pyrénées*, 189.

7. Eychenne, *Les Pyrénées*, 95–96. Eychenne points out that the Spanish border patrol's adherence to the Germans' demand, however, was far from consistent.

8. Poullenot, *Basses Pyrénées*, 122.

9. Eychenne, *Les Pyrénées*, 119.

10. Eychenne, *Les Fougères*, 195, has documented in her tally of successful escapes through the Basses-Pyrénées in this period that the number jumped from sixteen in October 1942 to ninety-six one month later.

11. Poullenot, *Basses Pyrénées*, 113. According to Ousby, *Occupation*, 250–55, German labor conscription policy in 1942 was a major impetus for rural segments of the population to join the resistance movement in France.

12. See Kedward, *Resistance in Vichy France*, 39–40.

13. Eychenne, *Les Fougères*, 143–44.

14. Eychenne, *Les Fougères*, 158–60.

15. Eychenne, *Les Fougères*, 158–60.

16. Poullenot, *Basses Pyrénées*, 41. As Kedward points out in *Resistance in Vichy France*, 39–40, many high-ranking officers of the organization (most notably General Georges Loustanau-Lacau) viewed the Légion as a mechanism for clandestinely continuing the war against the Germans. General Loustanau's tenure as a Vichy *légionnaire* was short-lived, however, and in November 1940 he organized his own escape and information service, the Alliance.

CHAPTER 10

1. Eychenne, *Les Fougères*, 65–66.

2. *Les fors* were a set of medieval laws that defined all rights to public and private lands. According to Manex Goyenetche, *Le Guide du Pays Basque* (Lyon: La Manufacture, 1989), 141, 66 percent of the land of the Pays de Cize was communal property to which resident landowners had certain grazing claims.

3. Poullenot, *Basses Pyrénées*, 113–15.

4. Ousby, *Occupation*, 253–55, discusses the important role that labor draft dodgers played in the formation of the *maquis* (guerrilla fighters) in 1943–44.

5. Gérard, *Les Grandes Heures*, 425–26, explains the elaborate financing scheme of the Belgian resistance. The stipends that were distributed by the government in exile to aid their underground railroad in occupied Europe actually originated in Belgium. Raymond Scheyven, a well-known Brussels banker, engineered a brilliant fundraising scheme: he enlisted 150 wealthy Belgians to loan two hundred million francs to the wartime government. To confirm receipt of the contributions in London and to inspire confidence among the lenders, each contributor wrote a message that eventually was aired on the BBC as part of its daily afternoon broadcasts to Belgians. The program was completely unknown to Pérot at the time.

CHAPTER 11

1. See William Ugeux, *Le Passage de l'Iraty* (Lyon: Armand Henneuse, 1962), 49–68, for a detailed account of the time between Ugeux's (alias Berthier's) departure from Grenoble until his arrival in Mendive.

2. See Ugeux, *Le Passage*, 84–103, for a dramatic account of their escapades from the time they landed at the Casa del Rei until they reached San Sebastian.

CHAPTER 12

1. According to Charles Schepens, though most of the beech trees being harvested from the Forêt d'Iraty were not of superior quality, occasionally a log of "first quality" lumber would appear. First quality logs would be designated for shipment to a plywood mill in Bordeaux. Also, trucks from a cement company in the region periodically would come to haul away the mountains of sawdust generated at the mill.

2. The transport of the cadaver via the cable was an unusual event. On other occasions, however, the cable crew and other workers in the mountains found the bodies of fugitives who had perished while unsuccessfully passing through the Forêt d'Iraty.

3. Elie Dyan letter to Cyrille Pomerantzeff, 22 January 1966, from Charles Schepens's private papers. Dyan actually addressed his correspondence to Cyrille, who forwarded the letter to Schepens.

CHAPTER 13

1. This climactic episode in the "épopée d'Iraty" has been mythologized in local oral tradition thanks largely to Jean Sarochar's storytelling. As one version of the story goes, when the Gestapo arrived at the factory office they approached Monsieur Pérot and demanded to speak to the factory director; the crafty Pérot replied, "I'll go get him," and then disappeared onto the factory floor. Another account explains that when the Germans mentioned the money in the safe, Pérot told them that he would go get the keys to prove his innocence and took the chance to escape. Ugeux also misinterpreted this scene in *Le Passage de l'Iraty* (109): in his description of the encounter Pérot told the Germans that he was going to go and get the documents that corroborated his story.

2. Various efforts have been made by French historians and those involved in the resistance effort to tally the number of fugitives who crossed the Pyrenees into Spain from 1940 to 1944. Their estimates have been based on both archival records (in France and in Spain) as well as attempts to locate and interview "les évadés de France." Most of the researchers agree that thirty to thirty-five thousand French people passed over the border (see Poullenot, *Basses Pyrénées*, 141–42),

with the total as high as fifty thousand (when citizens of other countries are included in the total). Eychenne documents that at least four thousand of those were in the Basses-Pyrénées (*Les Fougères*, 86), but contends that a total of fifteen thousand French citizens is a more realistic estimate (*Les Pyrénées*, 323–28).

CHAPTER 14

1. See M. R. D. Foot, *Resistance: European Resistance to Nazism 1940–1945* (New York: McGraw-Hill, 1977), 189–97.

2. See Poullenot, *Basses Pyrénées*, 139, where the author connects the 1943 release of prisoners to Franco's reevaluation of Hitler's chances of winning the war.

3. The young man's real name was Marcel Hitler; he was one of the young draft dodgers who, along with Pierre Harguindeguy, tried to escape from Mendive in March 1943.

4. The British were using American-produced TWA seaplanes developed during the 1930s to operate the special air service between Portugal and England.

5. In the last year of the war the Germans deployed the new V1 rocket against English targets, especially London; the new unmanned bomb enabled the Germans to launch them day and night.

6. Rémy, *Réseau Comète*, 124–25, describes an interview of Albert Greindl, one of the surviving agents of the Comet network, who was exposed by the same *passeur* and who described the circumstances of de Hepcée's capture and death.

CHAPTER 15

1. "Le Calvaire d'un Héros," *Bulletin Des IET* (n.d.): 3. An introduction to the article indicates that this unsigned eulogy was written by Pelfort's closest friend.

2. According to Madame Madeleine Faubert, the wife of the company's marketing agent, in order to meet the payroll Pelfort and her husband sold saccharine (smuggled from Spain) on the Parisian black market.

3. Pelfort's entire "Carnet de Route" is reproduced in "Le Calvaire," 4–5.

4. Pelfort, "Le Calvaire," editor's note, 3.

5. See Mark Kurlansky, *The Basque History of the World* (New York: Walker & Company, 1999), 220–21, for a description of the Spanish Basque refugees' participation in both the *maquis* and the special formal combat unit created in 1944 called the Guernica Battalion.

6. Poullenot, *Basses Pyrénées*, 226.

CHAPTER 16

1. Poullenot, *Basses Pyrénées*, 277–78.

CHAPTER 17

1. The prototype of Schepens's indirect binocular ophthalmoscope is part of the Smithsonian Institution's collection of medical instruments.

2. Bernard Duhourcau, *Guide Historique et Pittoresque de St.-Jean-Pied-de-Port et du Pays de Cize* (Bayonne: Editions Harriet, 1985), 50.

3. For an example of the ethnographer's transcription of Sarochar's narration of a Basque legend see José Miguel de Barandiaran, *Eusko-folklore, Obras Completas*, vol. 2 (Bilbao: Editorial La Gran Enciclopedia Vasca, 1974), 468.

CHAPTER 18

1. The name of the institute changed from the Retina Foundation to the Eye Research Institute in the 1960s.

2. Nestled into a stone niche outside the building is the folk carving of Chaindua, a young woman holding a pick in her left hand to symbolize the following story: Chaindua was a household servant in the village of Beyrie. One night during the corn harvest one of the farm hands offered ten sous to the person who located the pick that he had left in the fields. When she found it in the dark the man, regretting his offer, exclaimed, "The devil take you away," and with that Satan swooped down and carried the girl away in his claws. Members of the household and people from the village took up pursuit, but to no avail. As she was being carried over the Forêt d'Iraty she spied the Chapel of St.-Sauveur and prayed for help; the chapel bell began to ring, and immediately the demon dropped Chaindua to the ground.

The sound of the chapel bell was believed to have similarly saved a Basque farm hand, whose story provides the explanation for the mystic origin of the metal candelabra that is a permanent fixture of the interior of the chapel. According to the legend, while tending his animals the farm hand found a beautiful gold candelabra in the grotto of the Wild Ogress (Basa Andere), which he stole. The Wild Ogre (Basa Jaun) joined the Wild Ogress in the pursuit of the man, who took refuge in the Chapelle St.-Sauveur. The man immediately began praying, affirming that it was for the holy savior that he had acquired the object, and begged for pity. Immediately the sound of the bells sent the evil spirits running back to their forest lair.

3. The full text (in French) of the inscription on the plaque of the Chapelle St.-Sauveur reads: "De 1942 à 1944 Pour de nombreux patriotes belges rejoignant les forces alliées l'Iraty fut une halte sur le long chemin de la liberté. Les survivants ont choisi ce sanctuaire de paix pour redire leur gratitude à Dieu qui les protegea et à ceux qui en Pays Basque leur furent fraternels" (From 1942 to 1944 for numerous Belgian patriots seeking to join the Allied forces [the] Iraty [forest] was a stopover on the long road to liberty. The survivors have chosen this sanctuary of peace to

express again their gratitude to God who protected them and to those in the Pays Basque who acted as their brothers).

4. For his wartime service Charles Schepens was eventually awarded a French croix de guerre and two Belgian medals (the Officier de l'Ordre de Léopold and the Commandeur de l'Ordre de la Couronne).

5. While the social system within rural Basque villages is still anchored in the concept of the primacy of the family farmstead, the "first neighbor" relationship interjects an element of interdependence between households. The first neighbor (*lehen auzoa*) is designated as the closest property in the direction of the village church. It is the duty of the master or mistress of that household to serve as a witness in official transactions and provide aid in times of need, most particularly when a family member dies.

6. It is unclear whether the ceremony was to have taken place in Paris or Bayonne. Information taken from interviews conflicts with the contemporary newspaper account.

7. "Les autorités délivrent la Légion d'honneur à un berger basque sans savoir qu'il était mort," source unknown. From a newspaper clipping, Charles Schepens's private archives. The article, which includes Bonnet's homage to Sarochar, was sent to Schepens in January 1976 by Maitena Dabbadie (then proprietess of the Hotel Bidegain in Mauléon).

Selected Bibliography

Basque History and Culture
Europe, 1914–1945
French Rural Sociology
Oral History

BASQUE HISTORY AND CULTURE

Angulo, Miguel. *Randonnées en Pays Basque*. Biarritz: Editions Lavielle, 1986.
Barandiaran, José Miguel. *Eusko-folklore, Obras Completas*, Vol. 2. Bilbao: Editorial La Gran Enciclopedia Vasca, 1974.
Bernoville, Gaetan. *Le Pays des Basques*. Paris: Horizons de France, 1946.
Bidart, Pierre, ed. *Le Pays de Cize*. St. Etienne-de-Baigorry: Editions Izpegi, 1991.
———. *Société, Politique, Culture en Pays Basque*. Bayonne: Elkar, 1986.
Cerquand, Jean-François. *Légendes et Récits Populaires du Pays Basque*. Bordeaux: Editions Auberon, 1992.
Clark, Robert P. *The Basques: The Franco Years and Beyond*. Reno: University of Nevada Press, 1980.
De Foucher, L. *Un Mois aux Pyrénées*. Paris: Librairie Hachette, 1920.
Dendaletche, Claude. *Montagnes et Civilisation Basque*. Paris: Denoel, 1978.
Dufilho, André. *Docteur, Un Cheval Vous Attend*. Paris: Editions de la Table Ronde, 1989.
Duhourcau, Bernard. *Guide des Pyrénées Mystérieuses*. Paris: Editions Sand, 1985.
———. *Guide Historique et Pittoresque de St.-Jean-Pied-de-Port et du Pays de Cize*. Bayonne: Jean Curutchet les Editions Harriet, 1985.
Gallop, Rodney. *A Book of the Basques*. London: MacMillan, 1930.
Goyenetche, Manex. *Le Guide du Pays Basque*. Lyon: La Manufacture, 1989.
Jacob, James E. *Hills of Conflict: Basque Nationalism in France*. Reno: University of Nevada Press, 1994.
Kurlansky, Mark. *The Basque History of the World*. New York: Walker, 1999.
Laborde, Pierre. *Pays Basque Economie et Société en Mutation*. Bayonne: Elkar, 1994.
Laquet-Fiau, Henri. *Irati: Forêt mon amie*. Biarritz: Atlantica, 1999.
Laxalt, Robert. *In a Hundred Graves*. Reno: University of Nevada Press, 1972.
———. *A Time We Knew*. Reno: University of Nevada Press, 1990.
Ott, Sandra. *The Circle of Mountains: A Basque Shepherding Community*. Reno: University of Nevada Press, 1981.

Le Pays Basque. Paris: Hachette, 1926.

Reicher, Gil. *En Pays Basque — Saint-Jean-le-Vieux et le Pays de Cize.* Bordeaux: Editions Delmas, 1943.

Valéry, André. *Des Hommes dans la Forêt.* Portet-sur-Garonne: Loubatières, 1996.

Veyrin, Philippe. *Les Basques de Labourd, de Soule, et de Basse-Navarre: Leur histoire et leurs traditions.* Bayonne: Arthaud, 1975.

Viers, Georges. *Le Pays Basque.* Toulouse: Privat, 1975.

EUROPE, 1914–1945

Block, Gay, and Malka Drucker. *Rescuers: Portraits of Moral Courage in the Holocaust.* 3d ed. New York: TV Books, 1997.

Cobb, Richard. *French and Germans, Germans and French.* Hanover NH: University Press of New England, 1983.

Eychenne, Emilienne. *Les Fougères de la Liberté 1939–1945.* Toulouse: Editions Milan, 1987.

——. *Les Pyrénées de la Liberté 1939–1945.* Paris: Editions France–Empire, 1984.

Foot, M. R. D. *Resistance: European Resistance to Nazism 1940–1945.* New York: McGraw-Hill, 1977.

Gérard, Jo. *Les Grandes Heures de la Belgique.* Paris: Perrin, 1990.

Gérard-Libois, J., and José Gotovitch. *L'an 40: La Belgique occupée.* Brussels: CRISP, 1971.

Goris, Jan-Albert. *Belgium in Bondage.* New York: L. B. Fischer, 1943.

——, ed. *Belgium.* Berkeley: University of California Press, 1945.

——. *Belgium under Occupation.* New York: Moretus Press, 1947.

Guislain, Albert. *Bruxelles: Atmosphère 10–32.* Paris-Bruxelles: Eglantine, 1932.

Haestrup, Jorgen. *European Resistance Movements 1939–1945: A Complete History.* Odense: Odense University Press, 1981.

Hallie, Philip. *Lest Innocent Blood Be Shed.* New York: Harper & Row, 1979.

Jackson, Julian. *France: The Dark Years 1940–1944.* Oxford: Oxford University Press, 2001.

Kedward, H. R. *Resistance in Vichy France: A Study of Ideas and Motivation in the Southern Zone 1940–1942.* Oxford: Oxford University Press, 1978.

MacDonald, Nancy. *Homage to the Spanish Exiles.* New York: Insight, 1987.

Moore, Bob, ed. *Resistance in Western Europe.* Oxford: Berg, 2000.

Morgan, Ted. *An Uncertain Hour: The French, the Germans, the Jews, the Klaus Barbie Trial, and the City of Lyon, 1940–1945.* New York: William Morrow, 1990.

Motz, Roger. *Belgium Unvanquished.* London: Lindsay Drummond, 1942.

Ousby, Ian. *Occupation: The Ordeal of France 1940–1944.* New York: St. Martin's, 1997.

Paxton, Robert O. *Vichy France: Old Guard and New Order, 1940–1944.* New York: Alfred A. Knopf, 1972.

Poullenot, Louis. *Basses Pyrénées Occupation Libération, 1940–1945.* Biarritz: Editions J & D, 1995.

Rémy. *Réseau Comète.* Vol. 1–2, *La Ligne de Démarcation.* Paris: Librairie Académique Perrin, 1966–67.

Stéphany, Pierre. *1940: 366 Jours d'histoire de Belgique et d'ailleurs.* Brussels: P. Legrain, 1961.

Ugeux, William. *Histoires de Résistants.* Paris: Editions Duculot, 1979.

——. *Le Passage de l'Iraty.* Lyon: Armand Henneuse, 1962.

FRENCH RURAL SOCIOLOGY

Guillaumin, Emile. *The Life of a Simple Man.* Hanover NH: University Press of New England, 1983.

Hélias, Pierre Jakez. *The Horse of Pride: Life in a Breton Village.* New Haven: Yale University Press, 1978.

Tindall, Gillian. *Célestine: Voices from a French Village.* New York: Henry Holt, 1995.

Weber, Eugen. *Peasants into Frenchmen: The Modernization of Rural France, 1870–1914.* Stanford: University of California Press, 1976.

ORAL HISTORY

Frisch, Michael. *A Shared Authority: Essays on the Craft and Meaning of Oral and Public History.* Albany: State University of New York Press, 1990.

Pachter, Marc, ed. *Telling Lives: The Biographer's Art.* Washington DC: New Republic, 1979.

Portelli, Alessandro. *The Death of Luigi Trastulli and Other Stories: Form and Meaning in Oral History.* Albany: State University of New York Press, 1991.

Thompson, Paul. *The Voice of the Past: Oral History.* 3d ed. Oxford: Oxford University Press, 2000.

Index

Numbers in italics refer to the photographic insert; the first number is that of text page preceding the insert, the second that of the page in the insert.